Seven Weeks to Emotional Healing

By Joan Mathews Larson, Ph.D.

Seven Weeks to Sobriety:
The Proven Program to Fight Alcoholism
Through Nutrition

Seven Weeks to Emotional Healing:
Proven Natural Formulas for Eliminating Anxiety,
Depression, Anger, and Fatigue from Your Life

Seven Weeks to Emotional Healing

Proven Natural Formulas for Eliminating Anxiety, Depression, Anger, and Fatigue from Your Life

Joan Mathews Larson, Ph.D.

Ballantine Wellspring™

The Ballantine Publishing Group • New York

This book is intended to provide the reader with information only. As noted throughout the text, individuals should consult appropriate health care practitioners knowledgeable in the field of orthomolecular medicine prior to pursuing any particular course of treatment.

Names and identifying facts have been changed for all case studies included within this book so that individuals who may be described in the case studies will not be recognizable. Any similarities between the case study descriptions and actual, living persons are purely coincidental.

A Ballantine Wellspring™ Book
Published by The Ballantine Publishing Group

Mathews-Larson, Joan.
Seven weeks to emotional healing : proven natural formulas for eliminating anxiety, depression, anger, and fatigue from your life / Joan Mathews-Larson.—1st ed.
p.   cm.
Includes bibliographical references and index.
ISBN 0-345-43686-5 (hc.)
1. Mental health—Nutritional aspects. 2. Mental illness—Nutritional aspects.
I. Title.
RC455.4.N8 M37 1999
616.89'0654—dc21   99-012489

Text design by Ann Gold

Manufactured in the United States of America

First Edition: October 1999

10 9 8 7 6 5 4 3 2 1

This book is dedicated to my children,
Mark Mathews and Molly Mathews-Redden,
who work at my side and share my commitment
to a better future for us all.

CONTENTS

Seven Weeks to Emotional Healing

Finding Emotional Stability— Naturally

You are searching for answers to symptoms you have lived with all your life. You have gone into therapy hoping to talk these unstable moods away . . . and you now have great insights into your behavior—but the unwanted feelings are still there. You are beginning to doubt that there is any way to banish these goblins, yet coexisting with them is sapping the joy out of your life.

After all that you've been through, I expect you will feel skeptical when I assure you that you can free yourself from this state once and for all, that there is a way to banish these moods that have shadowed your life.

My promise is based on almost twenty years of work helping people overcome problems perceived as emotional that had previously gone unresolved. The principles in this book have been tested and fine-tuned at the Health Recovery Center since 1980. By using the same biochemical tools our clients have found so successful, you will effect the same positive results.

The research upon which each chapter is based is solid. I can say that because I have applied these methods to thousands of *real* people with *real* symptoms, and real lab work has confirmed, once and for all, what has gone wrong. Predictably, the anxiety or depression or paranoia or muddled moods or mind-racing or sullenness of clients have gradually faded away as their brains recovered a more optimal chemical balance.

These unstable feelings were *not* psychological in origin; they were the result of the unbalanced chemistry of their physical brains.

A large number of studies conducted worldwide have shown us what happens to thoughts, feelings, and behavior when key brain chemicals are unavailable or too plentiful. As a result of these studies, scientists have been able to show how a specific program of biochemical repair can restore stable "emotional" health ... and that is the essence of this seven-week program.

I have been involved in this approach since 1980, when I opened the Health Recovery Center in Minneapolis, Minnesota. Originally, we were licensed to treat alcoholism and drug addictions. Because these addictions destroy or block so many of the brain's important chemicals, our clients were also suffering from depression and anxiety when we first met. They seemed "emotionally" unstable, but conventional therapy did not turn them around. Looking back to our early days, I still shake my head when I remember how my traditionally trained counseling staff invariably felt that those clients had attitude problems, or just deliberately chose such negative behaviors. I had worked in traditional programs for six years before opening the Health Recovery Center, so I was aware of what the field considered "state of the art" treatment. I knew that four out of five treated alcoholics were expected to relapse within their first year out of treatment, and *one out of four of the deaths of these troubled alcoholics would be suicide*, also usually occurring within the first year after treatment.

My impetus to create a new treatment model came from a need to test a theory I had that treatment failure remained high because no one had addressed the *physical damage* that alcohol did to the human brain—damage that showed itself as unstable emotions.

My theory proved to be a winner! My not-so-profound idea that a chemical imbalance in the brain results in flawed thinking and behavior has proved itself repeatedly throughout the years. At the Health Recovery Center, we have consistently sustained a recovery rate of 75 percent or higher, despite a growing trend of attracting some of the neediest clients in the United States—many of whom have approached us as a result of reading my first book, *Seven Weeks to Sobriety.*

Over the almost twenty years of our existence, we gradually began to treat nonaddicted individuals who shared some of the same unstable emotional traits. In fact, their lab results looked amazingly like those of our substance-abusing clients! Yet they had never been addicted to alcohol or drugs.

The findings from the huge body of research are applicable to anyone whose brain biochemistry is causing emotional discomfort. Whatever the cause, your brain may be unable to maintain a state of optimal balance. If so, it may be telling you in the only way it can: *emotionally*. It is telling you with UNSTABLE EMOTIONS— these clue us in to an imbalance. What causes this to happen? Some of you may have gotten a bad shake genetically; some may be severely depleted by life stresses. Others may have unwittingly caused their own malnourishment through continually dieting or living on junk food! Regardless, in the end the result is the same: You feel as if you are operating on one cylinder. If, through good news or bad, you really don't feel any better, that is a major clue to search out solutions in the **physical** realm.

As you read through this book, I will help you to seek out the clues that your symptoms reveal, and *we will fix what's broken*!

We will accomplish our search by completing prescreens of symptoms, followed by confirming lab work, and finally by using well-tested repair formulas that are appropriate for you. However, unlike therapy, this program will concentrate entirely on *physical* repair. You will be learning about the body's *natural chemicals* and the proper amounts that are necessary to create our well-being, even our sanity. The difference in how you feel will be the strongest argument I can make. You have every reason to expect the same high rate of success that we have seen with clients at our center.

It is sadly ironic that I have benefitted from the findings of so many brilliant researchers, and yet at the time when *I* desperately needed such knowledge I had none of it. This was years ago, when the events of my life took a sharp turn and led me on a search that changed my life forever.

At a young age, my husband suffered a heart attack and died. Suddenly I was struggling to support three children. With all the chaos, I was slow to recognize that my teenager, Rob, was becoming hooked on alcohol and drugs. When I finally sought help for him, I assumed the "experts" knew what they were doing. I was wrong! A very depressed sixteen-year-old spent one month in a hospital setting reviewing all the mistakes of his young life—and it was devastating to him. Shortly after returning home he took his own life. In retrospect, I see the terrible harm counselors do by dwelling day after day on negative life events. Feelings of hopelessness and despair commonly result when perceived failures and weaknesses are continually filtered through a depressed brain. That Rob was unable to get the help he needed had a profound effect on me, and led me through an enormous body of research confirming how alcohol and even prescribed drugs, and/or stress, and/or poor nutrition, and/or poor absorption alter or destroy many of the natural substances the human brain needs in order to create and regulate emotions. As a result, our brains alter physically—but the changes are expressed *emotionally*.

Too late, I began to understand the chemical relationship between Rob's heavy alcohol use and his corresponding depression. The idea that counselors could "talk" his brain into repair began to seem idiotic; no amount of brilliant advice can change a brain's biochemistry one iota!

Eventually I began to think that many "psychological" symptoms may really be the result of a malfunctioning brain rather than a cause in themselves. And this understanding gave rise to more questions. Why not try to fix what's broken? Can we intervene to prevent similar tragedies? Can we undo the damage? After doing graduate work in human nutrition, I was eager to add a dimension of physical repair to a treatment that has always been entirely psychological. This was back in 1980.

It's sad to say, but in twenty years, the field of substance abuse treatment has made zero progress in recovery rates because it still clings to the belief that talk therapy will turn around damaged chemistry. This same belief system operates in many psychologists and psychiatrists today. It is a seriously flawed, unscientific belief. I tell you this based on years of watching spectacular emotional turnarounds through biochemical restoration. This book is written with a how-to approach to show exactly what we do at the Center and how you may apply these same principles to your own personal needs.

With these tools you will be able to make changes that measurably improve your quality of life. Briefly, here's an overall look at how this program will work for you.

1. First we do extensive symptom screening; these tests will offer clues to your underlying biochemical glitches.
2. You will be encouraged to pursue independent lab work based on what these clues suggest. Lab tests will confirm or cancel out your suspicions.
3. I will explain the way we repair these biochemical imbalances at the Center, presenting the research that supports the restoring of the brain's proper levels of natural chemicals. Then you will get clear instructions on specific formulas to correct biochemical mistakes and to reverse your symptoms.

    Please note: You won't need to worry about ingesting more than the maximum allowable amounts of each nutrient. I've made sure you cannot mistakenly take too much by providing the Nutrient Replacement List, page 56. Simply follow the easy instructions, and you will have no trouble keeping track of just how much to take.
4. And finally, you will learn the huge role that diet plays in maintaining emotional stability. There *is* a right diet for you, and I'll help you find it.

To boost your confidence in this approach, let me remind you that for almost twenty years the Health Recovery Center has been applying, in a clinical setting, the findings of many diligent researchers. We have been the "bridge" that takes their research and puts it into action with real people. The risk factor has always been low, as we only use substances that *belong* in the human body; we almost never use drugs to treat our clients.

While we have focused on rebuilding emotional stability in our clients, we have also continually been blessed with access to new research that we can test with our clients. Early on, we were rewarded by seeing some dramatic changes. After two years, we knew we were on to something, because our follow-ups continually showed high success rates. We have always done follow-ups, and from time to time we have collected data to document our results. (Currently, we are preparing a third study for journal publication.) Our scientific research project was the basis of my Ph.D. dissertation. The results were published in 1987 in the *International*

SYMPTOMS REPORTED BY HRC CLIENTS

Symptom	Before Biochemical Repair (%)	After Biochemical Repair (%)
Mood swings	70	5
Anxiety, fear	64	11
Exhaustion	67	3
Irritability	74	18
Poor memory	69	11
Magnify insignificant events	75	11
Reduced initiative	89	5
Tremors, shakiness	44	2
Dizziness	53	4
Depression	61	5
Headache	51	5
Insomnia	44	6
Chronic fatigue	77	15
Cry easily	42	4
Physically weak	44	2

Journal of Biosocial and Medical Research. Briefly, here are some highlights from that paper. The table on this page records the percentage of our alcoholic clients reporting symptoms when they first came for treatment, and six weeks later, after receiving biochemical repair.

The results underscore that dramatic changes are possible. And the same principles of physical repair that produced this success apply to all of us. Think about the alcoholic with these symptoms; is it any wonder alcohol looks appealing if it can cover up this misery? Or consider what happens when nonaddicted persons go to their psychiatrists complaining of anxiety, irritability, depression, exhaustion, insomnia, or fearfulness; usually they get *prescription drugs* to cover up their symptoms.

The bottom line is the same: *Our bodies—including our brains—are not designed to function well on toxic foreign substances.* These drugs may relieve or mask over your misery on a temporary basis, but many have long-term side effects and become less able to deliver relief unless the dosage continues to increase. No one wants to become a lifelong user of psychiatric drugs if there are other viable options. And believe me, you are about to discover the *mother lode* of options!

A doctor once said, "You can't diagnose it until you think of it." Well, for almost two decades, our clinic has been focusing on the causes of emotional instability that others do not consider. And now I can help you identify clues that point to *chemistry*, not personality, as the culprit that causes your emotional woes. It's a pretty safe bet that you have never come across this concept in your search for answers. You are in for a pleasant surprise.

In this book, I give you all that we have learned that can be useful to you. I know each of you readers has a different agenda, and so certain chapters will be more meaningful to some than to others. Still, I suggest that you begin by reading straight through the book, so you will not miss any valuable information. Then, go back to the beginning and use the book as a manual or study guide. Take all the tests, learn the signs that point to your body chemistry needing repair, and concentrate on making the appropriate dietary changes. Become familiar with what lab work is right for you and why. Consult with a doctor—I urge you to approach an orthomolecular physician if your traditionally schooled physician is not familiar with the approach I suggest (see Appendix B for contact information). Step by step, develop a lifelong regimen of nutrients that will bring you the stability you seek ... natural chemicals that you've always needed, but never knew you did!

One last word: I have saved the best for *last*. In Chapter 10 you will find answers that will change you in ways you never thought possible!

For today we have reached the brink of understanding aging— how to slow it down, and even how to *reverse* it. The most exciting and important replacement chemicals that do all this are the anti-aging hormones. Left to themselves, the levels of our various hormones gradually decline to almost zilch as we age. We are biologically programmed to peak early, procreate, then fade out and die. But by replacing these magical hormones, we can rejuvenate ourselves. *We can grow younger at any age.* Here are some direct results of hormone replacement:

- increased libido and restored sexual function
- rejuvenated immune system
- improved concentration, sharpened thinking
- elevated mood and energy levels

- lowered mental fatigue
- younger skin and appearance
- extended life span
- reduced stress
- reversal of deterioration caused by aging

Once you've worked to fine-tune your mind and body, you will want to maintain this high-quality state. Science has powerful new solutions that are clearly detailed for you at the end of this book.

No matter how skeptical you may feel now, I am certain that what you are about to experience will reassure you. Some of our most "doubting Thomases" have become true believers. Now it's *your* turn to benefit from today's cutting-edge research.

Welcome to the twenty-first century!

PART ONE

Feelings That Therapy Can't Heal

CHAPTER 1

It's Not All in Your Mind

As far back as he could remember, Peter had been fearful, but he covered it up extremely well. Now married, he supported his family adequately but felt shy and joyless most of the time. He drank beer occasionally to offset those feelings. Still, he seemed to become more of a loner with each passing year. Peter never considered himself a candidate to see a psychiatrist. He was simply living out his life of quiet despair until we met.

Meg was an excellent attorney with a very bright mind. Her facade was take-charge aggressive, and few crossed her. Yet at our first meeting she was in tears because of her angry, erratic behavior. She had no idea why she seemed to exist in a state of such high arousal. . . . This trait was hurting those she loved the most. She wanted to mellow out but knew her career couldn't afford the fog prescription drugs created.

An exceptional designer, musician, and musical director, Eric didn't have the emotional staying power to ignite his career into high gear. Despite his brilliance, his heart pounded with anxiety during performances. He drank a lot of caffeine and was a heavy smoker. His mood swings left him exhausted when he desperately needed extra energy. Ongoing psychological counseling did not change any of this. . . . Now he was considering taking prescribed drugs to relieve his depression and anxiety. He summed it up the *day we met, telling me, at age forty-two, "Some days my life feels entirely hopeless."*

Donna usually felt scattered. Her thinking was foggy, and her problems concentrating were affecting her job. Memories of her childhood were of a pale, listless little girl who had never felt the world was a friendly place. She had had frequent childhood illnesses— earaches, strep throats, and colds. Now as an adult, she still felt fragile. She told me she needed help to overcome her muddled thinking and get some joy in her life. But her number-one priority was finding relief from her fatigue, which made her tired right down to her bones. For Donna, life was an uphill battle—and she was slowly losing the war.

It is part of the human condition that we keep taking our own inventory and continually come up short, but it becomes a calamity if the missing pieces prevent us from enjoying a fulfilling, stable life. If, like Peter, Meg, Eric, and Donna, you are saying, "I wish I could feel better, think better, perform better," it is time to stop wishing and take heart! *This book will change your life.*

Like the case studies just cited, you, too, may be coexisting with an erratic nervous system or brain, and lack the energy, verve, joy, and confidence that are your birthright. Yet you may be hesitant about seeing a therapist. And, in fact, the idea that a good therapist can solve these problems by simply talking to you has been the great bane of the twentieth century! Untold millions are filling the coffers of psychologists and counselors who listen to the tales of misery that such lives produce but aren't able to effect real, positive, *lasting* changes in their clients.

Fortunately, in the last few decades, biochemists and medical doctors have begun to pinpoint scientific explanations for behavior that used to be labeled "psychological." These researchers have noticed that:

- many "psychological" symptoms often cluster in families.
- certain physical changes in the brain (and body) can create mayhem emotionally.
- an internal invasion of yeast parasites may create full-blown mental and physical illness.

- food intolerances strongly affect our emotions.
- airborne chemicals can alter our brains.
- angry outbursts are predictable from a brain in a chemical state of high arousal all the time.
- dozens of biochemical mistakes can result in bleak depression or anxiety.

All of these are fixable, *if we can identify them!*

A New Direction

In 1896, Sigmund Freud predicted that "the future may teach us to exercise a direct influence by means of chemical substances upon the amounts of energy and their distribution in the apparatus of the mind." By 1927 he had become "firmly convinced that one day all these mental disturbances we are trying to understand will be treated by means of hormones or similar substances." How right he was! Science now knows it can address such "mental disturbances" biochemically. It is no longer believed that talk therapy and good counseling advice can relieve the agony emanating from a chemically disrupted brain.

In fact, science has now taken off at a gallop in the direction of biochemical repair. One of the leaders in the field is a brilliant Canadian named Abram Hoffer who is both a biochemist and a psychiatrist. In the 1950s, he began to apply pellagra research to psychiatric patients. Earlier, vitamin B_3 (niacin) deficiency had been established as the cause of pellagra, a disease that causes confusion, disorientation, and memory disturbance. So here was a classic example of a *natural* substance that prevents a psychotic state. In fact, the prolonged absence of niacin in our bodies will ultimately result in death!

In 1962, Dr. Hoffer published the first double-blind study in the field of psychiatry. He found that, of ninety-eight schizophrenic patients receiving megadoses of niacin, the hospital readmission rate was 10 percent over three years with no suicides, while the placebo group had a 50 percent readmission with four suicides. Also in the 1960s, Dr. Hoffer treated about twenty-five former prisoners of war who had been imprisoned in Japanese concentration camps during World War II. He found that, in order to be free of the many physical and psychiatric symptoms (i.e., fears, anxieties, insomnia, depression) they developed during their internment, 90 percent of the former prisoners had developed a *permanent* need for large doses of niacin.

The Canadian Department of Health and Welfare also conducted a study to determine if the general chronic illnesses seen in the men held in Japanese POW camps, who underwent starvation and excessive stress, were present in their brothers who had served in Europe. The differences were remarkable! The men incarcerated by the Japanese suffered from serious ongoing psychiatric and neurological diseases throughout life, as well as heart disease, premature blindness, arthritis, and a high death rate. None of these symptoms was present in their brothers. Clearly, the starvation and stress endured in the Japanese camps had created chronic illness. Fortunately, Dr. Hoffer was able to treat some of these men, extending their lives and saving their sanity with niacin (B_3).

How Nutrient Deprivation
Cripples Us Emotionally

You may not see a connection between starving prisoners and our own poorly functioning health, but as you read on you will begin to understand how physical deprivation can trigger uncontrollable emotional behavior, all the way to madness. I expect many of you are protesting that you are not starving, by any means! But because of your unique, individual biochemical requirements or because of some glitches in how you absorb nutrients, or the fact that you live on junk food and colas, your brain may never get enough of what it needs. *Then you are in the same boat as the young men I am about to describe:*

During World War II, scientists in the United States also pondered the effects of starvation on captured GIs living in Japanese POW camps. To provide some answers, a six-month study was launched at the University of Minnesota using healthy young male conscientious objectors. This study produced incredible results (although, of course, this kind of study would not be conducted today).

The young men were deprived of more than half their normal food intake. Over the course of six months, many suffered severe physical and psychiatric changes, and most of these disturbances lingered long after the experiment had ended.

In the beginning, the men showed a high degree of tolerance and sociability with each other. But gradually they began to avoid group activities. There were frequent outbursts of anger and irritability, and many grew deeply depressed. Some finally required hospitalization in a psychiatric ward. One chopped off three of his fingers in response to stress; another became uncontrollably violent. Many expressed the fear that they were going crazy; others talked of suicide. They all cried a lot and displayed wild emotional disturbances. Because they felt increasingly socially inadequate, they now preferred to isolate themselves. Concentration and ability to comprehend became severely impaired even though IQ tests showed no drop in their intellectual abilities.

After the study ended, the emotional symptoms continued. In fact, researchers noted that some of the men grew even more negative, depressed, and argumentative, directly after the conclusion of the project!

What both the U.S. and Canadian studies show is that *"emotional" symptoms develop as a direct result of the unavailability of brain and body chemicals. These important chemicals create our stable emotions, behaviors, thoughts, and sanity.*

Of course, back in the mid-twentieth century, scientists were only beginning to discover the many natural vitamins, minerals, amino acids, essential fatty acids, enzymes, endorphins, and neurotransmitters needed for sanity and well-being. Even today, many people do not seem to grasp the concept that our emotional and physical health depends on having the proper concentration of the natural substances the human body needs to sustain life and normal emotional balance.

In fact, until only the last few decades, little was known about how brain chemicals influence emotions. Only a few scientists were dedicated to resolving chemically induced "emotional" problems by restoring adequate levels of the needed natural chemicals.

The growing awareness that natural substances are needed to create optimum brain functioning should have aroused tremendous interest in the scientific community. Unfortunately, the concurrent worldwide development of the drug industry, with its promise of far more lucrative rewards, lead researchers in another direction. Drug companies give university scientists generous grants to invent new, artificial, *patentable* chemicals. *There is no profit for them in developing promising nonpatentable natural brain/body chemicals.* And many of these artificial drugs have toxic side effects, because our bodies regard them as foreign invaders. According to the *Journal of the American Medical Association*, prescribed drugs cause 140,000 deaths yearly, yet *no drug has ever been able to totally duplicate the role of natural body chemicals.*

By pursuing these "patentable" avenues, the pharmaceutical industry today comprises some of the most powerful and profitable businesses worldwide!

Mind and Body—Intertwined

Luckily, in every generation there are a few truly dedicated geniuses who care more for science and humanity than for building their fortunes. Linus Pauling will be remembered as one such giant. He had already won two Nobel Prizes (in 1954 for chemistry, in 1962 for peace) when, in his sixties, he began studying mental disorders, focusing on underlying biochemical dysfunctions. This new interest grew out of his compassion for humankind:

> I like human beings. I like to think about the possibilities of decreasing the amount of their suffering. When I remember that 10 percent of the American people spend some part of their lives in a mental hospital and that *half* of all hospital beds in this country are occupied by mental patients, I do believe that it will be possible to get an understanding of the molecular and genetic basis of mental disease [and] therapeutic methods that will lead to the effective control of a very large part of mental disease.

Dr. Pauling's interest in disturbed mental function focused on physiology, not psychotherapy. He was the first to call mental disorders "molecular diseases," the result of a *biochemical* abnormality in the body. And he said, *"The mind is a manifestation of the structure of the brain itself."*

His involvement in brain research led him to coin his famous definition of *orthomolecular therapy*: "Orthomolecular psychiatric therapy is the treatment of mental disease by the provision of the optimum molecular environment for the mind, especially the optimum concentrations of substances normally present in the human body."

With that statement, Dr. Pauling gave a scientific identity to the role of nutrition in psychiatry. He challenged doctors to become aware of the overwhelming amount of information that was pouring in from all over the world, documenting the vital role natural chemicals play in brain function and other medical disorders. This book is based on those principles.

I bet you think Pauling's advice to medical doctors is obvious. Yet a recent study showed that while 74 percent of first-year medical students believed that a knowledge of nutrition is important to their career, by their third year of learning how to match drugs to symptoms, the number drops to 13 percent!

What Pauling is telling us is that the human mind cannot operate in a vacuum because it is totally dependent on the *brain* and its molecular function to create your emotional health. In the world of science, where two plus two always makes four, *a sane and stable mind is possible only with an organically healthy brain.*

Balanced Brain Chemicals = Emotional and Mental Health

The reward of getting the right chemicals into the brain at "optimum concentrations" is a joy to witness. Last year a friend complained to me that his three-year-old autistic son, Seth, refused to welcome him when he came home each evening. Instead, Seth sat there self-involved, shutting out the world. A therapist visited them twice weekly, but progress was poor.

I encouraged him to start Seth on B_6 and magnesium, both of which have been shown to work well for autistic children. Within two weeks I received an excited call: Seth was waking up to the world around him and starting to interact much more with his folks. Then, weeks later, his family stopped giving him the supplements, thinking perhaps the therapist was responsible for the breakthrough. It took very little time before Seth's autistic behavior reappeared. His parents ran for his nutrients.

For this child, B_6, which prevents the loss of dopamine from the brain, is critical, as is the magnesium. This is true for most autistic children. (It is speculated that the high upsurge of autism may be related to a modern medical practice; see Chapter 8.)

A number of years ago, a group of neuroscientists meeting at a Johns Hopkins symposium released a joint statement that I love: "Workings of the mind become scrambled when brain chemistry goes awry." They noted that specifically affected are:

- thoughts
- feelings
- self-awareness
- perception
- memory

How can we hope to act and feel normal if our "mental" balance is askew?

Another genius, the late Roger Williams, Ph.D., a University of Texas biochemist, discovered that actual optimal levels of natural brain chemicals can differ widely from person to person. This was an astonishing idea—that any two persons' requirements of these molecular chemicals might be vastly different, and so, on the same recommended daily allowance (RDA), one person stays healthy while the other limps through life never feeling normal!

The Safety of Our Natural Chemicals— and the Healing Power of Our Bodies

Dr. Pauling devoted much time to determining ideal doses of vitamins and other natural chemicals in the body. He concluded that there was great misrepresentation by some medical and scientific journals and by the media about the toxicity and harmful side effects of nutrients taken in greater quantities than the RDA. He called it "a bias based upon a lack of knowledge." An example he cited was about a toddler who swallowed the entire contents of a bottle of vitamin A and began to feel nauseous and headachy. The toddler was treated and then released from the local hospital. Newspapers across the country carried the headline POISONING BY VITAMIN A. Yet every day children *die* from aspirin poisoning—and these deaths go unreported.

Natural substances that belong in our bodies have remarkably *low* toxicity, especially when compared to drugs, which, in general, are highly toxic and sometimes prescribed in doses close to lethal levels. For example, a registered nurse in her forties came to my office recently to discuss her fear that she was becoming disabled from prescribed drugs. Between her physician and her psychiatrist, she was taking nine different drugs. Some of them were addictive; others were combining to create an unsafe level of toxicity. I couldn't believe it when she told me that her doctors were treating the side effects of her prescriptions with more drugs! Furthermore, I was horrified that even a registered nurse had unwittingly found herself on a regimen where she ingested enough toxic substances daily to systematically worsen her health!

Fortunately, there was another way to treat this woman's health problems, and it involved giving her body the nutritional means to heal itself. That's a very important concept: Our bodies are supposed to heal themselves. When we get an infection, the body is supposed to cure it. When we are injured, the body is supposed to heal. It does this innumerable times each day of our lives.

Dr. Albert Schweitzer put it eloquently: "We doctors don't do anything except help the doctor within." Our bodies are hardwired to be self-healing, but to do so they must be given the optimum natural substances needed. And compared to drugs, these natural chemicals are quite safe. So, you may wonder, why did the U.S. Department of Health and Human Services set the RDA levels so unrealistically low? Dr. Linus Pauling also asked that question, and answered it himself. After studying the RDA standards thoroughly, this famous Nobel Prize winner concluded that the RDA's daily nutrient allowances are "enough to keep people barely alive in ordinary poor health."

Repairing Biochemical Error and Reaching Organic Equilibrium

Once in a great while, a researcher with a doctorate in chemistry decides to become a medical doctor as well—a lucky break for mankind! Carl Pfeiffer, Ph.D., M.D., was such a scientist. In the sixties, Dr. Pfeiffer discovered that blood histamine levels were *elevated* in the lab tests of obsessive-compulsive individuals. As these patients improved, their histamine levels dropped and their depression lifted. In patients with very *low* levels of brain histamine, Pfeiffer found that they were likely to be paranoid and have hallucinations. Thus, individuals with either high or low levels of histamine showed some degree of thought disorder and overarousal. True to his chemistry background, Pfeiffer then began the search to determine which natural substances could make or block histamine in the brain. (Chapter 7 applies his valuable discoveries to your own needs.)

So, thirty years later, are psychiatrists systematically testing the histamine levels of their patients? *Not yet!* (You will see the array of abnormal histamine symptoms when you do the written screening tests for low/high histamine levels on page 219. You'll also learn what lab tests to take to confirm what you suspect, and last, how to repair this biochemical error.)

It makes much more sense to restore the natural levels of biochemicals, to re-create optimum balance. This organic equilibrium is called *homeostasis*. From that state you have the best shot at reaching your potential in life! And this is what we will try to achieve in *Seven Weeks to Emotional Healing*. The role of drugs in your emotional health should be *short-term*—a bridge until proper natural balance has been achieved.

In the seventies, Carl Pfeiffer confirmed the presence of what he called the "mauve factor." Sometimes the urine of normal individuals under stress or individuals suffering from mental illness changes to a mauve color after lab tests. He named this kind of anxiety disorder "pyroluria." A cluster of psychological and physical symptoms are identifiable in these people, not the least of which is a high level of inner tension and anxiety that steadily worsens with age. Pyroluria appears genetic, as it seems to run in families. Here is a description of an extremely pyroluric client:

Ted brought his mother with him to our appointment. His shyness was almost painful to behold as he let her answer my questions. This man was a computer whiz and a gifted writer. Still unmarried in his mid-fifties, he had never had a sexual experience because he was just too fearful to date women. He had worked at the same job all his life and kept a low profile. He still lived at home.

Ted had been separated from his family as a toddler, and blamed his deep-seated fears on that circumstance. But my thoughts went immediately to pyroluria. Judging by Ted's pale complexion and his answers to a list of symptoms, I was sure of it. He seemed so miserable that it was hard not to blurt out right then and there that there was probably a biochemical answer to his anxiousness.

Two weeks later his lab results confirmed my suspicions. (You'll find out more about pyroluria and how to treat it in Chapter 5.)

If doctors looked for such biochemical mistakes *before* writing prescriptions for benzodiazepine tranquilizers, treatment centers across this nation would not be full of miserable patients powerfully addicted to Librium, Ativan, Valium, and Xanax and struggling to endure the painful and long-lasting symptoms of withdrawal.

The Fats Our Brains Depend On

In the 1970s, another door opened to our understanding of the substances that are vital to our sanity and health: prostaglandins, which are made in the brain from omega-3 and -6 essential fatty acids (EFAs) and which regulate the neurocircuits throughout the brain and body.

According to researcher David Horrobin, M.D., "the level of prostaglandin E_1 (PGE_1) is of crucial importance to the body. A fall in the level of PGE_1 will lead to a potentially catastrophic series of untoward consequences including increased vascular reactivity, elevated cholesterol production, diabeticlike changes in insulin release, enhanced risk of auto-immune disease, enhanced risk of inflammatory disorders, and susceptibility to depression." At Health Recovery Center, we have consistently seen suicidal depression completely lift in only one week by normalizing PGE_1 levels in the brain! (I'll explain how in Chapter 6.)

Hyperactive children have long been involved in studies with the EFAs. Richard Passwater, Ph.D., describes one such study by Dr. Horrobin, at the Institute for Innovative Medicine in Montreal:

About 20 children were treated with substantial benefit in about two-thirds of them. Some responses were dramatic! In one case a boy who had been threatened with expulsion from school because of his impossible behavior was put on primrose oil (gamma-linolenic acid) without the knowledge of the school authorities. After two weeks on GLA, the teacher, who was unaware of the treatment, contacted the parents and said that in thirty years' experience *she had never seen such a dramatic and abrupt change for the better in a child's behavior* [emphasis added]. Some children do equally well no matter whether the oil is given by mouth or by rubbing into the skin. In others, there is the distinct impression that skin absorption, which will bypass malabsorption problems, may have a better effect.

In the last decade, we have seen an avalanche of exciting studies on essential fatty acids. During that time I heard molecular biologist Donald Rudin, M.D., present his research at a Huxley Institute training session in New York City. He spoke passionately about the connection between omega-3 fatty acid deficiency and mental illness. omega 3 is vital because it provides the base from which the powerful prostaglandin hormones are created. These hormones regulate every neurocircuit throughout the entire brain and body.

Rudin particularly urged using omega-3 fatty acid in the form of linseed oil to treat schizophrenia. Immediately he had my attention, as I was then attempting to stabilize a middle-aged man who was an alcoholic schizophrenic.

Carl had been referred to our clinic by our county's chemical and mental health unit, and was busy terrorizing my staff to the point where we were ready to part company with him. As soon as I returned from the New York conference I began giving him large doses of omega-3 fatty acid in the form of linseed oil (as per Rudin), along with megadoses of certain other nutrients.

What emerged was a soft-spoken, brilliant minister, who told me that, as a young man, his bishop had chosen him to study advanced theology in Switzerland because of his exceptional gifts. I could not believe the personality change! At this point in time he lived on welfare, but said he was going to approach his bishop to ask for support to reenter his chosen profession.

To make a long story short, the bishop knew Carl had had schizophrenia for many years, and turned him away. With his spirit crushed, and having no money or support, Carl stopped taking the omega-3 fatty acid replacement therapy. A year later he had regressed into his schizophrenic world.

Since that time we at the Health Recovery Center have pondered on much of the omega-3 and -6 essential fatty acids research, and we have applied it to those clients who showed marked deficiencies. The results have been rewarding, as you will see.

The Role of Amino Acids in Our Well-being

The eighties brought another explosion of exciting nutrient knowledge. Thanks to researchers like Eric Braverman, M.D., and Richard Wurtman, M.D., amino acids emerged as powerful tools for psychiatry because they convert to, or are our, brain neurotransmitters. These neurotransmitters create the chemical language of the brain, enabling it to function, to have memory, emotions, thoughts, feelings. They stimulate the mind, control depression, produce sleep, and create energy, excitement, and all manner of human responses.

I know this must seem somewhat complex, but it's important to take in the full meaning of that statement. *These natural brain substances are creating sanity and well-being.* And now, in many cases, the levels of these substances in our bodies can be measured by lab tests and supplemented as needed.

The impact of amino acid research on psychiatry should be monumental. But once again they have the misfortune of being created by Nature, not man; drug companies cannot patent and sell them at exorbitant prices. So there is little monetary reward for researchers who pursue the secrets of amino acids.

NATURAL SUBSTANCES VS. DRUGS: POLITICS FOR PROFIT?

The emphasis today seems to be on creating artificial drugs that mimic amino acids. For people who are depressed because of too little serotonin, the rush to *artificially* duplicate the work of the amino acid tryptophan, which converts into serotonin, has resulted in many SSRI-type* drugs that fail to increase serotonin but do play with it in the brain. What the SSRI drugs do is hot-wire the serotonin's neurotransmitter firing mechanism to artificially speed up the pumping of serotonin into the brain. In addition, they block serotonin from being reabsorbed back into the neurotransmitters, as it was designed to do. This results in serotonin accumulating within the brain, artificially creating what humans generally create naturally—that is, enough serotonin to avoid depression. The human body normally does this by supplying enough of the natural amino acid tryptophan, which then converts to serotonin, fully loading all our serotonin neurotransmitters. This is nature's design. Unfortunately, it is almost always true that our firing mechanism works fine, but there is just very little serotonin to fire in certain brains. (And many SSRI drugs can't increase the amount.) What depletes it? Ongoing stress, genetics, poor nutrition, alcohol, and drugs shortchange our natural supply of tryptophan to serotonin. And studies have correlated the depletion of tryptophan, and the decreased ratio between tryptophan and other amino acids, with suicide, depression, and even violence.

SSRI drugs cannot make serotonin. Nor can they supply serotonin. They can only play with the brain's uptake mechanisms—even though it is almost always true that the mechanism that fires serotonin into the brain is undamaged.

Taking SSRI drugs can lead to a myriad of unfortunate results, including severe agitation, violence, and suicide (such results were made public in hearings conducted by the U.S. Food and Drug Administration in September 1991). To better understand the SSRI drugs and their possible effects, I recommend *Talking Back to Prozac* by Peter Breggin, M.D. (St. Martin's Press, 1994). Dr. Breggin suggests another sinister outcome as a result of ongoing use of these antidepressants: To overcome an SSRI-induced glut of serotonin, the brain compensates by down-regulating, or shutting down, excess serotonin receptors. Dr. Breggin documents animal studies that show the numbers of receptors drastically diminished. The most likely explanation is that they have died off, but no one really knows if these serotonin receptor losses are permanent. Drug companies will not

---

* Serotonin-stimulating receptor inhibitors; for example, Paxil, Prozac, and Zoloft.

undertake this testing—undoubtedly because a finding of irreversible receptor loss could generate a rash of class action lawsuits.

The choice American consumers might have had to relieve depression was a $12 bottle of L-tryptophan capsules or a $200-a-month Prozac-type drug. But very shortly before Prozac made its debut, the FDA removed tryptophan from the U.S. market—because a limited supply of tryptophan had been contaminated by its manufacturer, Showa-Denka. While the rest of the world can still readily buy tryptophan, in the United States it has remained available only by prescription and is only dispensed from a few pharmacies in certain cities. The cost has increased to close to $55 per bottle as of this writing— plus your doctor's visit.* This is an example of politics played for profit. It also sheds light on why you may have little awareness of what science really knows about the natural chemicals creating your emotions. The good news is that we can measure our amino acid levels with lab testing—and once we attain a proper balance, we will experience huge improvements in terms of our emotional contentment.

Discovering the Chemistry of Emotions and Behavior

To sum up, many dedicated researchers have been burning the midnight oil for you. You'll get to know their work and apply their findings to your own problems in the pages ahead. While we all live with a neurosis or two, some are serious enough to interfere with our happiness. In *Seven Weeks to Emotional Healing* I'll help you to identify the clues that point to *chemistry*, not personality, as the cause of your emotional woes. The actual studies *and* the formulas we have tested at the Health Recovery Center are in the chapters ahead. You will soon have the tools you need to help yourself back into balance so that you are emotionally content, extremely well-balanced, and full of energy and vigor.

---

* A supposedly "safe" form of tryptophan, 5HTP, is now available over the counter, but while 5HTP raises the serotonin levels in the body, little is admitted to the brain unless another drug, carbidopa, accompanies it. (In Europe, 5HTP *is* used with carbidopa.) And too much serotonin around the heart will do the same damage as we saw with fen-phen (fenfluramine, diet pills), which raised serotonin levels in the body, causing serious heart damage and death! Warning: *Use tryptophan, not 5HTP, to be safe.*

PART TWO

Understanding the Chemistry Behind the Emotions

CHAPTER 2

Recognizing the Clues to Biochemical "Glitches"

Have you always longed for total mental clarity, a sense of joy and resiliency in living, and boundless energy? Have you had enough of up and down moods, anxiousness, tension, sadness, anger, irritability, muddled thinking, exhaustion, and feelings of powerlessness? You may doubt that a book can change any of this, but you will soon see that today's science has some new and powerful solutions for you. And the program you are about to begin will permanently impact your quality of life. This program is not asking you to change your thinking or reprogram your emotions, or to therapize yourself into wellness. I am proposing to fix that malfunctioning computer, your brain, so it will finally begin to serve you *normally*.

Your physical recovery, however, will depend on your strict adherence to the repair program that your body requires. You will find that you have to take many replacement nutrient supplements, based on the results of screening and lab tests. You will be making big changes in your diet and lifestyle. So expect your friends to tease you about becoming a health nut. (Smile; they only wish they had *your* discipline and results!)

On the Road to Your Personal Recovery

We all have our own specific emotional needs, but everyone should start with the basic repair program and diet. After that, we can assess your specific needs, one by one, and add only the appropriate formulas for your recovery. *As we begin, don't be tempted to casually read bits and parts of the chapters. To follow the program as it is laid out for you, read the entire book first. Then go back and, beginning with this chapter, study each chapter that the "Bio-Types of Emotions List" (page 33) has red-flagged for you.* I know you want to know what your specific symptoms mean biochemically—proof that there are underlying biochemical mistakes that are causing your grief. Well, the following section will help you feel more comfortable with this concept. Each symptom listed is connected to a *physical* cause, even though it may feel emotional in origin. Once you have completed the screen and tallied your results, you will know what specific biochemistry you need help with. The chapters ahead will provide you with specific answers. You will also come to know, through tracking your genetic history as well as your personal history, the conditions to which you are predisposed. Last, we'll lay out a basic formula that you should start taking immediately to begin to bring you back to optimal functioning. Let's get started.

BIO-TYPES OF EMOTIONS

Using the list on page 33, circle the corresponding number of each emotion that *sometimes* or *frequently* applies to you. Then take those circled numbers and circle them *wherever they appear* on the chart found on pages 34–36. Example: Number 1 on page 33 is the symptom of "some mental confusion." If *sometimes* or *frequently* you feel mentally confused, circle the #1. Then, circle *each* #1 appearing in the chart on pages 34–36. After you have finished circling all the numbers on both the list *and* the chart, count up how many numbers you have circled under each chapter on the chart (the vertical column) and put the total in the corresponding box under "Your Number Count." If your total for each chapter is at least as high as the bold number in the "Count per Chapter" box, you will particularly benefit from the chapter in question. For example: If the total numbers circled under chapter 9 are 10 or above, this chapter has important information for you.

The case studies in your special chapters will confirm that you are not alone in your travails, and that you can, and will, recover successfully, as many others have.

I know it is tempting to skip ahead to the chapters that sound important to you. *Don't!!!* I don't want you to miss important pieces of the puzzle. It will all come together for you very soon.

BIO-TYPES OF EMOTIONS LIST

1. Some mental confusion
2. Apathetic, "I don't care" attitude
3. Difficulty concentrating
4. Dizziness, light-headed at times
5. Sluggishness
6. Depression
7. Inner fearfulness
8. Suspicion, paranoia
9. Insomnia
10. Irritability
11. Exhaustion
12. Sleeps restlessly
13. Often feels withdrawn around people
14. Inner tension
15. Anxious, easily stressed
16. Tires easily, short on endurance
17. PMS symptoms
18. Feels better to skip breakfast
19. Don't handle stress well
20. Sadness
21. Poor dream recall
22. Muddled thinking
23. Paranoia
24. Poor memory
25. Panic attacks
26. Obsessive/compulsive behavior, feeling driven
27. Fatigue
28. Restlessness
29. Tenseness
30. Aggressive; lives in high arousal
31. Hyperactivity
32. Seeing or hearing what isn't there
33. Low vitality
34. Trembling, shakiness
35. Headaches
36. Weakness
37. Poor appetite, skips meals
38. Mood swings throughout the day
39. Easily angered
40. Mind often races
41. Impulsive
42. Violent outbursts
43. Short attention span
44. Sensitivity to chemical odors (i.e., perfumes)
45. Food bingeing
46. Task completion is hard
47. Very high or low libido (sexual energy)
48. Nervous exhaustion
49. Feeling unreal . . . perceptual disturbances
50. Talking or walking while asleep; or have nightmares
51. Suicidal thoughts
52. Easily agitated
53. Clumsiness, lack of coordination
54. Sighs a lot
55. Difficulty waking up in the morning

BIO-TYPES OF EMOTIONS

Chapter 9 Fatigue	Chapter 6 Depression	Chapter 3 Low Blood Sugar	Chapter 5 Anxiety	Chapter 8 Irritability, Anger, & Violence	Chapter 7 High Histamine, Manic	Chapter 6 Low Thyroid	Chapter 9 Candida, Food Allergies, Memory	Chapter 8 Chemical Sensitivities
1			1	1	1	1	1	1
2	2	1			2	2	2	2
3	3	2		3	3	3	3	3
		3						
4		4						
5	5			5		5	5	5
	6		6		6	6	6	6
			7			7	7	7
8		8	8	8		8	8	8
9	9	9			9		9	9
10	10	10	10	10	10		10	10
11	11	11	11			11	11	11
	12	12	12		12		12	12
14	14	14	14	14	14		14	14
15	15	15	15		15		15	15
16	16	16	16		16	16	16	16
17		17	17					
			18					
19	19	19	19	19	19		19	19
20	20	20	20			20	20	20

Chapter 9 Fatigue	Chapter 6 Depression	Chapter 3 Low Blood Sugar	Chapter 5 Anxiety	Chapter 8 Irritability, Anger, & Violence	Chapter 7 High Histamine, Manic	Chapter 6 Low Thyroid	Chapter 9 Candida, Food Allergies, Memory	Chapter 8 Chemical Sensitivities
			21					
22		22		22			22	22
23			23	23	23			23
24		24	24					
		25	25					
27	27	27	27		26	27	27	27
28		28	28	28			28	28
		29	29	29	29		29	29
30		30	30	30			30	30
		31		31			31	31
					32			32
33	33	33	33		33	33	33	33
		34	34			34		
35		35			35	35	35	35
36	36	36	36			36	36	36
	37	37	37	37				
38		38		38			38	38
39		39	39	39			39	39
	40				40			
41		41			41		41	41
42		42	42	42			42	42
43		43		43			43	43

Chapter 9 Fatigue	Chapter 6 Depression	Chapter 3 Low Blood Sugar	Chapter 5 Anxiety	Chapter 8 Irritability, Anger, & Violence	Chapter 7 High Histamine, Manic	Chapter 6 Low Thyroid	Chapter 9 Candida, Food Allergies, Memory	Chapter 8 Chemical Sensitivities
44								44
45	45	45					45	45
46	46	46	46	46	46	46	46	46
	47			47	47	47		
48	48	48	48		48		48	48
49		49	49		49			49
51	51	51	51		51	51		51
52		52	50	52			52	52
53		53	53			53	53	53
54	54	54	54			54		
55	55	55	55	55	55	55	55	55

COUNT PER CHAPTER

10	6	10	9	6	5	5	10	10
23	16	24	8	16	15	10	25	25

YOUR NUMBER COUNT

| CHAPTER 9 | CHAPTER 6 | CHAPTER 3 | CHAPTER 5 | CHAPTER 8 | CHAPTER 7 | CHAPTER 6 | CHAPTER 9 | CHAPTER 8 |

THE IMPACT OF YOUR GENETIC HISTORY

Abnormal brain function creates unstable mental and emotional states. A shortcut to reading the signals your body is giving you is to study the genetic history of your family. Filling out the "Genetic History" chart on page 39 will help you understand where and from whom these biological "gifts" have come. A recognition of your genetic history also proves useful in choosing the lab test that will be most helpful for you. Read the following instructions first before filling in your history.

To begin, record your paternal history on the left side of the chart and maternal history on the right. For each condition, list your immediate relatives (i.e., father, uncle) that apply, and then list what is specifically wrong (i.e., allergic to nuts, schizophrenic). Do not include relatives who are not *biologically related*. Before you fill out the list, review the paragraphs that follow so you will understand why these categories are important, and which of your relatives to list on the chart as bearers of the particular disorder(s).

NATIONALITY

You may not see your nationality as significant to your emotional complaint, but researchers have found some remarkable epidemiological patterns among certain groups. For example, the Irish seem to have more schizophrenia per capita than any other nationality. Scandinavians suffer from depression and have a high suicide rate. In the United States, the Midwestern states are known as the Goiter Belt because low levels of iodine in the soil create problems of hypothyroidism. The Irish, Welsh, Native Americans, Scottish, and Scandinavians seem to need extra prostaglandin E_1, a brain metabolite that lifts depression and creates a strong sense of well-being. Italians, Jews, and Native Americans are often vulnerable to diabetes. Northern Europeans have a greater susceptibility to alcoholism than southern Europeans, because northerners have used it for only fifteen hundred years, compared to more than seven thousand years of use for southerners. As Native Americans and Eskimos never had access to alcohol in their culture until a couple of hundred years ago, their vulnerability to alcoholism is very high— over 80 percent. (This is the "survival of the fittest" principle at work. In these instances, it works to eliminate, over many generations, those who were and are physically susceptible to alcohol's addiction and destruction.)

So be sure to list all known nationalities on both your paternal and maternal sides.

DEPRESSION

In addition to those relatives who sought formal treatment for their depression, also include the relatives who simply seemed to live with much inner sadness. Make sure to note any attempted or accomplished suicides here.

ANXIETY/PANIC ATTACKS

Some anxiety-riddled souls are so low-profile they are hard to identify. They avoid any and all stress like the plague. But if you can
identify them, list them here, as well as any others who may cling to
Valium or other tranquilizers, despite getting little relief.

VIOLENCE/UNPROVOKED ANGER

This kind of relative is easy to recognize. He or she seems to be in a
continual state of high arousal.

DIABETES OR HYPOGLYCEMIA

Few can identify serious blood glucose problems during the hypoglycemic years preceding diabetes. Still, look for the "sugarholics"—those who live on a six-pack of sugared colas daily or favor
junk-food diets laced with sugar. Eventually, the overproduction of
insulin this lifestyle triggers results in total exhaustion of insulin
supplies. At that point, blood sugar just keeps rising when carbohydrates are ingested, and full-blown diabetes is finally diagnosed.

MENTAL ILLNESS

This category would include relatives exhibiting symptoms of a nervous breakdown, schizophrenia, obsessive-compulsive disorders,
paranoia, or other ongoing abnormal mental states.

ALLERGIES

Take note of any relative who wheezes or sneezes around pollens,
dust, mold, or grasses. This is generally indicative of an allergy. Food
allergies often show themselves as addictions to certain foods. Chemical sensitivities to perfumes, formaldehyde, gasoline products, pesticides, and tobacco smoke usually run in families.

OBESITY/EATING DISORDERS

Look for relatives engaging in food bingeing and having weight problems leading to bulimia and/or anorexia. Young women are more
likely to become bulimic, but binge eating is a good sign of food
allergies/addiction in either sex at any age.

THYROID PROBLEMS

Low thyroid function shows itself as sluggishness, hair loss, weight
gain, and a slowness to warm up because of low body temperature. It

is a condition often found among members of the same family. Unfortunately, persons with similar amounts of energy usually tend to pair off in marriage, helping to perpetuate the high incidences of this trait.

ALCOHOL ADDICTION

Science has recognized the physical and genetic status of this disease for decades. To make an educated guess about some of the drinkers in your family, use this simple criterion: Does he or she have an unusually high tolerance for alcohol? Alcoholics perform better on alcohol, which energizes, not sedates them. The alcoholic feels a euphoria that non-alcoholics don't feel. Those who can and do put away a lot of drinks are most likely to have problematic chemistry, and over time their tolerance increases more and more.

GENETIC HISTORY

Paternal	Maternal
Nationality:	Nationality:
Depression (including manic depression):	Depression (including manic depression):
Anxiety / panic attacks:	Anxiety / panic attacks:
Violence / unprovoked anger:	Violence / unprovoked anger:
Diabetes or hypoglycemia:	Diabetes or hypoglycemia:
Mental illness:	Mental illness:
Allergies (foods or chemicals):	Allergies (foods or chemicals):
Obesity / eating disorders:	Obesity / eating disorders:
Thyroid problems:	Thyroid problems:
Alcohol addiction:	Alcohol addiction:
Other:	Other:

DETERMINE YOUR BODY'S WARNING SIGNS

Now that you have pondered the disease states that have surfaced in your family tree, it is time to look closely at *your* own life patterns.

The chart A History of My Symptoms (page 41) will make you aware of your own problematic symptoms and how enduring they have been in your life. Over half our clients, when questioned as to when they first saw signs of their symptoms, trace them back to their teens! That's because often this is the most destructive time of our lives nutritionally. Teens *live* on cola and junk food. I have seen many college students who became increasingly emotionally unstable, started failing in school, and lost their ability to function normally even before the end of their freshman year because they were literally living on refined sugars and take-out junk food. Being away from home and on their own for the first time and coping with college-level classes can create far too much stress and anxiety in a person whose brain chemistry is already precariously balanced. Thus the teen years are often the time that the first signs of emotional instability begin to appear.

In the next chapter you will learn specifically what "emotional" symptoms develop as a result of shortages of common vitamins, minerals, essential fatty acids, and amino acids. You will come to understand how systematically ignoring your nutritional needs may, over time, produce a wildly unstable person. Depending on how little reserve one has of certain life-giving elements, the resulting changes can range from panic attacks to exhaustion, from rage to suicidal ideation. For now, use your symptoms chart to confirm how your own symptoms have lingered and grown as your shortages of important natural chemicals worsened over the years.

Some of you may have taken medication to ease your symptoms. I won't deny that prescription drugs can be a short-term blessing when quick relief is needed. But the next step is to *eliminate for good* the cause(s) of your woes. In the chapters ahead, we will get to specifics about your individual biochemical needs. Right now, you'll obtain immediate benefits by starting to create a base of essential nutrients on which to build your emotional stability program.

A HISTORY OF MY SYMPTOMS

	Teens 10 to 20	Young Adults 20–30	PrimeTime Adults 30 to 40	MiddleAged Adults 40 to 50	Senior Adults 55 & Over
Depression or Manic Depression					
Thought Confusion					
Lack of Energy/ Fatigue					
Anxiety/ Inner Tension					
Irritability/ Uncontrolled Anger					
Suspicion/ Paranoia					
Poor Memory & Concentration					
Abrupt Mood Changes					
Cravings for Sugar, Food, or Alcohol					

Note: Put an X in each period of your life where the above symptoms were present.

Setting the Stage:
Basic Emotional Stability

Today, over 125 million Americans—more than half the population—take prescription drugs routinely, and many of these drugs interfere with the absorption and metabolism of essential nutrients. On top of this, few Americans eat a well-balanced diet. A recent USDA food consumption survey on twenty thousand people reveals that *none* of them consumed 100 percent of the recommended daily allowance for all the major nutrients. (This is made even worse when we remember Dr. Linus Pauling's comment that the RDA is "only enough to keep people barely alive in ordinary poor health"!)

The recommended daily allowance levels are barely adequate to prevent vitamin deficiency diseases such as scurvy (vitamin C deficiency) and beriberi (vitamin B_1 deficiency) in healthy people. And they seriously underestimate the needs of people suffering from depression, anxiety, dementia, schizophrenia, and other chronic and degenerative diseases.

Unfortunately, no one has ever recorded or documented the RDAs of people in pathological states. RDAs have only been set "for normal or average" persons (whatever that means).

So, if you live on a typical American junk-food diet, it is probable that you are far more undernourished than you suspect!

At Health Recovery Center (HRC), we often see, through hair analysis tests, that mineral levels are very low across the board. This is a certain sign of poor absorption and/or poor eating habits. Vitamins, minerals, amino acids, enzymes, and essential fatty acids must interact with each other to be properly utilized; no one substance works all by itself.

To correct these deficiencies, our approach has always been to start with a basic repair formula and then to add more potent levels of certain natural chemicals as lab tests confirm the need.

Unfortunately, except for amino acids, most natural substances do *not* act as quickly as drugs. They build more slowly, over days, weeks, or even months in people with poor absorption. But I can promise that the rewards of participating in this grand experiment to fine-tune your brain will prove a very pleasant surprise. As for your timetable, I am used to clients poking their heads in my office only a week or two into their new regimen to announce that their changes are unmistakable and they are ecstatic.

Is the Formula Safe?

The Balanced Emotions Basic Formula (on page 43) that I have designed for each and every one of you consists of a combination of amino acids, vitamins, minerals, and other nutrients that will provide the nourishment you need to establish a high level of health. For almost two decades I have used these substances with clients at these dosages with very few, if any, problems, and much measurable improvement. All of the substances in the following nutrient program are natural; your body already depends on them for life and

THE BALANCED EMOTIONS
BASIC FORMULA©

Nutrient	Dose	Directions
Free-form amino complex	700 mg	2 capsules at least ½ hour before breakfast 2 capsules at least ½ hour before supper
Tryptophan*	500 mg	2–4 capsules, ½ hour before bedtime
Vitamin C (Ester C)	675 mg	2 capsules with breakfast 2 capsules with supper
Multivitamin/mineral		2 capsules with breakfast 2 capsules with supper
Antioxidant complex		2 capsules with breakfast 2 capsules with supper
Cold-water Fish (EPA) (Omega-3 Fatty Acids)	360 mg	1 capsule with breakfast 1 capsule with supper
Gamma-Linolenic Acid (GLA) (Omega-6 Fatty Acids)	300 mg	1 capsule daily with food
Pancreatic enzymes	1,000 mg per capsule	1–2 capsules with breakfast 1–2 capsules with lunch 1–2 capsules with supper
Betaine HCl †	680 mg	1–2 capsules with breakfast 1–2 capsules with lunch 1–2 capsules with supper

Note: If you are already taking any of the above nutrients, do not exceed the amounts for your total dosage (see chart page 56).

Tryptophan is available by prescription in the United States and Canada. Your doctor can order it only from certain pharmacies. The two that we use are: Hopewell Pharmacy 1-800-792-6670 or College Pharmacy 1-800-888-9358.

† *Take only after determining need; see page 54, "Hydrochloric Acid Test."*

© *Copyright 1999 Health Recovery Center.™ All Rights Reserved.*

health. In fact, you'll find nutrient therapy is extremely safe, and especially so when compared to drug therapy.

Just look at these statistics, which were gathered between 1983 and 1987 and published in the *Journal of the American Medical Association* (January 1997):

- 0 deaths from nutritional therapy
- 1,132 deaths from prescription drugs used *correctly*, and 337 more deaths from over-the-counter aspirin and painkillers

Now, over ten years later, *JAMA* reports that *140,000 deaths occur annually from adverse drug reactions.* The same has not been true of nutrient therapy.

Note: Please bear in mind that when I constructed the HRC formulas, I did so with the best ingredients manufacturers could supply, knowing I'd have to watch the progress (or failure) of each client. I have consistently seen these formulas work. I know by continued observation and improved modifications that they *do* deliver what we expect. That's why today we at HRC send them out worldwide, from Singapore to Iceland. The easiest way to access whatever you will need from these formulas is to call our center at 800-247-6237.

The Balanced Emotions Basic Formula

Let me briefly explain about each substance in the formula so that you know what these nutrients are and are comfortable adding them to your diet.

AMINO ACIDS

Amino acids are getting the attention of newspapers across the country as science discovers their amazing roles in our brains and bodies. They are the building blocks of protein and the chief components of the brain's nutrition. Your central nervous system is almost entirely regulated by amino acids, but science is only just now beginning to understand how imbalances and shortages of them create "mental" illnesses such as depression, aggression, hostile behavior, anxiety, and paranoia.

All of the amino acids you will be taking in our program have therapeutic potential in regulating brain function. Each capsule contains eighteen separate free-form aminos, which is the preferred form for easiest absorption, and each capsule contains 700 milligrams.

This blend of amino acids has been developed and tested for several years at Health Recovery Center. We and our clients have been impressed with the results that loading amino acids produces in improving moods, memory, feelings, and energy.

For best absorption, these capsules should be taken on an empty stomach. An explanation of each amino's potential will be found in Chapter 4. Suffice it to say that entire books are being written extolling the effects of these magical substances. My favorite is *The Healing Nutrients Within* by Eric Braverman, M.D.

WARNING: If you have systemic lupus, erythematosus, are on methadone therapy, or have certain rare inborn genetic errors in amino acid metabolism (for example, phenylketonuria, or PKU), DO NOT take amino acids except under a doctor's supervision.

TRYPTOPHAN

Tryptophan is an essential amino acid that the human body can't manufacture itself. The brain uses it to produce the neurotransmitter serotonin, which maintains emotional calm, regulates sleep, and prevents depression. Suicidal patients show significant decreases in serotonin levels, and autopsies have shown that a very low brain level of serotonin is one biological marker to suicide. People who are depressed or agitated can often use tryptophan as effectively as antidepressants.

You may remember all the publicity surrounding the removal of tryptophan from the market in 1989 (see page 27). The FDA acted after several deaths and illnesses were traced to contaminated batches of the amino from Japan. The investigation of the exact nature of the chemical contaminant responsible was completed, but so far there has been no indication of when the FDA will permit the reintroduction of over-the-counter tryptophan (it has only approved 5HTP, which for the reasons cited earlier I do *not* recommend); the FDA has now allowed the sale of tryptophan by prescription only. Your doctor can order it only from certain pharmacies. The two we use are: Hopewell Pharmacy, 1-800-792-6670, and College Pharmacy, 1-800-888-9358.

VITAMIN C (ESTER C)

The newest form of vitamin C has been named Ester C. It enters the bloodstream twice as fast, penetrates the cell walls more efficiently, and is held in the body twice as long as the ascorbate form of vitamin C. It is also buffered with calcium to be easy on your stomach. Today, vitamin C is the most popular vitamin supplement in the United States.

Vitamin C is a powerful detoxifier. At high-dose levels, it kills invading viruses and bacteria. At 200 grams daily intravenously, it has cured hepatitis and the mononucleosis virus within days, according to researcher Fred Klenner, M.D. Almost every animal on our planet manufactures its own ascorbate, except humans. Mankind lost that luxury somewhere in our early development. A serious depletion of vitamin C results in frequent infections, fatigue, and "mental" disorders such as depression. In earlier centuries, scurvy was a common killer before we came to understand the body's need for vitamin C. Ascorbate is one of the least toxic substances known. Linus Pauling tells us, "People have ingested 125 grams at one time with no harm." He notes that, while it has been suggested that a high intake of vitamin C can cause kidney stones, "not a single case of such kidney stones exists in medical literature."

How much vitamin C a person can take by mouth is limited by the onset of diarrhea. The level at which this occurs is called "bowel tolerance," and it differs, depending on your state of health. If you are treating a virulent flu, you may load 50 to 75 grams of vitamin C with no sign of diarrhea. But on a healthy day, you may find you reach bowel tolerance at only 12 grams.

Vitamin C has been our most powerful weapon in detoxifying our clients at Health Recovery Center, whether it is against drugs, alcohol, or viral or bacterial problems. There is no better safeguard against disease than adequate amounts of vitamin C in your body.

MULTIVITAMINS/MINERALS

The following formula is used at HRC. It is the best combination of vitamins and minerals we can offer our clients. This combination contains no yeast, corn, soy, dairy products, preservatives, or chemical dilutants. Every mineral is chelated to (combined with) an amino acid to greatly increase absorption. (*Note:* If you choose to buy one of the multivitamin formulas currently on the market, make sure the doses are comparative and that the minerals are chelated for absorption.)

CONTENTS OF OUR MULTIVITAMIN-MINERAL CAPSULES

Nutrient	Dose per 2 capsules	Dose per 4 capsules
Vitamin A (palmitate)	4,000 IU	8,000 IU
Vitamin B_1 (thiamine)	50 mg	100 mg
Vitamin B_2 (riboflavin)	25 mg	50 mg
Vitamin B_3 (niacinamide)	50 mg	100 mg
Vitamin B_5 (pantothenic acid)	100 mg	200 mg
Vitamin B_6 (pyridoxine)	50 mg	100 mg
Vitamin B_{12} (cobalamine)	100 mcg	200 mcg
Folic acid	150 mcg	300 mcg
Biotin	80 mcg	160 mcg
PABA (para-aminobenzoic acid)	40 mg	80 mg
Vitamin D_3	30 mg	60 mg
Vitamin E (DL-alpha-tocopherol acetate)	80 IU	160 IU
+ Calcium (carbonate/citrate)*	100 mg	200 mg
+ Magnesium (magnesium oxide)	100 mg	200 mg
+ Potassium (potassium chloride)	95 mg	190 mg
+ Manganese (manganese sulfate)	3 mg	6 mg
+ Zinc (zinc sulfate)	6 mg	12 mg
+ Boron	100 mcg	200 mcg
+ Copper (copper sulfate)	300 mcg	600 mcg
+ Selenium (sodium selenite)	60 mcg	120 mcg
+ Vanadium (vanadium pentoxide)	40 mcg	80 mcg

Nutrient	Dose per 2 capsules	Dose per 4 capsules
+ Molybdenum (sodium molybdate)	40 mcg	80 mcg
+ Chromium picolinate (amino acid chelate)	60 mcg	120 mcg
Bioflavonoids	20 mg	40 mg
Choline	20 mg	40 mg
Inositol	10 mg	20 mg
Hesperidin	5 mg	10 mg
Iodine (kelp)	50 mcg	100 mcg
Rutin	5 mg	10 mg
Octacosanol	50 mcg	100 mcg
Betaine HCl	10 mg	20 mg
Papain (papaya)	5 mg	10 mg
Lipase	2 mg	4 mg
Bromelain	5 mg	10 mg
Licorice root	10 mg	20 mg

* Plus sign (+) means mineral is chelated with glutamine for increased absorption.

A word about the B complex vitamins in the multivitamins formula above: The B vitamins in this formula are particularly valuable. B vitamins play a vital role in maintaining a stable nervous system and a balanced brain, and a deficiency of these vitamins can have severe effects on your body. Here are some highlights:

- *Thiamine* (B$_1$): The loss of thiamine causes neurological damage, such as numbness and tingling in the arms and legs, as well as many mental symptoms, including memory loss, mental confusion, nervousness, headaches, and poor concentration. Severe deficiency causes beriberi or Wernicke-Korsakoff syndrome, an irreversible brain deterioration seen in alcoholism.
- *Niacin* (B$_3$): Abram Hoffer, M.D., a pioneer in niacin research, notes that symptoms of anxiety neurosis are strikingly similar to those that occur in *mild*-niacin deficiency (subclinical pellagra). These include: depression, fatigue, apprehension, headache, hyperactivity, and insomnia.

- *Pyridoxine* (B_6): We use B_6 for the formation of fifty different enzymes. B_6 is essential to metabolize all the amino acids and convert them into neurotransmitters. It is also vital for maintaining a stable immune system. Deficiency results in anxiety, nervousness, and depression. A severe lack of B_6 can bring on convulsions, severe anxiety, and extreme nervous exhaustion.
- *Pantothenic acid* (B_5): B_5 plays a major role in adrenal function. It has long been called the antistress vitamin. In one study, prison volunteers who were deliberately fed a diet lacking pantothenic acid became increasingly irritable, depressed, tense, dizzy, sullen, and quarrelsome. All symptoms disappeared when this nutrient was resupplied.
- *Folic acid:* Symptoms of deficiency are agitation, moodiness, headaches, depression, and fatigue. A severe deficiency affects libido (sex drive).
- *B_{12}:* Cobalamin depletion causes difficulty in concentration and memory, and a stuporous type of depression. Many emotional disorders, including insanity, result from a severe B_{12} deficiency. B_{12} is poorly absorbed in people over fifty. Weekly injections make a huge difference in the lives of many people.
- *Inositol:* This B vitamin is required for the proper action of brain neurotransmitters such as serotonin and acetylcholine. Thus, low inositol levels induce depression. Furthermore, inositol has been shown to be effective in stopping panic disorders. Unlike drugs, this water-soluble vitamin has no significant side effects.
- *Choline:* This improves learning capacity and protects against memory problems.

Before we move on, let me remind you that all of the trace elements included in this multivitamin/mineral formula are essential for life. *Our emotional and physical well-being depends on the availability of the proper amounts of these substances.* The chart Minerals That Affect the Brain (page 50) shows the roles some of the minerals have in the body and how their deficiencies seriously affect the brain and nervous system. In the following chapters we will delve into the signs and symptoms of mineral depletion in the body, but in the lab, hair analysis is an excellent way of determining mineral and toxic metal levels.

MINERALS THAT AFFECT THE BRAIN

Nutrient	Effect on the Body	Deficiency
Chromium	Regulates blood sugar	Hypoglycemia, diabetic neuropathy
Copper	Neurotransmitter control	Neurological problems, anemia, hypothyroidism, weakness
Zinc	Controls smell and taste	Lethargy, anxiety, pyroluria (zinc & B_6 deficiency), loss of taste & smell, hypogonadism
Iron	Energy production	Neurological problems, poor memory, depression, poor concentration
Magnesium	Neurotransmitter control	Nervous exhaustion, anxiety, depression, insomnia, tremors

ANTIOXIDANT COMPLEX

The role of antioxidants in the body has only recently been fully understood. Oxidation ages us and irreversibly damages the intricate workings of our brains. Brain cell membranes are the most susceptible to *lipid* peroxidation. This type of damage comes from exposure to toxic fumes from paint, cigarette smoke, gasoline, cleaning fluids, solvents, rancid food, and chemicals of all sorts. Certain vitamins (B_6, C, E, A), minerals (selenium, zinc), aminos (glutathione, methionine, cysteine, dimethylglycine), and herbs (gingko, silymarin) can protect the body's cells and nerves from being damaged by oxidation. In general, such antioxidants slow the aging process and protect our mental faculties against deterioration. Antioxidants are also our first line of defense in protecting us against cancer and heart attacks. The following shows the contents in the capsules at Health Recovery Center.

CONTENT OF OUR ANTIOXIDANT COMPLEX CAPSULES

Nutrient	Dose per 2 capsules	Dose per 4 capsules
Beta-carotene	20,000 IU	40,000 IU
Vitamin E	150 IU	300 IU
N, N Dime- thylglycine	200 mg	400 mg
Vitamin C	200 mg	400 mg
L-Cysteine	200 mg	400 mg
Silymarin	200 mg	400 mg
Glutathione	120 mg	240 mg
Methionine	100 mg	200 mg
B_6 (pyridoxal 5 phosphate)	20 mg	40 mg
Zinc	20 mg	40 mg
Selenium	150 mcg	300 mcg
Co-enzyme Q 10	20 mg	40 mg

OMEGA-3 FATTY ACIDS

Essential fatty acids (EFAs) are required for our survival, but they are not produced by our bodies. We have to ingest them. Unfortunately, the average diet has few foods that are high in omega-3 fatty acids (cold-water-fish oils, certain seeds, and green leafy vegetables). Also, the food industry removes omega-3 fatty acids whenever possible—they become rancid easily—and replaces them with hydrogenated oils. Researcher Donald Rudin has documented the declining intake of omega-3 fatty acids in the twentieth century, and correlated it to the sharp increase in such modern illnesses as cardiovascular disease! In 1982 a Nobel Prize in Medicine was awarded for the discovery of how the metabolism of omega-3 EFAs help to prevent heart problems.

The role of omega-3 fatty acids in the brain is impressive. We need it for steroid hormone production, for immune system functioning, and for the neural actions that affect our thinking and moods. Besides helping to regulate body temperature, it serves as the messenger for all hormone secretions as well as the uptake of those B vitamins that stabilize our emotions.

Cold-water-fish oils—from salmon, tuna, and cod—are not likely to be eaten daily. But taking those oils in capsule form is just as effective.

EPA (eicosapentaenoic acid) omega-3 capsules are preferred over

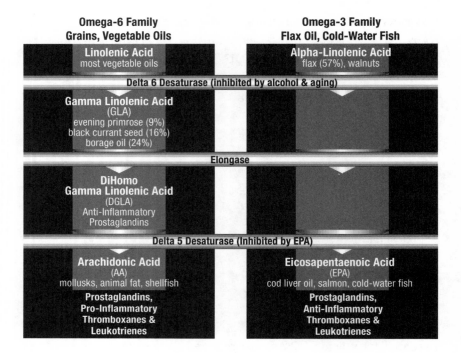

Omega-6 Family Grains, Vegetable Oils	Omega-3 Family Flax Oil, Cold-Water Fish
Linolenic Acid most vegetable oils	**Alpha-Linolenic Acid** flax (57%), walnuts
Delta 6 Desaturase (inhibited by alcohol & aging)	
Gamma Linolenic Acid (GLA) evening primrose (9%) black currant seed (16%) borage oil (24%)	
Elongase	
DiHomo Gamma Linolenic Acid (DGLA) Anti-Inflammatory Prostaglandins	
Delta 5 Desaturase (Inhibited by EPA)	
Arachidonic Acid (AA) mollusks, animal fat, shellfish	**Eicosapentaenoic Acid** (EPA) cod liver oil, salmon, cold-water fish
Prostaglandins, Pro-Inflammatory Thromboxanes & Leukotrienes	**Prostaglandins, Anti-Inflammatory Thromboxanes & Leukotrienes**

flax or flax oils for many people, since the conversion of flax's ALA (alpha-linolenic acid) into EPA is blocked in people with low levels of delta 6 desaturase. Individuals of Scandinavian or Celtic ancestry and Native Americans, as well as alcoholics and those with the markers found in the chart on page 41, are likely candidates for this flaw.

With this glitch, the omega-3 chain of conversion breaks down, so the brain never gets enough omega-3 fatty acids to provide adequate mood regulation, or control hormone levels, and to stabilize emotions.

Fish oil capsules are easy to take but are dependent on adequate stomach acid (HCL) for easy digestion. If you find yourself burping fish oil, it means you need more hydrochloric acid (see page 54 for determining amount).

OMEGA 6 (GAMMA-LINOLENIC ACID)

Gamma-linolenic acid (GLA) is the other "good" oil that many people lack. Despite the high fat intake in our diets today, the conversion in the brain of GLA to the important prostaglandins is often inadequate, and the result can be disastrous. Dr. David Horrobin, GLA researcher at the Institute for Innovative Medicine in Montreal, has found that inadequate levels of prostaglandin E_1, which is made in the brain from GLA, can produce auto-immune disease, inflammatory disorders, coronary thrombosis, spasm types of heart attacks, angina, and serious depression.

For the past ten years, the Health Recovery Center has promptly eliminated the type of suicidal depression that PGE_1 deficiency creates in clients who claimed to have tried everything with no success. (In Chapter 6, I will describe clues to look for in yourself to determine this deficiency if you are experiencing depression.)

PANCREATIC ENZYMES

If your pancreas fails to deliver adequate digestive enzymes to your intestinal tract, your absorption of fats and proteins will be gravely impaired. Even the uptake of B vitamins will partially suffer. The old saying "You are what you eat" really should be updated to "You are what you *absorb*." This entire program rests on that premise.

BETAINE HYDROCHLORIDE

Insufficient stomach acid is another reason why nutrients are not absorbed. This can be a significant health problem. More people have too low gastric acidity than too much stomach acid, and this deficiency shows itself by the following symptoms:

- feeling bloated after eating (waist expands)
- gas or belching immediately after a meal
- nausea after taking supplements
- indigestion
- diarrhea or constipation
- fingernails are weak and peeling
- adult acne
- undigested food in stools
- iron deficiency

Low stomach acidity is common in older people and in those with food allergies, candidiasis, hepatitis, lupus, frequent hives, pernicious anemia, rosacea, eczema, diabetes, autoimmune disorders, and alcoholism.

A note about antacid intake: Some people feel they have too much stomach acid and take antacids. If this is you, please be careful because *you are seriously interfering with the absorption of the minerals from your foods.* Antacids also block pancreatic enzyme release, so they ultimately interfere with almost all nutrient absorption. *Of course, those who are concerned about heartburn or other evidence of too much stomach acidity should not take hydrochloric acid (HCl).*

To determine whether your body produces sufficient HCl acid, take the following test.

HYDROCHLORIC ACID TEST

1. Start with one HCl capsule—10 grains—with a full meal. If you notice a tingling pain or a burning sensation in your stomach *you do not need hydrochloric acid.*
2. If there are no reactions, after two days of taking a single capsule with meals, increase the number of capsules with each meal to two.
3. Continue increasing every two days, taking up to ten capsules at a time, if necessary. Cut back by one capsule per meal when you reach a state of tingling or other discomfort, such as a sensation of heaviness or a feeling of warmth in the stomach or lower sternum. *Note:* These dosages may seem large, but a normally functioning stomach manufactures considerably more.
4. Once you have established a dose (ten capsules, or less if warmth or heaviness occurs), continue this dose.
5. With smaller meals, you may require less HCl, so you may reduce the number of capsules taken.

Individuals with a very moderate HCl deficiency generally show rapid improvement in symptoms and have early signs of intolerance (tingling, burning, heaviness, warmth) to the acid. This typically indicates a return to normal acid secretion.

Individuals with hydrochloric acid deficiency typically do not respond as well to supplements, so to maximize the absorption and benefits of the nutrients you take, it is important to be consistent with your HCl supplementation.

WARNING: *If, at any time, you experience a burning sensation, discontinue HCl supplementation. Administration of HCl is contraindicated in people with peptic ulcer disease. Also, HCl can irritate sensitive tissue and can be corrosive to teeth; therefore, capsules should not be emptied into food or dissolved in beverages.*

When you have adequate HCl, you will have good absorption of all your nutrients, and you can then watch the rapid regeneration of health in every system of your body.

Keeping Track of Your Nutrient Use

Now's the time to familiarize yourself with the Nutrient Replacement List (page 56), which will help you keep track of every nutrient you're taking. In the weeks ahead, you will probably find other formulas that are right for you and the list of nutrients that you are taking will grow. If you simply follow these easy instructions, you will have no trouble keeping track of what you take so that you never exceed recommended intakes:

1. *To add a nutrient,* find it on the nutrient replacement list. If it is not there, enter it in the blank space provided at the end of the list.
2. *If you already are taking a nutrient called for in one of the formulas,* increase the amount you presently take to the **level of the new formula. DO NOT ADD THE FULL FORMULA DOSE TO WHAT YOU ARE ALREADY TAKING.** Here is an example: Your vitamin/mineral formula includes a daily dose of 100 milligrams of B_6. The formula for pyroluria calls for a B_6 intake of 250 milligrams. So rather than start taking 350 milligrams (250 mg plus 100 mg), you should be taking 250 milligrams—the new higher level of the new formula.
3. *If a formula calls for the **same dose** of a nutrient you already take,* remember not to double the amount. Your current dose should serve the purpose.

Bear in mind that what may seem a high dose to you, is a *needed level* for certain brains. We have monitored such situations for twenty years, and I assure you that erring on the side of *too little* rather than *too much* will be far more disappointing to you.

THE HRC NUTRIENT REPLACEMENT LIST

Combination Total	Nutrient	Daily Dose Limit*
_____	Free-form amino acids (700 mg)	2,800 mg
_____	Tryptophan‡ (500 mg)	1,000 mg to 3,000 mg
_____	Vitamin (Ester) C† (675 mg)	as determined by need
_____	GLA (300 mg)	900 mg
_____	Omega-3 EFA (cold-water fish) (360 mg)	1,080 mg
_____	Pancreatic enzymes (500 mg)	3,000 mg
_____	Betaine HCl (680 mg)	as determined by need
_____	Glutamine (500 mg)	3,000 mg
_____	Niacinamide† (450 mg)	400 mg to 500 mg
_____	Melatonin (3 mg)	3 mg to 6 mg

MULTIPLE VITAMIN & MINERAL

TOTAL	FOUR CAPSULES CONTAIN	DAILY DOSE LIMIT*
_____	Vitamin A (palmitate)	8000 IU
_____	Vitamin B_1 (thiamine)	100 mg
_____	Vitamin B_2 (riboflavin)	50 mg
_____	Niacinamide†	100 mg
_____	D-Calcium Pantothenate	200 mg
_____	Vitamin B_6 (pyridoxine HCl)	100 mg
_____	Vitamin B_{12} (cyanocobalamin)	200 mcg
_____	Folic Acid	300 mcg

TOTAL	FOUR CAPSULES CONTAIN	DAILY DOSE LIMIT*
_____	Biotin	160 mcg
_____	PABA	80 mg
_____	Vitamin E (d-alphatocopheryl)	160 IU
_____	D$_3$	60 IU
_____	Calcium (95% carbonate/ 5% citrate)	200 mg
_____	Magnesium (amino acid chelate)	200 mg
_____	Potassium (amino acid chelate)	180 mg
_____	Manganese (amino acid chelate)	6 mg
_____	Zinc (amino acid chelate)[†]	12 mg
_____	Boron (amino acid chelate)	200 mcg
_____	Copper (amino acid chelate)	600 mcg
_____	Selenium methionine	120 mcg
_____	Vanadium (amino acid chelate)	80 mcg
_____	Molybdenum (amino acid chelate)	80 mcg
_____	Chromium picolinate (amino acid chelate)	120 mcg
_____	Bioflavonoids	40 mg
_____	Choline	40 mg
_____	Inositol	20 mg
_____	Hesperidin	10 mg
_____	Iodine (kelp)	100 mcg
_____	Rutin	10 mg
_____	Octacosanol	100 mcg
_____	Betaine HCl	20 mg
_____	Papain (papaya)	10 mg
_____	Lipase	4 mg
_____	Bromelain	10 mg
_____	Licorice root	20 mg

ANTIOXIDANT COMPLEX

TOTAL	FOUR CAPSULES CONTAIN	DAILY DOSE LIMIT*
_____	Beta-carotene	40,000 IU
_____	Vitamin E (d-alphatocopheryl)	300 IU
_____	N,N Dimethylglycine	400 mg
_____	Vitamin C (calcium ascorbate)[†]	400 mg

TOTAL	FOUR CAPSULES CONTAIN	DAILY DOSE LIMIT*
_____	L-cysteine	400 mg
_____	Silymarin (milk thistle extract)	400 mg
_____	Glutathione	240 mg
_____	Methionine	200 mg
_____	B$_6$ (pyridoxal-5 phosphate)§	40 mg
_____	Zinc picolinate†	40 mg
_____	Selenium	300 mcg
_____	Co-enzyme Q10	40 mg

ADDITIONAL NUTRIENTS

_____

_____

_____

_____

_____

_____

_____

_____

_____

_____

_____

_____

_____

* See point #2, page 55.
† This nutrient appears more than once on this chart. Please be sure to take the *highest amount* called for by any one formula. Do NOT add up all the dosages.
‡ Tryptophan is available by prescription only.
§ B$_6$ converts into pyridoxal-5 phosphate; pyridoxal-5 phosphate is a form of B$_6$.

Practical Advice for Obtaining and Managing Your Nutrients

The nutrients used at Health Recovery Center are the best quality we can find. They are in capsules, rather than difficult-to-digest hard-pressed tablets. To obtain the ingredients in the Balanced Emotions Basic Formula and all other formulas in this book, call Bio-Recovery at 1-800-247-6237.

If you are traveling, the easiest way to carry your nutrients is in a plastic dispenser, which we will send with your nutrients at no charge. You should take your amino acids one half hour before breakfast and supper. For your noon meal, you need to carry only your digestive enzymes and HCl, if needed. If you will be away for breakfast or supper, pack your aminos (2), vitamin C (2), multivitamin/minerals (2), antioxidant (2), GLA (1), pancreatic enzymes (1 or 2), EFA (1), in your plastic dispenser compartments, and you won't miss a beat. Tryptophan should be taken before bedtime.

Optimizing Your Program

You are now ready to swing into action. Consider yourself the star of an experiment that will benefit *you*. With balanced brain chemicals, you can and will create superior mental and emotional health.

As we move into the healing weeks ahead, be patient and open-minded. It takes time to identify and alter the causes of your imbalances, and it takes perseverance on your part to assimilate these concepts and put them to proper use. Physical/emotional imbalances often seem to affect us spiritually, in that we may feel disconnected from our deeper selves when we are biochemically out of "sync." So let me make a few general suggestions:

- Start exercising one half hour every day—or at least every other day.
- Take time to relax.
- Commune with nature through some outdoor activity—take up gardening or go for a walk.

- Take time each day to be still and meditate, or pray, or just to feel your connection to all of life everywhere.
- Remember that your thoughts affect your health, so choose to expect the best.
- And, of course: start taking the Balanced Emotions Basic Formula.

CHAPTER 3

Feeding Your Famished Brain
How Diet Affects Emotions

P eg enjoyed a six-pack of cola daily and loved ice cream. She didn't correlate her dietary habits with her complaints of no energy and feeling weak, light-headed, shaky, and anxious. But the results of her five-hour test for hypoglycemia were spectacular—spectacularly abnormal, that is! Starting with a normal fasting level, her blood sugar rose within half an hour to the diabetic range and then came plunging down 175 points, putting her in a state of insulin shock. At the lowest point, Peg felt faint from weakness and dizziness and was overcome with confusion.

All of Peg's symptoms disappeared once she began a diet that corrected her acute response to refined sugars.

Paul was on Prozac but experiencing little relief from his moodiness and anxiety. He lived on coffee and cigarettes all day long, interspersed with cans of cola. His concentration was so poor, he could no longer read a book. Paul's wife accompanied him during his appointment to see me. Her concern was that his frequent mood swings and mental confusion were affecting his success as a salesman, as well as their family life. Paul loved sweets as snacks, and ate his only meal of the day at suppertime. When he was tested for hypoglycemia, the fall in his blood sugar was astonishing. As his brain lost its fuel (glucose), he began to experience all of the familiar symptoms—fatigue, headache, faintness, internal trembling, rapid pulse, and especially anxiety and confusion. After our consultation, Paul knew he was faced with a major

*overhaul in lifestyle. He willingly gave up caffeine, refined sugars,
and nicotine, and the trade-off has proved well worth the effort. He
loves having a stable brain and being on an even emotional keel.
He is thriving in his sales career, and once more is a hero at home.*

*Mary's complaints ranged from fatigue and anxiousness to
frequent crying and flying off the handle. Lab tests showed her
fasting glucose levels were low, which is not true for most hypoglycemics. After the sugar challenge, Mary lost even more brain
fuel, which gradually increased her light-headedness and disorientation. In her effort to supply her brain with glucose, Mary had
a daily regimen that included eight Mountain Dews and a high-
carbohydrate diet. But it was a battle she couldn't win until she
gave up refined sugars. For the next nine months she stayed on a
strict hypoglycemic diet. We retested her. Remarkably, her fasting
blood sugar rose to the normal range, and after the sugar challenge, her blood sugar dipped only slightly instead of falling pre-
cipitously. Most important, Mary's "emotional" symptoms had all
disappeared (along with twenty-five unneeded pounds!).*

*Tim came to HRC at the request of his employer. He had been
unable to work for six months due to anxiety, depression, dizziness, mental confusion, and insomnia. He was currently taking
two well-known antidepressants, to no avail. He complained of
trembling and feeling cold much of the time. Because his cholesterol was close to 300, Tim had received from his family doctor a
prescription to lower cholesterol. He refused to take it, knowing
that deaths among those using these drugs are significantly higher
than those refusing to take them. He informed me that he ate several candy bars and eight bananas every day. His grandmother
had diabetes. A five-hour glucose tolerance test for hypoglycemia
proved revealing. His blood sugar rose to prediabetic levels and
then plunged 150 points, leaving him anxious, shaking, light-
headed, and confused. That experience made Tim a believer. He
was willing to switch to a whole-foods diet and abandon all refined
sugars and caffeine. He exchanged his antidepressant drugs for
thyroid medication, which he needed, and the essential fatty acids
that lifted his depression. Within six weeks he was completely
free of his symptoms. Tim's high cholesterol also came down*

dramatically, despite his never having filled his anticholesterol prescription.

Years ago, as a busy young wife and mother of three, I [the author] often skipped meals. To make up for this, I snacked on cookies and mugs of coffee all day long for energy. Eventually I began to get "spells" of light-headedness. I felt anxious and jumpy. By early evening I hardly had enough go-power to make supper before collapsing. Finally, I saw several different physicians, seeking answers. None of them asked about my diet. Instead, I was given assorted prescriptions for tranquilizers and antianxiety drugs that only made me feel worse. One internist even told me I needed cortisone. His high-dose prescription sent me to the medical section of the public library for more facts. I discovered I could expect cortisone to bestow its usual symptoms: a round moon-face, a buffalo hump on my upper shoulders, and a very unstable mental state. As my original symptoms were still with me despite my use of cortisone, I quickly discontinued the prescription. At that point, this same medical doctor called my husband to advise him that if I would not continue his prescription, I should see a psychiatrist.

Fortunately, by that time I had found a book on hypoglycemia by endocrinologist Dr. John Tintera. As he described the symptoms of unstable glucose metabolism and its corresponding adrenal exhaustion, I felt as if I was reading my biography. His message was clear: no more cookies, sweet snacks, or caffeine. Clean up my act, or the medical doctors would have me drugged up and miserable.

I know how hard it is to get off refined sugars with no support. It's a miserable struggle! But just at that time in my life, my husband suddenly died from a heart attack. I knew then I had to have a clear head and some energy to support my three young children on my own.

So I found another M.D.—who himself was hypoglycemic— and he agreed to test me. My glucose level soared into the diabetic range and then plunged downward to insulin-shock levels. During this six-hour test I was trying to read, and after three hours I kept rereading the same lines over and over with no comprehension. The insight I got from that lab test saved me from becoming a lifelong diabetic. I immediately took the refined sugars out of my cupboards and my mouth. Slowly my light-headedness faded and my energy returned. My shakiness and loss of concentration disappeared. At a time when I had to work, go back to college, and raise my family, my brain was up to the task. It seemed like a miracle. I began to read extensively about hypoglycemia—and the rest is history!

What the Research Shows

Here, in a nutshell, are the facts: Our brains have two absolute requirements for energy, development, and survival: glucose and oxygen. Without oxygen being pumped to the brain, we would soon become mindless vegetables. With no glucose to fuel the brain, the effect is the same. As Govind Dhopeshwarkar, M.D., says in *Nutrition and Brain Development*: "Short disruptions in blood supply to the brain are either fatal or produce lasting damage. Even in the presence of adequate blood circulation, severe hypoglycemia (low level of blood sugar) produces similar effects."

The rise in popularity of processed sugars like sugar-coated cereals, cookies, colas, and candy bars has occurred quickly in the last half of the twentieth century, and our bodies' biochemistry hasn't adapted well. To understand how the symptoms of hypoglycemia can develop, you need to know how our glucose metabolism works. Our bodies convert *all* foods to glucose, but the change from refined sugars and white flours (starches) happens at a much faster rate. Ideally, when too much sugar floods the bloodstream, the pancreas pumps out just the right amount of extra insulin to counteract the overload. But if you have frequent, excessive meals or snacks of refined sugars and starches, your oversensitive pancreas gets trigger-happy and pours too much insulin too fast. That insulin removes too much sugar, causing your blood sugar levels to fall far below normal. And your brain does poorly on reduced glucose (fuel). You may develop headaches, feel anxious, irritable, tired, dizzy, confused, forgetful, uncoordinated, and unable to concentrate. You may even feel and act antisocial.

Eventually, as glucose levels drift downward, your body has to stop the fall. Otherwise you will plunge into deep shock—and if the drop were to continue with no interruption, you would die! Fortunately, the physical stress being produced will eventually release the adrenal hormone epinephrine. This hormone signals the liver to break down its emergency sugar, glycogen, into glucose and release it into the bloodstream. This sugar stops further insulin shock and protects your brain by providing emergency glucose. But the epinephrine (adrenaline) release brings its own unpleasant reactions. You may suddenly feel shaky, sweaty, and weak, and you may be aware of a rapid heartbeat. Caffeine produces these same symptoms and is associated with a temporary rise of blood sugar levels. This is the lift you demand every morning.

The seesawing of blood glucose all day long creates many uncomfortable symptoms, and most Americans interpret those signals as a need to grab a sweet snack or cola. Are some of the symptoms that appear in the list on page 66 familiar to you? They are from a research paper compiled by Stephen Gyland, M.D., based on his study of twelve hundred hypoglycemic patients.

Dr. Gyland himself experienced many of these symptoms as a young man beginning his medical practice. When he became so incapacitated that he could no longer work in medicine, he began a futile search for help from major medical centers across the United States, including the famed Mayo Clinic. Finally, he pieced together, on his own, the correct diagnosis of hypoglycemia, which he then verified with a six-hour glucose tolerance test.

If, when you finish a meal, you are still looking in the refrigerator for more, you are probably seeking something sweet because your high-carbo meal has set off a hypoglycemic drop in your blood sugar. A meal high in refined carbohydrates may induce "postprandial fed-state hypoglycemia," which triggers an intense craving for more sweets and/or coffee. This same postprandial hypoglycemia often triggers psychological symptoms. A 1982 report in *Biological Psychiatry* describes sixty-seven subjects given a glucose tolerance test who were measured throughout for psychological symptoms as a result of the loss of glucose in the nerve cells. Says this study, "Their mental stability, clarity, and agility were seriously affected if glucose levels fell below sixty mg per deciliter." This study concluded that "mental confusion does occur with postprandial hypoglycemia," and suggested that "those complaining of fatigue or depression one to four hours after meals have their blood sugar evaluated with a five-hour glucose test."

SYMPTOMS REPORTED BY HYPOGLYCEMICS*

Symptom	Frequency (%)
Nervousness	94
Irritability	89
Exhaustion	87
Faintness, dizziness, tremors, cold sweats	86
Depression	86
Vertigo, dizziness	77
Drowsiness	73
Headaches	72
Digestive disturbances	71
Forgetfulness	69
Insomnia	67
Constant worrying, unprovoked anxieties	62
Mental confusion	57
Internal trembling	57
Heart palpitations, rapid pulse	54
Muscle pains	53
Numbness	51
Indecisiveness	50
Antisocial behavior	47
Crying spells	46
Lack of sex drive (females)	44
Allergies	43
Uncoordination	43
Leg cramps	43
Lack of concentration	42
Blurred vision	40

Symptom	Frequency (%)
Muscle twitching & jerking	40
Itching & crawling skin sensations	39
Gasping for breath	37
Smothering spells	34
Staggering	34
Sighing & yawning	30
Impotence (males)	29
Unconsciousness	27
Nightmares, night terrors	27
Rheumatoid arthritis	24
Phobias, fears	23
Neurodermatitis (painful red skin rash)	21
Suicidal intent	20
Nervous breakdowns	17
Convulsions	2

*Taken from a study of 1,200 hypoglycemia patients by Stephen Gyland, M.D.

How Likely Is It That You Are Hypoglycemic?

Hypoglycemia is a word many medical doctors hate. Some call it a fad disease and refuse to do the lab tests necessary to prove or disprove your suspicions.

I have never been able to understand this block in their scientific thinking, especially since the American Medical Association awarded its Distinguished Medal of Honor to Seale Harris, M.D., in 1929 for the discovery of hypoglycemia. At that time, the sugar intake in the United States was modest. Now we are averaging, per person, 140 pounds per year, and our carbohydrate-sensitive (hypoglycemic) population is at an all-time high!

Even mental health professionals often fail to recognize hypoglycemic symptoms. They attempt to explain them as psychological phenomena. If you have puzzled over noticeable changes in your moods, thoughts, and feelings, don't be so quick to accept them as psychological disorders. Hypoglycemia *can* cause severe metabolic changes in your brain and nervous system, creating altered moods, emotional instability, and behavior changes. The HRC Hypoglycemic Symptometer on page 71 will help you evaluate your own symptoms and decide if you want to seek verification with a lab test.

Some of the items on the symptometer checklist are self-explanatory, but most need some clarification. *Be sure to read the following section clarifying the symptoms before beginning the test.*

1. *Unstable moods, frequent mood swings:* Frequent changes in mood are a symptom of hypoglycemia. As brain levels of glucose fluctuate, so do moods. But the mood changes that occur are in the course of *twenty-four hours*, in contrast to the mood swings of manic depression, which occur over weeks or months.

2. *Bad dreams, sleepwalking or -talking.* These are signs of low levels of vitamin B_6, which is destroyed in metabolizing refined sugars.

3. *Crying spells:* Self-explanatory.

4 and 5. *Blurred vision* and *frequent thirst:* These symptoms suggest diabetes; a five-hour glucose tolerance test is in order.

6–9. *Headaches, forgetfulness, muscle aches,* and *bingeing on sweets:* Self-explanatory.

10. *Confusion:* Difficulty in thinking clearly. Health Recovery Center clients have described this as feeling like they have to "think through peanut butter."

11. *Nervous stomach:* Heavy caffeine users often complain of this problem.

12. *Poor sleep, insomnia, etc.:* Difficulty falling asleep (insomnia); waking often during the night; not being able to fall asleep again easily.

13. *Nervous exhaustion, excessive fatigue:* This means feeling as if you are coming apart at the seams, or are strung out emotionally.

14. *Indecision:* Not being able to make up your mind about everyday matters.

15. *Can't work under pressure:* Self-explanatory.

16. *Craving for sweets:* Besides the obvious sweets, nondiet carbonated beverages often contain up to ten teaspoons of sugar. So if you're drinking a lot of these sodas, you may be satisfying an unrecognized craving for sweets.

17. *Depression:* This problem sometimes goes unrecognized, especially in men. Measure depression by asking yourself if, when you take your emotional temperature, you often feel sad inside.

18. *Feelings of suspicion, paranoia:* Hypoglycemics may experience these feelings as a result of altered brain chemistry.

19. *Light-headedness, dizziness:* These are symptoms of hypoglycemia; you may have noticed them in the late mornings or afternoons, when your blood sugar drifts too low. Some hypoglycemics also have abnormally low blood pressure and may feel light-headed when they stand up suddenly.

20. *Anxiety:* In this context, anxiety refers to an ongoing state rather than concern about specific events.

21. *Fearfulness:* Fear of people and places is usually rooted in the biochemical status of the brain.

22. *Tremors, shakes:* This means involuntary shaking.

23. *Night sweats:* This indicates exhausted adrenal glands due to the continual demands for emergency adrenaline to raise falling blood sugar levels.

24. *Heart palpitations:* Pounding heart or rapid pulse.

25. *Noticeable lift after one alcoholic drink:* Alcohol is more potent than other sugars, and acts faster to reach the brain and relieve hypoglycemic symptoms.

26. *Hunger after meals:* Self-explanatory.

27. *Antisocial feelings:* Avoidance of social situations, or feeling withdrawn around people.

28. *Irritability, sudden anger:* The sudden outpouring of adrenaline to stop the fall in blood sugar can, and does, trigger sudden irritability and anger.

29. *Lack of energy:* This is a common symptom of hypoglycemia.
30. *Magnifies insignificant events:* Think about whether you blow things out of proportion.
31. *Poor memory:* By this I mean short-term memory. Do you forget why you came looking for something? Do you continually have to write down appointments and make other notes to yourself? Sugar is a destroyer of vitamin B$_1$ (thiamine), a key nutrient for memory recall.
32. *Inability to concentrate:* Do you have trouble reading a book or sticking to a project?
33. *Sleepy after meals or late in the afternoon:* A meal should give you a lift, not make you sleepy. Sleepiness in the late afternoon may also be caused by declining glucose levels (hypoglycemia).
34. *Chronic worrier:* Self-explanatory.
35. *Difficulty awakening in the morning:* This problem occurs among nutritionally malnourished persons. (It may also be a symptom of low thyroid function.)

Instructions for scoring your symptometer appear at the top of the chart. Don't feel discouraged if your score is high; it is only a barometer of your *present* emotional and physical state. Once your specific problems are identified, we will get on with the job of repairing the damage. In fact, I expect many of you will score significantly high. You can then choose one of two courses:

1. Adopt the hypoglycemic diet and formula explained in this chapter and follow them faithfully for three weeks. You absolutely will be able to see your moods and energy gradually improving. With this approach you bypass the lab work but accomplish the same goal.
2. For those who need a powerful push to make changes, the reality of looking at the results of your own five-hour glucose tolerance test is invaluable. You can see the actual roller-coaster ups and downs you live with, and you can take heart that your unstable moods are a product of your chemistry, not your personality . . . and that it is, of course, correctable!

The HRC Hypoglycemic Symptometer

Instructions: Check off each symptom in one of the columns to indicate the degree of severity that applies to you. Zero means never, one means mild, two means moderate, and three means severe. Add up the number of the checks in each column and multiply each of those totals by the number printed at the top of each column. Your total score then equals the sum of all the column scores. (Scores over 35 are significant indicators of hypoglycemia.)

Symptom	Never 0	Mild 1	Moderate 2	Severe 3
1) Unstable moods, frequent mood swings	____	____	____	____
2) Bad dreams, sleepwalking or -talking	____	____	____	____
3) Crying spells	____	____	____	____
4) Blurred vision	____	____	____	____
5) Frequent thirst	____	____	____	____
6) Headaches	____	____	____	____
7) Forgetfulness	____	____	____	____
8) Muscle aches	____	____	____	____
9) Bingeing on sweets	____	____	____	____
10) Confusion	____	____	____	____
11) Nervous stomach	____	____	____	____
12) Poor sleep, insomnia, etc.	____	____	____	____
13) Nervous exhaustion, excessive fatigue	____	____	____	____
14) Indecision	____	____	____	____
15) Can't work under pressure	____	____	____	____
16) Craving for sweets	____	____	____	____
17) Depression	____	____	____	____
18) Feelings of suspicion, paranoia	____	____	____	____
19) Light-headedness, dizziness	____	____	____	____

Symptom	Never 0	Mild 1	Moderate 2	Severe 3
20) Anxiety	____	____	____	____
21) Fearfulness	____	____	____	____
22) Tremors, shakes	____	____	____	____
23) Night sweats	____	____	____	____
24) Heart palpitations	____	____	____	____
25) Noticeable lift after one alcoholic drink	____	____	____	____
26) Hunger after meals	____	____	____	____
27) Antisocial feelings	____	____	____	____
28) Irritability, sudden anger	____	____	____	____
29) Lack of energy	____	____	____	____
30) Magnifies insignificant events	____	____	____	____
31) Poor memory	____	____	____	____
32) Inability to concentrate	____	____	____	____
33) Sleepy after meals or late in the afternoon	____	____	____	____
34) Chronic worrier	____	____	____	____
35) Difficulty awakening in the morning	____	____	____	____

THE LAB TEST

At Health Recovery Center, we urge our clients to take the glucose tolerance test because actual lab evidence seems to propel clients into action better than if we force the diet on them with no scientific confirmation. However, if you are unable, financially or geographically, to take advantage of lab work, you should accept the written screen and move forward with the program. It will result in the same solution.

For those of you who want to take the lab test but find that your personal physician is unresponsive to your testing needs, the following national organizations make referrals of caring physicians in the United States and Canada:

American Holistic Medical Association (AHMA)
4101 Boone Trail
Raleigh, NC 27607
1-703-556-9728
(A list of AHMA physicians in your area will be mailed to you for a small donation.)

American College for Advancement in Medicine (ACAM)
23121 Verdugo Drive #204
Box 3427
Laguna Hills, CA 92654
1-714-583-7666
(A list of ACAM physicians in your area can be yours by sending a self-addressed, stamped envelope.)

For a list of orthomolecular physicians in Canada and the United States, contact the:

Journal of Orthomolecular Medicine
16 Florence Avenue
Toronto, Ontario M2N 1E9, Canada
1-416-733-2117

Glucose Tolerance Test Preparations

1. For three days before testing, eat your usual diet.
2. Do not take nutritional supplements for forty-eight hours before the test.
3. Do not eat or drink (except water) after 10:00 P.M. the night before the test.
4. Because cigarettes are cured with three different kinds of sugar, smoking invalidates test results. *Do not smoke* (or chew gum) before or during the test.
5. Be aware that various conditions will influence your test results:
    Conditions or medications that will INCREASE blood glucose levels: chlorpromazine, diuretics, epinephrine, general

anesthetics, indomethacin, marijuana, nicotine acid, ACTH, adrenal steroids, androgens, estrogens, glucagon, growth hormone, oral contraceptives, thyroid, emotional stress, infection, overfeeding, pregnancy, starvation followed by refeeding, aldosteronism, anacidity, arthritis, gastrectomy, hypertension, jejunectomy, liver disease, myocardial infarction, nephritis, obesity, pheochromocytoma, advanced age, coffee, prolonged inactivity, and smoking.

Conditions or medications that will DECREASE blood glucose levels: aspirin, barbiturates, bishydroxycoumarin, chloramphenicol, MAO inhibitors, oxyphenbutazone, phenylbutazone, phenyramidol, probenecid, propranolol HCl, propylthiouracil, fever, islet-cell tumors of the pancreas, Addison's disease, strenuous physical exercise, alcohol, Valium, Librium, and other benzodiazepams.

6. Bring this book with you so you can use the chart on this page to keep a record of any symptoms that occur during the test.
7. When the test is over, *and before you go home*, have some fruit or orange juice to restore your blood sugar levels.

HYPOGLYCEMIA TEST SYMPTOMS

	Fasting	½ Hour	1st Hour	2nd Hour	3rd Hour	4th Hour	5th Hour	6th Hour
Gasping for air								
Headaches								
Fatigue								
Shaky								
Irritable								
Anxious								
Weak								
Paranoia								
Depression								

	Fasting	½ Hour	1st Hour	2nd Hour	3rd Hour	4th Hour	5th Hour	6th Hour
Nervous								
Sweating								
Digestive disturbance								
Worrying								
Clumsiness								
Lack of concentration								
Suicidal thoughts								
Exhausted								
Heart palpitations								
Forgetfulness								
Ears ringing								
Restlessness								
Light-headedness								
Indecisiveness								
Cold hands/feet								
Blurred vision								
Joint pain								
Loss of appetite								
Sugar cravings								
Alcohol cravings								
Food cravings								
Other								

Glucose Patterns

The normal range of fasting blood sugar values (measuring only glucose and not saccharoids) is 70 to 100 milligrams. Most fasting blood sugars are within the normal range, so a simple fasting test taken after simply not eating the night before is useless.

Figure 1 on page 77 depicts the shape of a normal glucose tolerance test curve. You can use it to plot your own test numbers and then compare where your numbers fall to the normal range.

Figure 2 on page 78 shows other types of curves:

• *Diabetic.* To determine your risk level, add the first four figures from your test:

fasting _____
½ hour _____
1 hour _____
2 hour _____
TOTAL   _____

If the total is under 500, you are not diabetic. If the total is over 800, you are definitely diabetic. The group with numbers between 500 and 800 typically has problems with a delay in their production of insulin and being overweight. Their glucose curves may best respond to a nutritional (diet) adjustment and weight loss.

• *Prediabetic/hypoglycemic.* A sharp climb in blood sugar levels into the diabetic range in the first hour is followed by a release of a substantial amount of insulin that dramatically drives the elevated reading down—into a hypoglycemic state—before adrenaline stops the fall and saves the day. Any drop totaling 100 points or more is indicative of hypoglycemia.

• *Reactive hypoglycemia* (up and down rapidly). A rapid rise in blood sugar within the first half hour of the test that is followed by a flood of insulin that usually bottoms out during the third hour (a drop more than 20 points below fasting) is usually accompanied by anxiety, sweating, and heart-pounding.

• *Flat allergy curve hypoglycemic.* This low flat curve fails to rise to a normal high of around 150. Instead, it shows very little rise of blood sugar in response to glucose loading. Here the levels seem to drift along in a flat pattern. This curve is characteristic of many young

FIGURE 1: NORMAL GLUCOSE TOLERANCE TEST

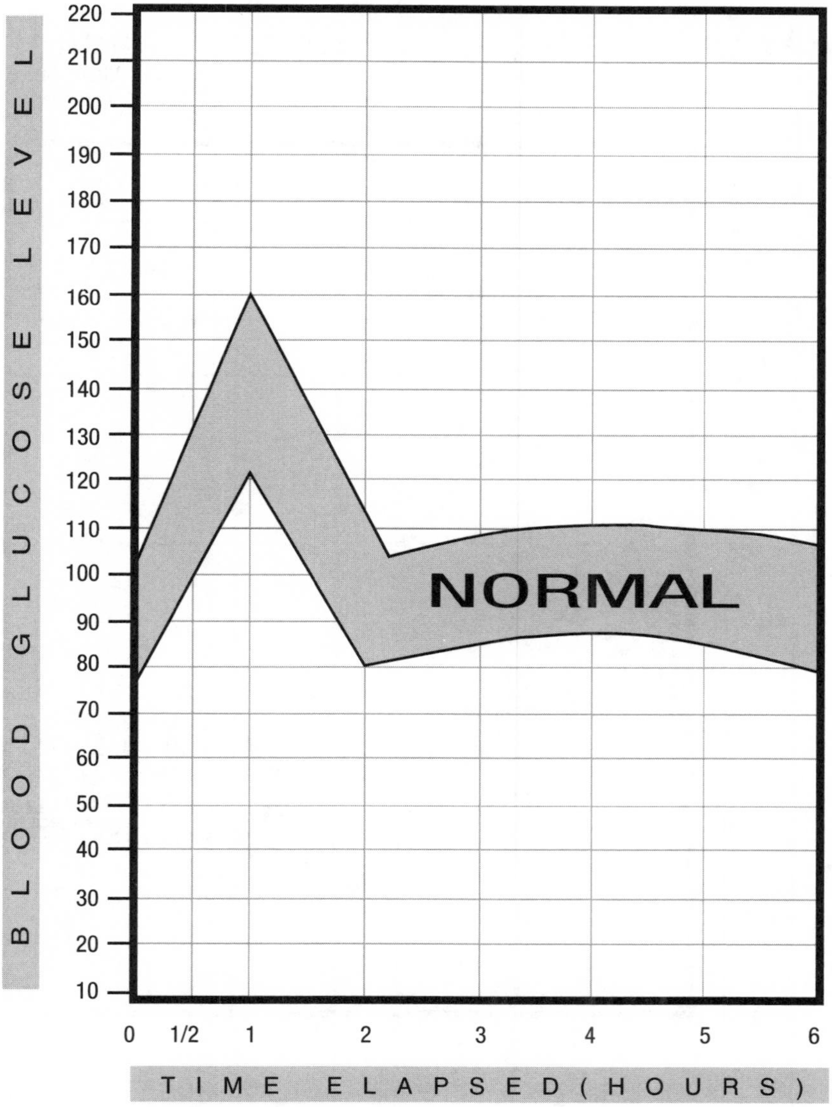

FIGURE 2: SIX-HOUR GLUCOSE TOLERANCE TEST

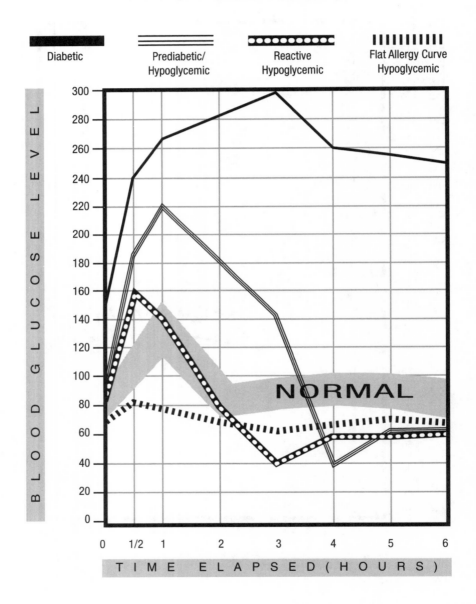

people. It indicates exhaustion; poor absorption (of glucose) from the gastrointestinal tract; possible thyroid, adrenal, or pituitary/adrenal insufficiency; or automatic nervous system disturbances.

All of these patterns call for a major overhaul in your diet to normalize your glucose metabolism and banish your hypogly-cemia symptoms.

Treating Hypoglycemia

There is no magic pill that cures hypoglycemia. The quickest and most effective treatment is through changes in your diet. In the seventies, when I began working with this population, there were two distinct camps of thinking about diet. The first was to feed all hypoglycemics a complex carbohydrate diet, spacing "small" meals every three hours.

The second was to reduce all carbohydrates radically and replace them with proteins and fats. The odd thing was that each of these diets had successes and failures. Of course, there was little or no research then on determining levels of carbohydrate sensitivity, or eating a diet corresponding to blood type characteristics and the rate at which you metabolize foods. Today, we can zero in on all of these factors so that your food choices fit you like a glove (and keep you at your best weight). By the end of this chapter, you will have the clues you need to select your ideal diet.

AM I REALLY CARBOHYDRATE ADDICTED?

- According to recent government figures, weight gain in the U.S. population over the past twenty years has increased by *31 percent* despite the food industry removing fat from so many of the products on grocery store shelves!
- The percentage of overweight children has *doubled* in the last decade!
- The weight loss industry bilks *$33 billion* out of overweight Americans yearly despite the dangerous rebound effect that sends individual weight scales even higher within two years.
- A 1995 Harris Poll found *71 percent of Americans over age*

twenty-four are overweight—up from 64 percent in 1990, and from 58 percent in 1983. (Overweight determinants are based on the Metropolitan Life tables of recommended weight averages.)

Before the low-fat diet craze started forty years ago, far fewer people were fat. What is creating such hunger in us? *Trying to live mostly on carbohydrates!* Unlike fats and protein, carbohydrates always trigger the release of insulin, which fattens us up. It destroys the brain's fuel. It plays havoc with energy and emotional stability. The more you look at the list of hypoglycemic symptoms, the angrier you should get that you have been encouraged to go down this path by the food industry and by some nationally respected health institutions like the American Heart Institute, the AMA, and the National Institute of Health.

Here is how the wrong belief got started.

In 1953, Ancel Keys, M.D., a leader in promulgating the mistaken belief about saturated fats, proclaimed that *all* dietary fats raise serum cholesterol. Dr. Keys based his statement on the atherosclerosis seen in rabbits fed diets high in cholesterol. He did not take into account that rabbits not only do not eat saturated fats naturally, but that they have *no* compensating feedback mechanisms that reduce their liver's daily cholesterol production whenever dietary cholesterol is eaten.

Humans, however, automatically make from 10,000 to 14,000 milligrams of cholesterol daily. *If dietary intake of cholesterol goes up, our livers make less, and vice versa.* Thus, limiting dietary cholesterol will have only a *trivial* effect on our overall cholesterol level. Many studies have proved that people develop coronary heart disease even though they eat more carbohydrates and little fat (cholesterol). Although Dr. Keys drew from the World Health Organization's report on estimated fat intake and incidences of death from coronary heart disease, he only selected the seven national studies that agreed with his theory; he omitted data from *fifteen* studies that did not fit his preconceived notions.

From 1955 to 1960, the famous Framingham (Massachusetts) Heart Study investigated coronary heart disease extensively. Their data shows *no* relationship between dietary fats, cholesterol, and heart disease. Since that time, thirty-three other clinical trials have shown a similar lack of relationship.

In August 1991, Dr. Keys finally wrote in the *New England Jour-*

nal of Medicine, "Dietary cholesterol has an important effect on the cholesterol level in the blood of *chickens and rabbits,* but many controlled experiments have shown that dietary cholesterol has only a *limited effect in humans*" (emphasis added).

Dr. Keys has finally come full circle in acknowledging that dietary cholesterol is insignificant in regard to heart disease. Unfortunately, mistakenly believing otherwise, this nation has now traded all kinds of fats for all kinds of sugar. It is critical that we undo this thinking.

FATS ARE ESSENTIAL TO OUR DIET

Some of the most renowned scientists now agree that the high-carbohydrate/low fat way of eating is not only wrong but dangerous. In 1993, a group of respected scientists collaborated on *Coronary Heart Disease: The Dietary Sense and Nonsense,* in which they published the studies the general public never sees. Their graphs show how the popular anticholesterol drugs **increased** death rates in six of eight randomized blind studies, rather than saving lives.

There is also a sinister result to lowering the availability of fats in our brain: The brain's gray matter is predominantly composed of fats—it is 60 percent essential fatty acids. Cholesterol-lowering drugs dramatically reduce availability of these fats where they are most needed: *in our brains!* And essential fatty acids have a powerful effect on our emotional stability. They permit the brain to utilize all of the B vitamins as well as many mood-altering natural chemicals. Studies are showing consistently rising death rates from suicide and violence in the population taking EFA-blocking, anti-cholesterol drugs.

It's hard to believe that informed consumers would prefer lower cholesterol levels to stable emotional health. Studies of cholesterol-lowering drugs show repeated evidence of high toxicity and of lowering the essential fatty acid levels in our brains. And these drugs are not accomplishing anything lifesaving; most heart attack victims have normal, or even low, cholesterol. *What fat-phobic Americans need to learn quickly is that essential fats are vital to our health.* Cholesterol is important to our nervous system, our endocrine system, and to every cell in our bodies. And foods naturally high in fat are healthy to eat.

But the key word here is "natural." Once they are tampered with, their nature is altered, and they should be avoided at all costs. We call these "trans-fatty acids" and "partially hydrogenated" oils. Hydrogenation destroys essential fatty acids, but the food giants still use this process to achieve longer shelf life for their products. Trans-fatty acids deplete your real fatty acids, and they manage to get stuck in many parts of the body. They line our arteries, adrenals, liver, heart, spleen, and kidneys, and damage these organs. *Over two thirds of the population die from degenerative diseases involving fats!* If you read food labels, you will see that almost every fat is "partially hydrogenized."

So, you should make every effort to avoid foods heavy in manmade fats: margarine, vegetable oils, processed cheeses, deep-fried foods, lard, shortening, hot dogs, sausage, brats, pork rinds, bologna, peanut butter with hydrogenated fat, potato chips, mayonnaise, and bakery goods.

The following foods contain natural (good) fats and can be eaten freely: almonds, avocados, macadamia nuts, olives, beef, Brazil nuts, butter, hard cheese, feta cheese, cottage cheese, chicken, duck, eggs, filberts, goat's milk, goose, hazelnuts, lamb, organ meats, peanut butter, unroasted or raw peanuts, pine nuts, pecans, pistachios, pumpkin seeds, rice germ, sesame seeds, sunflower seeds, walnuts, wheat germ, yogurt (whole milk).*

Remember, fats are a source of energy—our most efficient source! Not only are they easy to absorb but they contain *twice* the caloric energy of carbohydrates and proteins. Fats are a secret weapon in the diet of hypoglycemics—and the foods you've been avoiding are probably exactly what you *need*!

TREATING YOUR HYPOGLYCEMIC SYMPTOMS

Life is always a trade-off: you give up what you like for something you want even more. Ridding yourself of roller-coaster emotions is accomplished by trading in the refined sugars and caffeine in your diet. This sacrifice will pay enormous dividends in mental stability and increased energy.

*Both lists are taken from *Eat Right to Live Long* by Dr. Cass Ingram, N.D. (Hiawatha, Iowa: Cedar Graphics, 1989), p. 142.

You'll find your new diet (with modifications to suit you to a tee) at the back of this chapter. But before you get on the bandwagon, I want to make it as easy as possible to succeed. The biggest stumbling block for sugarholics has always been the intense, and very real, cravings for sweets. *This can sabotage all your plans unless these cravings are laid to rest.* The Hypoglycemia Formula we have developed and which is currently used at Health Recovery Center can do this for you (see page 84). But first an explanation of the substances in the formula.

CHROMIUM

This mineral is essential for sugar metabolism. It helps to stabilize the glucose tolerance curve for both hypoglycemics and diabetics by raising levels that are too low and lowering levels that are too high. Eating refined sugars forces a 20 percent increase in the loss of chromium from the body, depleting the stores needed to control abnormal glucose fluctuations. *Note:* It is important to take a type of chromium that is easily absorbed, such as chromium picolinate, and not inorganic chromium salts.

MAGNESIUM

A double-blind study done with hypoglycemics proved that 600 milligrams daily of magnesium stabilized blood sugar and blocked the plunge into a hypoglycemic state in all persons receiving this daily dose.

VITAMIN C (ESTER C)

Vitamin C is magnificent against stress. The adrenal glands use large amounts of it for hormone production. But adrenal supplies of vitamin C become severely depleted as a result of the overproduction of adrenaline needed to stop the disastrous drop in blood glucose. Adrenal exhaustion and ongoing anxiety develop as a result. (We will talk about undoing this state in Chapter 5.)

NIACIN (B₃)

This vitamin is essential for the regulation of blood sugar and the production of energy. Because niacin seems to lift the entire glucose curve, it stems the fall into insulin shock. "Time released" niacin avoids the uncomfortable flushing effect that occurs when straight niacin is used. Niacin is safe to take without medical supervision.

The Health Recovery Center Formula for Hypoglycemia©		
Nutrient	**Dose**	**Directions**
Chromium picolinate	200 mcg	1–2 capsules at breakfast
Magnesium	400 mg	1 capsule at breakfast 1 capsule at supper
**Vitamin C (Ester C)	675 mg	2 capsules at breakfast 2 capsules at supper
*Niacin (B$_3$)	500 mg	1 capsule at breakfast 1 capsule at supper
Pantothenic acid	500 mg	1 capsule at breakfast 1 capsule at supper
Glutamine	500 mg	2 capsules ½ hour before lunch (on empty stomach) 2 capsules ½ hour before supper (on empty stomach)

Note: If you are already taking any of the above nutrients, do not exceed these amounts for your total dosage (see chart page 56).

Do not use if you are diabetic or have liver damage.
**You are already taking this as part of your Balanced Emotions Basic Formula. Do not duplicate.*

© Copyright 1999 Health Recovery Center.™ All Rights Reserved.

However, *high doses may affect a damaged liver*, so if your lab test or medical history shows liver function abnormalities, do not use niacin without medical monitoring.

PANTOTHENIC ACID

This B vitamin is essential for restoring adrenal gland hormones, always exhausted from coping with hypoglycemic ups and downs. Replacing lost pantothenic acid will help repair this damage and restore your natural buffer against stress.

GLUTAMINE

This is a fabulous amino acid when it comes to blocking sugar cravings. I call it "God's gift to hypoglycemics" because, in emergencies, it can be absorbed directly into the bloodstream, bypassing the intestinal tract. You'll find relief from your cravings comes swiftly by opening a glutamine capsule and letting it dissolve in your mouth under your tongue (it tastes mildly sweet). Inside your brain, glutamine converts to glutamic acid, the only other source of glucose available to the brain. So it becomes a great alternative source of brain fuel that will stop the cravings set off by glucose levels that are dropping too low. (Alcoholics using glutamine this way can, and do, successfully stop cravings for alcohol, which speaks loudly to these cravings having a hypoglycemic basis.)

SAYING "NO" TO CAFFEINE

I've rarely met a "practicing" hypoglycemic who still doesn't cherish his or her pots of coffee. Younger people punctuate their day with Surge or Mountain Dew, which combines a sugar blast with a caffeine fix. They have discovered that their blood sugar comes shooting up like a rocket, energizing them temporarily. Caffeine does this by stimulating your (overworked) adrenals to release adrenaline—and thereby emergency sugar—into your bloodstream. Never mind that your real level of energy is nil. Continually doing this to your adrenals is akin to beating a dying horse. Adrenaline circulating in your bloodstream makes you irritable, anxious, shaky, and restless. Your heart may pound, and you may even have panic attacks. Eventually the surge of energy is reduced to *temporarily* alleviating your ongoing fatigue.

Neal, a young carpenter, told me that no woman cared to date him for long because of his wild bursts of temper and mood swings. He was drinking a six-pack of Mountain Dew on the job every day, and needed a pot of coffee every morning "to get going." After I convinced Neal to give up his caffeine "fix" and to follow a sugar-free diet, his disposition slowly mellowed, and his tremors and snappishness disappeared. No longer "wired," he has finally been able to sustain a caring relationship, and his life has turned around.

If you are drinking several cups of coffee or caffeinated colas daily, don't try to stop cold turkey, or you will go into withdrawal from this addictive drug. You will get a powerful headache, and feel listless and jumpy for days. The better approach is to cut your intake over a week's time. Trade caffeine for herbal teas, or just drink sparkling water with lime or lemon. Your reward for dumping caffeine will be evident in your increased energy levels and reduced sugar cravings.

SAYING "NO" TO NICOTINE

Since nicotine is cured with sugar—corn, beet, or cane—there is a link between hypoglycemia and nicotine addiction. You can temporarily raise your blood sugar by lighting up a cigarette. Nicotine has many health hazards, but the fact that it keeps you hypoglycemic by adding one more source of sugar to your diet should be the final straw! *You can kick this habit, and you will, but don't attempt it for a few weeks.* Once you are off refined sugars and caffeine, you will be ready for that last step. In Chapter 9, I'll give you our Smokers Formula to reduce your cigarette cravings and increase the brain's calming waves. By that time, your immune system and general health will be high enough to confront cigarettes and win.

CHOOSING THE RIGHT DIET FOR YOU

Three factors will influence how you select your ideal diet:

> Your fast or slow oxidation of foods.
> Your blood type (O, A, B, AB).
> Your sensitivity to carbohydrates.

Fast or Slow Oxidation

By oxidation, I mean how fast or how slowly your body changes food to energy. *Slow oxidizers* live with thyroid and adrenal glands that are relatively underactive. Adrenal insufficiency creates poor production of glucocortical hormones. When more blood sugar is needed, this person can't secrete enough adrenal hormone to trigger a fast conversion of glucose from the liver's stored emergency sugar, and hypoglycemia results. The slow oxidizer also cannot transport enough glucose across the cell membrane because of too little sodium and potassium. And the actual burning of glucose within the cells is inefficient. It is not metabolized adequately due to low thyroid hormone activity and/or a lack of co-enzymes.

The slow oxidizer often has chronic symptoms of fatigue, constant craving for sweets, depression, and/or mental confusion.

As one's oxidation rate slows even more with a diet high in dairy and fat or low in protein, a slow oxidizer should choose a high-protein diet with very little dairy and only modest amounts of good fats. Needed supplementary nutrients are vitamins A, C, E, and B complex and manganese, as these enhance adrenal function. Zinc is needed for protein metabolism. Potassium helps lower the high calcium levels, which improves thyroid function. Omega-3 and -6 fatty acids should also be added to boost the brain's supply of its important fats. But slow oxidizers must eat sparingly from the fats listed on page 82. It is better for them to take EFA oils specifically on a daily basis.

Fast oxidizers have low calcium and magnesium levels. Their high sodium-to-potassium ratio is linked with the alarm stage of stress and produces the rapid metabolism of foods and overactive thyroid and adrenal glands. This adrenal activity produces a continual conversion of stored sugar to blood glucose, and severely depletes glycogen reserves. Hyperactive thyroids rapidly burn glucose and further deplete reserves. Under stress, such people experience precipitous falls in blood sugar levels, and are said to have "reactive" hypoglycemia. Activities and foods that worsen their rapid oxidation state are exercise, overwork, stresses of all kinds, sweets, and caffeine and alcohol.

This group benefits from eating *frequent*, small meals high in fats and proteins. Fat slows the excessive oxidation rate and does not trigger an insulin response. Restoring calcium, magnesium, and zinc will also slow the oxidizing rate. Vitamins A, D, B_2, B_{12}, choline, and inositol also slow an excessive rate of oxidation.

The Importance of Your Blood Type

Science has recently unlocked new chemistry clues from our blood types. Research by James D'Adamo, M.D., and his son, Peter D'Adamo, M.D.—detailed in the book *Eat Right 4 Your Type*—examines how different blood types relate to the body's chemistry, diet, and disease susceptibility. Once you know which blood group you are (O, A, B, or AB), you also know and can apply the same code (O, A, B, AB) to your skin cells, lung cells, and intestinal cells. In fact, all body cells are the same "type" as your blood. Dr. D'Adamo has identified cell-type "lectins," or markers, that are unique to each individual. These lectins (proteins) can be matched to similar food lectins that are compatible to you. *For in fact, the chemical reactions between your blood and the foods you eat can be healing or poisoning* (although many foods have a neutral effect). The trick is to adjust your diet to the needs of your blood type so as to increase your health and correct your weight. The lectin activity of incompatible foods has the following effect, according to *Eat Right 4 Your Type*:

1. Hormonal balance is upset, causing water retention and thyroid disorders.
2. Production of insulin is compromised.
3. Food-burning metabolism rate is slowed, so you can't efficiently turn calories into energy.
4. Digestive tract lining becomes inflamed.
5. Digestive process is disrupted, causing bloating.

Each blood type has its own good and bad foods. Here is a thumbnail sketch of each one:

TYPE O
Because they possess high levels of stomach acids, people with this type thrive on high-protein diets of fish, animal meats, and poultry. Our type O ancestors—and the first humans were type O—had no exposure to dairy products or grains, including gluten (found in wheat, oats, rye, and barley). Consequently, modern type O's lack these digestive enzymes. Overweight type O's will discover they can lose pounds rapidly by removing dairy from their diets. People with this blood type tend toward hypothyroidism because they produce too little iodine (symptoms of an underactive thyroid include fatigue, weight gain, chilling easily, and retention of fluids).

Type O's should exercise vigorously to ward off fatigue and depression. An intense exercise program may be critical to maintaining ideal weight and controlling stress. The sluggish metabolism of type O's responds well to taking daily high-potency B complex capsules.

About 46 percent of Americans have type O blood.

TYPE A
This blood type—the second oldest—emerged as the wild meat supply dwindled and agriculture first appeared. These individuals have

lower levels of hydrochloric acid and digestive enzymes than type O's, and find it hard to digest protein. They probably have difficulty with dairy products. Type A's thrives on vegetables, eggs, fruits, nuts, and seeds and do poorly on any form of wheat and certain seafood—shrimp or lobster.

Exercise requirements are much less strenuous than for type O, and relaxation is important.

Type A blood is found in 42 percent of Caucasian Americans and 27 percent of Black Americans.

TYPE B

This type—less than ten thousand years old—appeared after domestic grains were introduced into the human diet, so people with this blood type are well-adjusted to large amounts of dairy, animal protein, and grains. The first type B's were nomads from central Asia and eastern Europe, and were known for their longevity, which they claimed was due to their devotion to yogurt. Olives, olive oil, and feta cheeses are second nature for this ancestry. Pineapple is especially good to stop any bloating from their lack of digestive enzymes.

Type B's ideally combine strenuous exercise with meditative exercises (i.e., yoga or tai chi.)

Only 10 percent of Caucasians and 20 percent of Black Americans are type B.

TYPE AB

The most recent blood type—within the last one thousand years—this type is best adjusted to newer dietary food groups such as grains, dairy, vegetables, and fruits. Digesting and metabolizing meats is a problem because of insufficient stomach acid. Thus, most meats eaten by AB's tend to get stored as fat. Another weight-loss trigger for this group (besides avoiding meat) is avoiding wheat, which tends to make body muscles acidic. Calories are more easily burned when muscle tissue is alkaline, so high-alkaline fruit juices like cranberry, grape, and cherry are recommended.

AB types need sea salt to increase sodium levels. Green tea is very beneficial as a daily beverage choice. Daily use of an antioxidant is important as this group has the highest susceptibility to cancer. Substances like vitamins A, C, E, B_6; and zinc, selenium, cysteine,

teine, and methionine will inhibit free radicals from damaging cells, thereby causing disease and aging. Light exercise and increased relaxation suits this group best.

Only 2 to 5 percent of the population has the AB blood type.

Sensitivity to Carbohydrates

Is your daily diet laced with refined sugars? Does just reading about parting with your daily cola, doughnut, cookie, roll, sugar-sweetened cereal, ice cream, candy bar, and sweetened coffee and tea put a frown on your face? Then you likely are consuming enough sugar to guarantee heart disease, diabetes, cancer, obesity, and other degenerative diseases. Your thyroid and adrenal glands are busy working overtime to deal with your continual sugar loading and will eventually burn out.

You are in desperate need of a diet that tricks your body into feeling satisfied and full without all that sugar! The test on page 91 will separate the sugarholics from the rest of the population and determine which diet is right for you. If you score high (8 to 12 points) you are a perfect candidate for the low-carbo diet, but any score over 5 suggests you need to consider the diet that follows.

The Low-Carbohydrate Hypoglycemic Diet

The object of the low-carbo diet is to reduce your intake of insulin-triggering carbohydrate foods. Without insulin to plunge your blood sugar into a hypoglycemic state, your brain will stop signaling wildly to resupply its fuel (sugar). Once this happens, you will see your sugar cravings stop. This diet requires keeping track of how many grams of carbohydrate you eat, so you should buy a carbohydrate counter at your local drugstore. Usually 75 grams is adequate to control sugar cravings. You may be able to load up to 100 grams, but if you are extremely carbohydrate-sensitive, you may only get by with 50 grams a day of carbohydrates. Your body will decide for you . . . too many carbos and you will start craving sugar.

Please note: Blood types O and B will thrive on the low-carbo diet because their ancestors existed mostly on meat protein and their bodies still prefer it. *Types A* and *AB* have problems digesting

CARBOHYDRATE ADDICTION TEST

Instructions: If your answer to each question is yes, please put a check mark in the column.

___ 1. When eating sweets, starches, or snack foods, is it hard to stop?

___ 2. At a restaurant, do you eat several rolls of bread before the meal is served?

___ 3. Do you ever hide food or eat food secretly?

___ 4. While eating carbohydrates, do you feel out of control?

___ 5. Does your diet consist mainly of breads, pastas, starchy vegetables, fast foods, and/or sweets?

___ 6. Do you binge on snack foods, candy, or fast foods?

___ 7. Do you often feel hungry and unsatisfied after a meal, no matter how much you eat?

___ 8. Does eating a sweet snack lift your spirits?

___ 9. Do you feel sleepy or groggy after a high-carbohydrate meal (i.e., breads, potatoes, pastas, desserts)?

___ 10. *Which would you prefer:

__spaghetti	or	__steak
__sandwich	or	__salad
__potato	or	__broccoli
__cookie	or	__strawberries
__cracker	or	__raw vegetables
__chips	or	__raw nuts
__breaded fish	or	__baked fish

___ 11. Do you get tired or hungry by mid- or late afternoon?

___ 12. When dieting, is it easier for you to skip breakfast and avoid food for most of the day than to eat small diet meals?

*For question 10, consider your overall response to be yes if you checked more items in the left-hand column than in the right-hand column.

Score: Total the number of checked responses. Then determine which of the following categories you fit into:

    1–2 doubtful addiction
    3–5 mild addiction
    6–7 moderate addiction
    8–12 severe addiction

If you score over five, you are a candidate for the low-carbohydrate diet.

protein, but this resolves itself when they increase their much needed digestive enzymes and hydrochloric acid. *All four types* will be able to adjust to either this diet or the one that follows by paying careful attention to their own special characteristics as they choose their food menus. Also, this diet is preferable for *slow oxidizers*, but it can be essential for both slow and fast oxidizers if they are carbohydrate-reactive.

ALLOWABLE FOODS

MEAT AND FISH

beef

chicken

clams

duck

fish (all kinds)

goose

lamb

lobster

oysters

pheasant

pork

scallops

shrimp

turkey

DAIRY

butter

cheeses, all aged or fresh goat or cow

cottage cheese (plain)

cream, half and half

eggs

kafir

sour cream

yogurt (plain, nonsweetened)

VEGETABLES

asparagus

avocado

beans (wax or green)

bean sprouts

broccoli

brussel sprouts

cabbage

carrots

cauliflower

eggplant

kohlrabi

  leeks
  onions
  pea pods
  scallions
  soy beans (tofu)
  spinach
  squash (zucchini or summer)
  tomato
  turnips

SALADS

  alfalfa sprouts
  bean sprouts
  bok choy
  chives
  cucumber
  endive
  jicama
  lettuce
  mushroom
  olives
  parsley
  peppers, red and green
  radish
  romaine
  spices without sugar, all

GRAINS

  Wasa breads (flat breads)

FRESH FRUITS

  apricots (3)
  grapefruit
  grapes (green, 10)
  honeydew melon
  kiwi fruit, 1
  lemons
  orange, 1 medium
  peaches

pineapple, 1 slice fresh
prune, 1 small
raspberries (1 cup)
strawberries (1 cup daily)
tangerines

BEVERAGES

Dilute all fruit juices, three parts spring water to one part juice.
apricot juice
carrot juice
clear broth
club sodas
cream (but no milk—cream has no carbs)
green tea (mild)
herbal teas
lemon juice
lime juice
orange juice
pineapple juice
seltzer water
sparkling waters (flavored, no sugar added)
tomato juice
V-8

SWEETENERS

inositol powder (do not exceed 5 teaspoons daily)
stevia

FATS

Brazil nuts
filberts
hazel nuts
macadamia nuts
olive oils
pecans
pine nuts
pistachios
pumpkin seeds

raw almonds
sunflower seeds
walnuts

SALAD DRESSINGS

blue cheese (soybean oil, egg yolks, vinegar, lemon juice)
guacamole (avocado, lemon juice, onion)
mayonnaise (no sugar) (flax seed oil, olive oil, egg, lemon juice)
ranch (soybean oil, egg yolk, buttermilk)
salsa
vinaigrette (olive oil, egg yolks, vinegar)

WARNING: Avoid dressings containing any form of refined *sugars and/or* partially hydrogenated *oils, meaning they have been altered for longer shelf life. Partially hydrogenated oils are the* **bad** *fats that are linked to coronary heart disease and cancer.*

FOODS TO AVOID

MEATS

The following are usually laced with some form of sugar as a preservative. Check the labels for exceptions.
bacon
canned meats
cold cuts, all
deli meats
hot dogs
salami
sausage with additives

VEGETABLES

corn
french fries
ketchup
potatoes, white
potato chips
sweet pickles
sweet relish

GRAINS

Most are high in carbohydrates and must be avoided. This means all:

breads

cereals

crackers

pasta

pizza

pretzels

rice cakes

rolls

FRUITS

All dried fruits (e.g., raisins, figs) and fruits canned in syrup.

applesauce   (unsweetened 1 cup = 28 grams of carbohydrates)

banana   (1 = 27 grams of carbohydrates)

blueberries   (1 cup = 20 grams of carbohydrates)

cantaloupe   (½ = 22 grams of carbohydrates)

cherries   (1 cup = 24 grams of carbohydrates)

pear   (1 = 21 grams of carbohydrates)

watermelon   (4×8 = 35 grams of carbohydrates)

The carbohydrate levels on fruits are given because they are so high. Adding too much fruit to your diet, therefore, will often put your otherwise okay low-carbohydrate count over allowable levels before you've had all your meals.

SWEETS

artificial sweeteners, including aspartame

candy

caramel

chewing gum

honey

jam and jelly

malt

maple syrup

marmalade

molasses

sugar (refined, corn, beet, cane)

And other forms of sugar: dextrose, fructose, glucose, hexitol, lactose, maltose, mannitol, sorbitol, sucrose.

BEVERAGES
  alcoholic beverages
  cocoa
  coffee
  colas
  milk (skim, 2%, or whole)
  Ovaltine
  soft drinks
  teas (except mild green tea)

SUGGESTED DAILY MENUS (Low-Carbohydrate Diet)

Please note: The protein portions throughout this diet can be as much as you can eat.

Breakfast
one half grapefruit, 1-egg cheese omelet, 1 cup green tea
  or
scrambled tofu with onion and green pepper, handful of raw almonds or other unroasted nuts, sparkling water with fresh lemon squeeze or diluted with ⅓ fruit juice.
  or
scrambled eggs and turkey breakfast sausage*, 2 apricots, 1 cup green tea or glass of V-8

Lunch
chef's salad with 3 tomato slices or 3 cherry tomatoes, cooked turkey, chicken strips, and feta cheese; 1 cup vegetable beef soup, 1 cup green tea
  or
hamburger patty; tossed salad with mushrooms, tomatoes, peppers, and sprouts; sparkling water with a lime twist
  or

*Sugar-free, nitrate-free sausage is sold at whole-food stores or co-ops.

tuna or chicken salad on half an avocado; 1 slice of Wasa bread, buttered; a glass of sparkling water

or

shrimp or seafood salad with hard-boiled eggs, green tea or sparkling water

Supper

broiled Norwegian salmon, buttered broccoli, mixed greens with tomato and cucumber, ½ cup fresh strawberries with cream, sparkling water or V-8 juice

or

meatloaf (hamburger, onion, mushrooms, and tomato paste), asparagus or any acceptable vegetables, 1 slice of Wasa bread (buttered), 8 green grapes, a chunk of hard cheese, and sparkling water

or

roasted beef or chicken, steamed cauliflower or other acceptable vegetable, carrots and cabbage salad with fresh onion, one peach, acceptable beverage

Snacks

a piece of hard cheese

one slice Wasa bread with butter or peanut butter

raw nuts (unroasted), one handful

V-8 juice, 1 glass

Stay with the low-carbo diet for one to three months, until your cravings are a thing of the past. Then, as your chemistry becomes better suited for more carbohydrates (based on blood type and oxidation type), you can make the switch to the moderate-carbohydrate diet.

The Moderate-Carbohydrate Hypoglycemic Diet

Please note: This diet allows a higher intake of complex carbohydrates that better suits the *fast-oxidizer* and blood types A, B, and AB. Most important, it is designed for those *who are not presently trapped in their addiction to simple and refined sugars and white flours*. If you are hopelessly hooked on sugar, do not attempt to get free of your addiction with the moderate-carbo diet.

ALLOWABLE FOODS

PROTEIN

chicken and other fowl

eggs

fish

meat

shellfish

tofu (soy)

CHEESES

All hard cheeses. Cream cheese and cottage cheese can be eaten but have roughly half the protein value of most other cheeses. Do not use processed cheese, cheese spreads, or squeeze-bottle cheese. Cheese has high fat and sodium content.

VEGETABLES

artichokes (globe or French)

asparagus

beans (green or wax)

beets

broccoli

cabbage

carrots

cauliflower

celery

cucumbers

lettuce

mushrooms

olives

onions (green or raw)

parsley

peppers

pickles (dill or sour)

pimientos

peas (green or edible pod)

potatoes

radishes

rutabaga

sauerkraut

soybeans
spinach
squash (hubbard or winter)
tomatoes
water chestnuts
zucchini

SPROUTS
alfalfa
bean

WHOLE GRAINS
barley
buckwheat
millet
oatmeal
rice (brown or wild)
whole wheat

FRESH FRUITS
apples
apricots
avocados
banana, one (although bananas contain 23 percent fructose carbohydrates, one banana a day is permitted because of its high potassium content)
blueberries
cantaloupe
casaba melon
cherries
coconut (fresh)
fruit salad (without grapes)
grapefruit
grapes (eat sparingly, as these are high in fructose)
honeydew melon
lemons
limes
muskmelon

oranges
peaches
pears
pineapple
plums
raspberries
rhubarb (no sugar added)
strawberries
tangerines

NUTS AND SEEDS

Nuts are good sources of protein, but use raw nuts and seeds *only*. The roasting process changes the fat content of nuts and seeds to form free radicals, which are potential carcinogens. Avoid roasted products.

almonds
Brazil nuts
peanuts
pecans
pumpkin seeds
sesame seeds
sunflower seeds
walnuts

BEVERAGES

Dilute all fruit juices, two parts spring water to one part juice.

apricot juice
carrot juice
clear broth
grapefruit juice
herb teas
lemon juice
lime juice
loganberry juice
milk
orange juice
pineapple juice
raspberry juice
sauerkraut juice

tangerine juice
tomato juice
V-8 juice
vegetable juice

FATS

Fats are essential for steroid production, and the fats in butter, cream, milk (if tolerated), and salad oil contribute to a well-balanced diet, as do fats present in other natural foods.

SALT

Allowed in moderate amounts. Consider Morton's Lite Salt, which has half the potassium and half the sodium of regular salt.

FOODS TO AVOID

MEATS

All these are usually packed with some form of sugar as a preservative. Check labels for exceptions.
bacon
canned meats
cold cuts
hot dogs
salami
sausages

VEGETABLES

pickles (sweet)
potato chips or fries
relishes (sweet)
rice (white)

GRAINS

Avoid "enriched white flours" in any form. Use only whole-grain flours.
breads
cereal (dry)
crackers (white)
grits
pancakes (from white flour)

pizza
pretzels
rolls
waffles

FRUIT

dried fruits (raisins, dates, etc.)
fruits canned in syrup

PASTA*

macaroni
noodles
spaghetti

SWEETS

artificial sweeteners
candy
caramel
chewing gum
honey
jam
jelly
malt
marmalade
molasses
sugar
syrup
And other forms of sugar: dextrose, fructose, glucose, hexitol, lactose, maltose, mannitol, sorbitol, sucrose.

BEVERAGES

alcoholic beverages
caffeinated beverages
cocoa
coffee
cola
decaffeinated beverages

*Unless made with whole grains.

diet soft drinks
Ovaltine
soft drinks
strong tea

DESSERTS
cake
chocolate
cookies
custard
dessert topping
ice cream
Jell-O
pastry
pie
puddings

SUGGESTED DAILY MENUS (MODERATE-CARBOHYDRATE DIET)

Breakfast
2 eggs or yogurt; 1 slice protein bread or ¼ cup oatmeal, millet,
buckwheat, or whole-wheat cereal; 1 glass of milk or other acceptable beverage
  or
1 pat butter, 1 slice natural cheese on whole grain bread, a piece of
fresh fruit in season (one piece or small bowl), handful of raw nuts
(almonds, sesame seeds, pumpkin seeds), 1 cup of yogurt, tomato,
or V-8 juice (8–12 oz.)
  or
1 cup cooked cereal (millet, buckwheat, whole wheat, or oats), 1 pat
sweet butter, 8 oz. glass of fruit juice

Midmorning Snack
(On this diet, your carbohydrate breakfast will trigger insulin, lowering
your blood sugar. This snack will resupply your brain fuel, glucose.)
5 to 10 raw almonds or other raw, unroasted nuts
  or

1 piece fresh fruit (pear, pineapples, papaya, melon, or a bowl of cherries) and 1 slice cheddar or other natural cheese
   or
½ large or 1 small avocado
   or
Tomato or V-8 juice (8–12 oz.)
   or
Orange juice or grapefruit juice

Lunch

1 slice whole-grain bread with 1 pat butter, 1 slice natural cheese, 1 cup green tea
Beans and brown rice with fresh tomato, onion, and garlic
   or
½ cup fresh grilled or drained, canned salmon or tuna; small vegetable salad; sparkling water
   or
Any breakfast choice
   or
Hamburger patty with melted cheese, tossed salad with natural dressing or avocado, sautéed mushrooms with butter, 1 cup green tea or fruit juice, fresh peach
   or
Bowl of freshly prepared vegetable, mushroom, pea, or lentil soup; sparkling water
   or
Any other cooked or steamed vegetable dish (green beans, carrots, broccoli, cauliflower, zucchini), 1 cup of herbal tea

Midafternoon Snack
Same choices as midmorning snack

Dinner
Broiled chicken (skin removed), ½ baked potato, green or wax beans, 1 slice whole-grain bread (with 1 or 2 pats butter), mixed raw vegetables, strawberries, herbal tea

After-Dinner Snack
Same as midmorning snack

SHOPPING TIPS FOR EVERYONE

- Choose foods that are as close to their natural state as possible: fresh vegetables and fruits; fresh meats, fish, chicken, and eggs; raw nuts and seeds; fresh salad greens.
- Avoid canned, processed, dyed, chemically flavored, frozen, or additive-laden foods.
- If you can't find millet bread or brown rice bread at your supermarket, try a food cooperative. Some health food stores also carry these whole-grain substitutes for wheat bread. Before you buy rye or oat bread, read the label carefully. Wheat is usually the first ingredient listed.
- Don't buy *roasted* nuts. The process of high-heat roasting causes undesirable changes in the natural oils the nuts contain. In the body, this altered oil can promote formation of free radicals—dangerously unstable molecules capable of damaging healthy tissue and promoting the development of cancer. Choose only raw nuts and seeds.
- Pass up luncheon meats (Spam, bacon, ham, bologna). They are loaded with refined sugars and cancer-causing nitrates.
- You can find fruit-sweetened jams at a food co-op or health food store.
- Drink flavored sparkling water (read the label to confirm that it is sugar-free).
- Cut your salt intake by using lite salt, which contains half the potassium (needed for cellular energy) and half the sodium of regular salt.

HOW MUCH TIME BEFORE I FEEL GOOD ON THE DIETS?

At Health Recovery Center, we see our clients' progress as having three stages:

Stage 1. Many of our clients lament, as they withdraw from refined sugars, "I'm so wiped out and tired all the time." Well, you are getting a look at your energy levels without artificial stimulants. Luckily, this stage usually lasts only a week to ten days.

Stage 2. This brings a noticeable but not consistent improvement in overall energy. You will experience periods during the third

---

MEAL PREPARATION TIPS

- Peel fruits and vegetables, or remove outer layers, to avoid pesticide residues.
- Steam your vegetables until they are almost tender, not soggy (if you cook them in water, you will lose much of their vitamin and mineral content). Your best choice, nutrition-wise, is raw vegetables.
- Use fruit juice on cereal if you don't have soy, rice, or goat's milk. (The ban on cow's milk is only a temporary measure until you have had your allergy test.)
- Keep a lot of assorted nuts, sunflower seeds, apples, oranges, carrot sticks, celery, and other raw vegetables on hand for snacking.

---

and fourth weeks when many days are greatly improved, but your newfound energy and mood stability is not an everyday thing.

Stage 3. Now there's a marked improvement in energy, with mood stability and ongoing mental clarity. It is common to have this stage happen by or after the fourth week on the diet.

It's Your Choice

One last word about diets and food: It takes a little reprogramming to know what to put in your mouth for the ultimate value rather than the sixty-second taste. You need to decide whether to build vitality, energy, mental clarity, and top-notch health, or to choose the short-lived, sweet tastes of sugars.

The only way to fight your cravings for refined sugars is not to eat any at all. Even a little sugar turns on intense desires for "more, more, more" that last all day . . . and you see yourself trading mental equilibrium and a competitive edge for colas, cookies, candy, and ice cream.

Your body will change food to energy more efficiently when you adjust your intake to your unique blood type and oxidation metabolism. And as you stay on the hypoglycemic diets, with every passing day, you will grow more stable and healthy. There are many ways to perk up besides caffeine and refined sugars. The next chapter tells you all about them . . . and what they can do for you.

CHAPTER 4

Shopping for Relief at
Your Natural Pharmacy
Amino Acids, Vitamins, and Minerals

I t has taken mankind thousands of years to uncover important secrets about that most important organ, the brain. Folklore long
held that the brain's functioning depended on what we ate; it wasn't
until the last part of the twentieth century that we had any true
grasp of how the brain really works.

We now know that the human brain transmits thoughts and creates emotions and memory partly by means of neurotransmitters
that load and fire and reload continually. Communication within the
brain and between the brain and the rest of the central nervous system occurs by means of these chemical messages that are exchanged through our neurotransmitters; their precursors, the amino
acids; and co-enzyme vitamins and minerals. Eight amino acids are
essential to life, and many others are conditionally essential, meaning their requirements are greatly increased by disease or inborn disorders. The proper functioning of our brains and emotions depends
on an adequate supply of all of these vital natural substances.

Understanding the
Biochemical Basis of Our Emotions

Past generations have believed that biochemistry and emotions are
separate. Today we are seeing that all human emotions have a biochemical basis, that body and mind are totally intertwined. In *Expressions of the Emotions in Man and Animals*, Charles Darwin

observed that all people share common emotional facial expressions (as do some animals). We also all experience the emotions of sadness, fear, anger, joy, disgust, contentment, pleasure, and pain. Our facial expressions for these emotions are the same whether we are Asian, African, or European. Because of this universal phenomenon, Darwin concluded that mankind must have an inborn genetic mechanism that governs these emotional expressions, a universal chemistry for emotions. As far back as the 1920s, Wilder Penfield, M.D., at Montreal's McGill University found that by stimulating certain areas in the brain, he could automatically produce different emotional reactions, such as weeping, laughing, and anger.

Candace Pert, M.D., a former National Institutes of Health researcher, explains in her book *Molecules of Emotions* that emotion-carrying peptides (made from aminos) continually circulate and communicate throughout our brains and bodies. Receptors for these peptides and neurotransmitters are present not only in the brain but in the endocrine system, spinal cord, and even immune system. She says: "What we experience as an emotion or feeling is also a mechanism for activating a particular neuronal circuit SIMULTANEOUSLY THROUGHOUT THE BRAIN BODY—which generates a behavior with all the necessary physiological changes that behavior would require." (My emphasis.)

She found that brain peptides and substances like the pituitary hormone ACTH are present in many other parts of the body. For most of us it is a strange idea that the emotional and mental activity in our brains is actually present throughout our entire bodies. But a network unites our endocrine, immune, and nervous systems, connecting them through receptors called neuropeptides. Dr. Pert proved that virtually *every* peptide found in the brain has duplicate receptors throughout the body. Thanks to this work, it is clear that *the brain is not the seat of our emotions.*

Since our emotions originate as amino acids, we are at a disadvantage when we are denied normal amounts of them. Amino acids alone, or by their transformation into neurotransmitters and neuropeptides, supply us with the chemicals necessary to generate pleasure, alleviate pain, protect against radiation, and combat the aging process. They thereby can treat our depression, anxiety, memory loss, and many other seemingly "psychological" states.

As you begin to understand these remarkable substances, you

will quickly tune in to the connection between their deficiencies and changes in your brain's equilibrium. A serious depletion will likely be labeled a "disease" or called a "mental illness," and in today's common medical thinking, disease equals taking drugs to relieve symptoms. But often a safer approach is to measure and supply the right amounts of our missing natural chemicals rather than to use foreign, synthetic, and sometimes toxic substances to try to duplicate nature. We will see how this can happen by *treating* ourselves with amino acids; minerals; and vitamins, EFAs, enzymes, and so on.

AMINO ACID REPLACEMENT

Amino acid therapy is fast becoming a viable means for healing and repairing our bodies and minds. These substances are not only much safer than drugs, but they can be selectively supplemented according to individual need. And this kind of treatment does not create deficiencies in other amino acids—which is not always the case with drug therapy.

Science has been recognizing amino acid patterns and correlating their deficiencies to disease for about three decades. In *The Healing Nutrients Within*, Dr. Eric Braverman, who has pioneered amino acid therapies in treating an array of physical and "mental" disorders, points out that "at present, less than 20 percent of all drugs administered by a physician are effective. All the healers a physician needs are in the body, there for the harvesting by future generations of physicians and scientists. Amino acids are an example of this harvest."

In *Elemental Nutrients*, Dr. Carl Pfeiffer, founder of the Princeton Bio Center and another pioneer in amino acid research, offers us Pfeiffer's Law:

We have found that, if a drug can be found to do the job of medical healing, a nutrient can be found to do the same job. For example, anti-depressants usually enhance the effect of serotonin and the epinephrines. We now know that if we give the amino acids tryptophan or tyrosine, the body can synthesize these neurotransmitters, thereby achieving the same effect. Nutrients have fewer, milder side effects, and the challenge of the future is to replace or sometimes combine drugs with the natural healers called nutrients.

Happily, all individual amino acids in their free (predigested) form can effectively be supplied by mouth. They also enter the brain/body network quickly, unlike vitamins and minerals, which slowly build their levels over days or weeks.

Free-form aminos are predigested to absorb immediately, without any need of digestive enzymes. They go to work at once in all the metabolic pathways where they are needed. In the United States, most amino acids are available without a prescription because they do not fall under the classification of drugs. These essential substances were designed by Nature, not drug companies. So while in many cases they act like medicine, they are classified as foods.

A Crash Course in Amino Acids

Some of the biggest biological tasks of amino acids are:

1. creating your actual cells and body tissues.
2. promoting the growth and repair of all parts of your body.
3. creating the enzymes needed for the production of all hormones as well as for digestion.
4. promoting the proper functioning of the blood.
5. making possible the intricate communication within the brain and between the central nervous system and the endocrine and immune systems.
6. creating energy by converting to glucose, blood sugar, and glycogen (a sugar stored in the liver and used for emergency energy).

Eight amino acids are classified as "essential," meaning that we would die if we could not ingest them daily. The friendly bacteria living in the intestinal tract need to provide us with small amounts continually, to keep us alive and in balance. The rest of the aminos are considered "conditionally essential," meaning they can be manufactured within the body if you don't get them in your diet. But that creates another problem: Your body must then divert its important essential amino acids from their lifesaving tasks to form these missing substances.

Let's first discuss in general the potential worth of amino acids to your *emotional* health and stability. Then I'll provide a brief explanation of each amino and its effects on the body. Later in this chapter I will give you more details about identifying your symptoms with lab tests (including an amino acid assay) and matching the results to the right amino acids and the cofactors that trigger their performance.

Easing Your Moods with Aminos
DEPRESSION
A common cause of depression is catecholamine deficiency in the brain. *Phenylalanine, tyrosine,* and *dopa* are the amino precursors of these catecholamines. In one double-blind study, phenylalanine proved comparable to the antidepressant drug imipramine in relieving depression.

Tryptophan's benefits in loading the brain with serotonin to lift depression are well documented. For example, back in 1985, the *Journal of Affective Disorders* described how abnormally low serotonin metabolism can cause impulsive acts of suicide. (Chapter 6 explains how to use these aminos to combat biochemical depression.)

ANXIETY
The adrenaline outpouring that occurs when we are stressed is what creates our anxious feelings. That alarm system heightens mental alertness and may cause stomach queasiness, sudden sweating, shakiness, and a racing heart. Certain amino acids can strengthen the inhibitory (quieting) system in the brain, reducing these intense, alert beta brain waves and promoting calm alpha waves. (Alpha waves, which are quieting and relaxing, also increase gastric juices in the stomach, solving digestive problems.)

Glycine is an inhibitory neurotransmitter. It quiets the nerve cells in the spinal cord, brain stem, and central nervous system.

Taurine, another calming amino, suppresses the release of excitatory neurotransmitters like norepinephrine. Taurine acts like a light tranquilizer throughout the body. It is found in large amounts in the central nervous system, as well as in the excitable tissues, such as the heart. The amino *histidine* also reduces beta waves in the brain and encourages calming alpha waves.

The neurotransmitter *GABA* (gamma-aminobutyric acid) has a

powerful, soothing effect on the brain. In fact, benzodiazepine tranquilizer drugs (like Valium, Librium, and Ativan) work by stimulating the brain's GABA receptors. At HRC, we successfully free clients from tranquilizer addiction by substituting GABA to reload their depleted GABA neurotransmitters. (Chapter 5 explains how to use these aminos to combat anxiety.)

OBSESSIVENESS AND COMPULSIVITY

Genetically, some of us inherit naturally high levels of histamine, a brain neurotransmitter made from the amino histidine. It can speed up the brain's metabolism and create feelings of being driven or feeling compulsive, and crying easily. Another amino acid, *methionine*, helps to control this biochemical error by reducing excessive amounts of histamine. (Chapter 7 describes how histamine affects us emotionally.)

EXHAUSTION AND HIGH LEVELS OF STRESS

The physical and emotional stresses of life deplete us, and eventually cause great losses in our amino acid supply. Phenylalanine is used in large amounts to make adrenaline as is tyrosine and methionine. By supplementing these aminos, we can circumvent the exhaustion that ongoing stress produces in us.

Stress not only causes an increase in the breakdown of protein, but it creates increased amounts of toxic ammonia. The amino acid that clears this poison from our brain and bodies is *glutamine*. (Chapters 6 and 9 offer treatment for high stress levels and the inevitable exhaustion that follows.)

IRRITABILITY AND SUDDEN VIOLENCE

Certain aminos have a tranquilizing effect on the brain. In fact, a rise in these substances will shift brain activity from an alert, aroused beta state to a calm, relaxed alpha state. (Chapter 8 discusses this amino formula.)

MUDDLED THINKING AND FOGGINESS

We can increase our alertness by supplying the brain with more fuel, glucose. We do this by taking the amino glutamine, which converts to glutamic acid, an alternate source of the brain's only fuel, glucose. Glutamic acid also rids the brain of ammonia, the chemical that accumulates from a breakdown of worn-out protein. This is removed from the body through the urea cycle, by combining the ammonia with glutamic acid. A shortage of glutamic acid means that toxic ammonia remains in the brain and body, doing harm. So taking glutamine that quickly converts to glutamic acid lets you rapidly reverse ammonia buildup. The result is improved mental alertness and mental clarity. (Chapter 9 describes amino use to combat muddled thinking and fogginess.)

These are just a few examples of the diversity of amino acids in creating and maintaining emotional stability. They work best in certain combinations and with certain supportive vitamins and/or minerals. I have watched the amino acids perform their miracles for *over fifteen years*. The formulas in this book are based on what Health Recovery Center clients have taught us—the combinations to use, and how much to take. Their success stories clearly validate the worth of applying all this research to the actual needs of human beings.

How to Assess Your Current Amino Acid Levels

Many labs now measure amino acid availability through either plasma or urine. The following conditions suggest a problem in your amino acid metabolism:

- Chronic fatigue that is refractory to conventional treatments
- Frequent headaches
- Mental disperceptions
- Neurological disorders
- Learning disabilities

If you identify with any of these categories, it would be worthwhile to invest in a lab test. They cost around $250 as of this writing but provide a wealth of information.

The abnormal amino acid patterns that are revealed can suggest a number of things, such as:

- a functional deficiency of certain vitamins and minerals.
- inborn metabolism errors.
- the availability of the key aminos that influence sleep, moods,

PRECAUTIONS TO OBSERVE WITH AMINO ACIDS

In general, taking amino acids is quite safe, as aminos are the body's building blocks of protein. However, there is no substance—including water—that cannot, when incorrectly used, cause harm. With this in mind, let's review the red flags that will tell you an amino supplement is *not* for you:

- **Phenylalanine:** Do not use if you are taking MAO inhibitors for depression or suffer from any of the following conditions: phenylketonuria (PKU), cirrhosis or any other liver damage, melanoma, or migraine headaches. Monitor blood pressure when taking this supplement, as L-phenylalanine may elevate blood pressure.
- **Tyrosine** and **Tryptophan:** Do not use if you are taking MAO inhibitors. Do not take tyrosine if you have liver damage, including cirrhosis. Monitor blood pressure when taking this supplement, as tyrosine may raise blood pressure.
- **Histidine:** Do not use if you have a history of schizophrenia.
- **COMBINATIONS OF AMINOS:** Do not take blends of several amino acids if you have liver damage or if you are restricted from taking phenylalanine, tyrosine, tryptophan, or histidine.

and behavior. Some abnormal amino acid patterns are red flags for impaired ammonia detoxification. (Elevated ammonia leads to mental and behavioral dysfunctions, headaches, and central nervous system disorders.)

These assays also offer insight into degenerative disease, susceptibility to occlusive cardiovascular disease, liver and kidney detoxification impairment, and more. Some of the labs doing this testing are found in Appendix C. After completing this book, ask your doctor to run this test for you so you can confirm, once and for all, what your symptoms seem to suggest. If your doctor is unfamiliar with reading amino assays, or refuses to run the test, use Appendix B to find alternative medicine resources.

THE AMINO ACIDS: OUR NATURAL PHARMACY

Alanine: Converts quickly to usable glucose and prolongs blood sugar stability (helpful for hypoglycemics). Reduces elevated triglycerides in diabetics; may be helpful in preventing seizures. Combined with high doses of B_6, plays an important role in reversing immune deficiency by reproducing lymphocytes.

Arginine: Triggers release of growth hormone from the pituitary; increases sperm count; detoxifies excess ammonia, which is helpful in cirrhosis of the liver; stimulates the immune response by enhancing production of T cells.

WARNING: Use carefully in schizophrenic conditions.

WARNING: May cause replication of herpes simplex virus; keep intake low in affected individuals.

Aspartic Acid (Asparagine): Highly concentrated in the brain, low levels are frequently found in those suffering from unipolar depression. Protects the liver; helps detoxify ammonia; promotes uptake of trace minerals in the intestinal tract. New research points to aspartic acid as having a bigger role in creating brain energy metabolism than as a neurotransmitter.

Carnitine: Helps mobilize cellulite and other surface fats; helps combat fatigue and muscular weakness; helps provide energy for tissues by promoting oxidation of long-chain fatty acids; useful in clearing triglycerides from the blood.

Citrulline: A precursor of amino acids arginine and ornithine; plays a role in the detoxification of ammonia; stimulates growth hormone.

Cysteine: Helps repair tissues damaged by alcohol abuse, cigarette smoke, and air pollution through detoxification of acetaldehyde; helps maintain skin flexibility and texture; promotes red and white blood cell reproduction and tissue restoration in lung diseases; promotes iron absorption; helps prevent formation of harmful peroxidized fats and free radicals; protects the lungs against damage from cigarette smoke; used in treatment of bronchial disease and asthma.

GABA (Gamma-aminobutyric Acid): Induces calm and tranquility; may be useful in treatment of schizophrenia, epilepsy, depression, high blood pressure, high-stress disorders, manic behavior, and acute agitation.

Glutamic Acid: Precursor of GABA and glutamine. Taken by mouth, glutamic acid cannot cross the blood-brain barrier. *Do not substitute for glutamine.*

Glutamine: Antistress effect; useful in treatment of alcoholism and hypoglycemia by reducing cravings for alcohol and sugar. Improves memory and dexterity. Increases alertness by ridding the brain of excess ammonia.

Glycine: Can be used as a beverage sweetener; decreases uric-acid levels to reverse gout; useful in epilepsy and other conditions characterized by abnormal nerve firings.

Histidine: Creates an antianxiety effect in the brain; promotes good hearing by stimulating auditory nerves; may be a promising answer for rheumatoid arthritis; releases histamines from body stores for sexual arousal.

WARNING: Use carefully; do not use in manic-depressive patients or those with elevated histamine levels.

WARNING: Take with vitamin C.

Isoleucine and **Leucine**: Involved in stress, energy, and muscle metabolism, and useful in stress states associated with surgery, trauma, cirrhosis, fever, and starvation. Leucine also stimulates insulin release and inhibits protein breakdown.

Lysine: Controls viral infections; inhibits growth and recurrence of herpes complex; stimulates secretion of gastric juices; controls muscle contractions and spastic disorders.

Methionine: Removes excess brain histamine that can cause depression and obsessive-compulsive disorders; prevents deposits and cohesion of fats in the liver; acts as memory builder by synthesizing choline.

WARNING: Must be taken with vitamin B_6.

WARNING: Avoid if you have low histamine levels.

Ornithine: Reduces fat and increases muscle mass by promoting fat metabolism and stimulating production of growth hormone; helps detoxify ammonia.

D-Phenylalanine: Controls pain; elevates moods by increasing endorphins.

WARNING: Should not be taken by those using MAO inhibitors for depression.

L-Phenylalanine: Helps manage certain types of depression by increasing levels of the neurotransmitter norepinephrine, a precursor of epinephrine (adrenaline); increases blood pressure in individuals with low blood pressure.

WARNING: Should not be used by anyone taking MAO inhibitors for depression.

WARNING: Do not take if you have high blood pressure. Monitor blood pressure if headaches develop, and stop using phenylalanine.

Proline: Can help lower blood pressure; promotes wound healing.

Serine: A derivative of glycine; can cause psychotic reactions and elevated blood pressure. Serine enhances the effects of opiates (morphine, etc.) and may be useful for pain relief. A high serine-to-cysteine ratio is a clinical marker for psychosis.

Taurine: Can help inhibit epileptic seizures; helps repair muscle and tendon damage; helps promote skin flexibility; stops alcohol-withdrawal tremors. Is valuable in its potassium-sparing ability and it keeps the heart muscle adequately supplied with potassium.

Tryptophan: Helps alleviate depression by increasing levels of the neurotransmitter serotonin; induces sleep; has an anti-anxiety effect; appears to aid in blood clotting. Deficiency causes insomnia, depression. (Should be taken with vitamin B_6, niacin, and fruit juice to maximize uptake by the brain.)

Tyrosine: Useful in combating depression because it is a precursor of the neurotransmitters norepinephrine and adrenaline; a precursor of thyroid hormone.
WARNING: Should not be used by anyone taking MAO inhibitors for depression or by those with malignant melanoma.
Valine: Promotes muscle coordination and proper functioning of the nervous system; promotes mental vigor. Low serum valine is consistently found in patients with anorexia nervosa.

MISSING MINERALS THAT DISRUPT EMOTIONS

Life on earth originated in a solution rich in *minerals*. We cannot grow life without adequate amounts of these minerals, and deficiencies in them produce impaired functioning or death. Minerals and trace elements help produce energy and control the many chemical reactions in our bodies. An alarming problem in the United States today is the loss of minerals in the topsoil. Of the forty-four minerals and trace elements still found in the sea, twenty have already disappeared from the land! Fertilizers further deplete our minerals. Soils deficient in minerals such as magnesium, iron, and manganese can still yield bountiful crops, but the humans who eat these crops then develop severe deficiency diseases!

Food processors also strip much of the nutrition that remains by refining, processing, and inventing artificial substitutes that pose as eggs, orange juice, and other foods. Thus you are probably being shortchanged in terms of minerals in your diet. Now research is gradually linking an excess or deficiency of certain minerals to "emotional" symptoms. The following are examples of just how mineral availability can result in "emotional" symptoms.

ZINC

Serious zinc deficiency will affect brain function, creating severe mental problems, including learning and behavioral disorders and an inability to handle stress.

Animals in the last trimester of pregnancy with zinc deficiency produce offspring with smaller than normal brains and less than half the learning ability. Female offspring born to zinc-deficient mothers were violent and aggressive.

When zinc supplementation was given to zinc-deficient twenty-year-old students, they showed a marked difference in scholastic performance after one year, compared to a matched group not receiving zinc.

MAGNESIUM

Magnesium deficiency is seldom recognized because it isn't looked for. Symptoms may include irritability, confusion, personality changes, memory impairment, and learning disability. Also, magnesium prevents and corrects heart arrhythmias, although an ongoing deficiency ultimately results in cardiomyopathy.

IRON

An *overload* of iron is fairly common, and can cause depression and chronic, disabling fatigue. The FDA has attempted, unwisely in my opinion, to increase the amount of iron in our foods. Already, white flour has been "enriched" with additional amounts of iron, which can lead to a serious buildup of iron levels in the body.

MANGANESE

A deficiency can lead to glucose intolerance (diabetes). Manganese is required to make acetylcholine, a neurotransmitter. Also, antipsychotic medications (major tranquilizers) bind to manganese, causing a deficiency that results in tardive dyskinesia (contorted facial twitching) in about one quarter of schizophrenics taking antipsychotics. Taking manganese daily helps to prevent or reverse this toxic reaction. Abnormally high manganese levels often result in episodes of violence.

COPPER

Excess copper may result in paranoia, aggressiveness, and fearfulness.

LITHIUM

Lithium in high doses is used to treat manic-depression psychosis. At HRC, we have used 300 to 400 milligrams of lithium to improve mood and lift depression.

SELENIUM

This mineral has antidepressant properties at 200 micrograms twice daily. It is an antagonist to heavy metals, helping to remove mercury, aluminum, and cadmium from the body. It is needed in the production of thyroid hormones.

CHROMIUM

In the form of chromium picolinate, this helps to correct glucose intolerance in hypoglycemics thus stabilizing mood swings and energy levels.

The following table will familiarize you with minerals and trace elements—specifically their deficiency symptoms, toxicity levels, and ideal dosages.

MINERALS AND TRACE ELEMENTS

	Symptoms of Deficiency	Symptoms of Toxicity	Found in	Recommended Daily Allowance (Adults)	Maximum Therapeutic Repair Dosage for Adults
Calcium	Leg and feet cramps, anxiety, numbness, tenseness, insomnia, irritability, nervousness, periodontal disease, osteoporosis	Bone and tissue calcification	Dairy products, sunflower seeds, parsley, almonds, bonemeal, watercress, whole grains	800 mg	1,500 mg
Chromium	Diabetes, hypoglycemia, heart disease	No oral toxicity ever reported	Brewer's yeast, meats, beef liver, shellfish, whole wheat, rye, butter, oysters, margarine, cornmeal, shrimp	10 mcg to 30 mcg	480 mcg
Copper	Anemia, weakness, hypothyroidism	Paranoia, fears, hallucinations, aggressiveness, hyperactivity, stuttering, premature aging	Oysters, Brazil nuts, soy lecithin, almonds, walnuts, beef liver, clams, cod liver oil, lamb, rye, butter, garlic	2 mg	1 mg to 3 mg

MINERALS AND TRACE ELEMENTS, CONTINUED

	Symptoms of Deficiency	Symptoms of Toxicity	Found in	Recommended Daily Allowance (Adults)	Maximum Therapeutic Repair Dosage for Adults
Iron	Anemia, dizziness, weakness, inability to concentrate, poor memory, depression	Bronzing of skin, liver toxicity, cardiac insufficiency	Kelp, brewer's yeast, meats, eggs, green vegetables	10 mg (men) 20 mg (menstruating women)	Ferric citrate: up to 50 mg (Supplement iron with E because E is destroyed by iron supplements)
Magnesium	Memory impairment, insomnia, tremor, weakness, numbness, fatigue, anxiety, personality change, rapid heartbeat, hyperactivity, muscle aches, depression, delirium tremens	Drowsiness, stupor	Kelp, green leafy vegetables, peas, molasses, whole grains, soybeans, brown rice, almonds, cashews	350 mg	1,000 mg

MINERALS AND TRACE ELEMENTS, CONTINUED

	Symptoms of Deficiency	Symptoms of Toxicity	Found in	Recommended Daily Allowance (Adults)	Maximum Therapeutic Repair Dosage for Adults
Manganese	Reduced levels of dopamine, slow bone healing, disk problems in the back, sore knees due to cartilage damage, impaired glucose tolerance, reduced brain function and inner-ear balance; severe deficiency produces skipped heartbeats and convulsions	Schizophrenic-like symptoms, tremors, muscular rigidity	Turnip greens, rhubarb, Brussels sprouts, oatmeal, millet, cornmeal, carrots, eggs, pork and lamb, tomatoes, cantaloupe, whole-grain cereals	5 mg	20 mg
Potassium	Muscle cramps, fatigue, weakness, constipation, edema, headache, heart arrhythmia, joint pain	Cardiac arrest, apathy, kidney failure or dehydration can elevate potassium to toxic levels	Oranges, dark green leafy vegetables, legumes, avocado, bananas, squash, tomatoes, sunflower seeds	2 g to 6 g	Usually not needed; can use light salt or no salt to boost potassium intake

MINERALS AND TRACE ELEMENTS, CONTINUED

	Symptoms of Deficiency	Symptoms of Toxicity	Found in	Recommended Daily Allowance (Adults)	Maximum Therapeutic Repair Dosage for Adults
Selenium	Contributes to cancer and heart disease	Loss of hair and nails, paralysis, lassitude	Butter, smoked herring, wheat germ, bran, liver, eggs	50 to 200 mcg	300 mcg
Sodium	Low blood pressure, hot weather weakness, weariness	Swelling, tension, irritability, high blood pressure, PMS symptoms	Kelp, green olives, dill pickles, cheddar cheese, table salt, soy sauce, potato chips	4 g	Not needed except for sunstroke or exhausted adrenals
Zinc	Cold extremities, poor peripheral circulation, loss of taste and smell, poor wound healing, lethargy, poor appetite, prostate problems, acne, toxic copper levels, hypothyroidism	Drowsiness, vomiting, copper deficiency	Oysters, lamb, round steak, gingerroot, pecans, peas, shrimp, parsley, potatoes	15 mg	25 mg to 50 mg

Measuring Mineral Availability in Your Body

Testing of mineral levels can be done through blood, urine, or hair analysis. An inexpensive but accurate test choice is to submit a hair sample to any of the laboratories listed in Appendix C. All of the labs cited have voluntarily accepted the guidelines for hair element analysis established by the Hair Analysis Standardization Board of the American Holistic Medical Institute. *Please note:* it can prove misleading to accept all of your mineral levels at face value, because certain high readings may indicate storage of the mineral in the hair and soft tissues, and yet it will still be unavailable in blood and bone. Therefore, it is important to have the tests interpreted by a *knowledgeable physician or nutritionist.*

VITAMINS THAT AFFECT YOUR BRAIN

In Chapter 2 (on pages 48–49), we talked specifically about the B vitamins and their powerful effect on the brain and nervous systems, so I won't get into detail here again. The following table of vitamins gives you a complete account of vitamin deficiency, toxicity, and ideal therapeutic dosages.

VITAMINS

	Symptoms of Deficiency	Symptoms of Toxicity	Found in	Recommended Daily Allowance (Adults)	Maximum Therapeutic Repair Dosage for Adults
A (palmitate; beta-carotene)	Frequent colds, respiratory illness, calcium phosphate kidney stones, acne, dry skin, night blindness, burning eyes, eye infections, poor nails and dull hair, insomnia and fatigue	Aches and pains, poor appetite, yellowing of skin, weight loss, sore eyes, enlarged liver, decalcification of bones	Green leafy vegetables, liver, eggs, whole milk, cream, carrots, fruits, cod liver oil	6,000 IU (adults) 3,000 IU (children)	25,000 IU
B₁ (thiamine)	Mental confusion, depression, fatigue, apathy, anxiety, inability to concentrate or tolerate pain, sensitivity to noise, low blood pressure, heart palpitations, numbness or burning in hands and feet	Water soluble; excess is not stored in the body	Dairy products, brewer's yeast, bran, mushrooms, dark green vegetables, and organ meats	1 mg to 1.5 mg (0.5 mg per 1,000 calories of food)	300 mg daily

VITAMINS, CONTINUED

	Symptoms of Deficiency	Symptoms of Toxicity	Found in	Recommended Daily Allowance (Adults)	Maximum Therapeutic Repair Dosage for Adults
B$_2$ (riboflavin)	Red tongue, cracks in corners of mouth, dizziness, watery or bloodshot eyes, hair loss, brain and nervous system changes, mental sluggishness, depression	Water soluble; excess is not stored in body	Dairy products, organ meats, brewer's yeast, poultry, fish, eggs, dried beans, peanuts	10 mg	100 mg
B$_3$ (niacin)	Fear, suspicion, depression, insomnia, weakness, mental confusion, red-tipped tongue, sore mouth, dermatitis, excessive gas, irritability	Large doses of niacin should be avoided by those with liver disease; may cause a marked drop in blood pressure; raises blood sugar levels; can irritate ulcers because of its acidity; raises uric acid levels and so can trigger gout	Lean meats, peanuts, brewer's yeast, wheat germ, desiccated liver, fish, poultry	18 mg (men) 13 mg (women)	100 to 3,000 mg

VITAMINS, CONTINUED

	Symptoms of Deficiency	Symptoms of Toxicity	Found in	Recommended Daily Allowance (Adults)	Maximum Therapeutic Repair Dosage for Adults
B₅ (pantothenic acid)	Fatigue, sleep disturbances, depression, adrenal exhaustion, recurrent respiratory illness, constipation, low blood pressure, irritability, burning feet	Water soluble; excess is not stored in the body	Organ meats, bran, peanuts, brewer's yeast	10 mg	100 to 1,000 mg
B₆ (pyridoxine)	Mental confusion, irritability, depression, anxiety, numbness or cramping in hands and feet, insomnia, nausea in the morning, anemia, water retention, PMS symptoms	Extended use at levels over 1,000 mg has resulted in numbness of extremities	Meats, fish, peanuts, soybeans, bananas, whole grains, spinach, broccoli, legumes	2.2 mg	100 to 1,000 mg

VITAMINS, CONTINUED

	Symptoms of Deficiency	Symptoms of Toxicity	Found in	Recommended Daily Allowance (Adults)	Maximum Therapeutic Repair Dosage for Adults
B$_{12}$ (cobalamin)	Pernicious anemia, numbness, neurological changes, poor reflexes, apathy, poor concentration, confusion, paranoia, poor memory	Water soluble; excess is not stored in the body	Eggs, meat, poultry, fish, dairy products, brewer's yeast	6 mcg	1 mg
Folic acid	Anemia, poor digestion, constipation, diarrhea, deterioration of nervous system, apathy, withdrawal, irritability, poor memory	Masks B$_{12}$ pernicious anemia. Water soluble; excess is not stored in the body	Green leafy vegetables, wheat germ, dried beans and peas	400 mcg	800 to 3,000 mcg
Choline	Low levels of phosphatidylcholine prevent adequate conversion to memory neurotransmitter (acetylcholine)	Unknown	Lecithin, egg yolks	None established	10 g daily to treat memory

VITAMINS, CONTINUED

	Symptoms of Deficiency	Symptoms of Toxicity	Found in	Recommended Daily Allowance (Adults)	Maximum Therapeutic Repair Dosage for Adults
Inositol	Poor sleep, anxiety, panic attacks, depression	Unknown	Whole grains, lecithin, liver, brewer's yeast	None established	Up to 20 grams (20,000 mg)
Biotin	Fatigue, depression, skin disorders, muscle pain	Unknown	Yeast, pork and lamb, liver, egg yolks, nuts (especially peanuts)	None established (our own bodies make about 300 mg daily)	
C	Fatigue, loss of appetite, sore gums, slow wound healing, aching joints, bruising easily, frequent infections, mental disorders	Rare; water soluble; high doses will eventually cause diarrhea; ascorbic acid form of vitamin C can activate peptic ulcer in susceptible people	Citrus fruits, cauliflower, Brussels sprouts, broccoli	20 mg	3,000 to 6,000 mg daily, for viral or bacterial infections, take to bowel tolerance (the point where diarrhea begins)
D	Rickets, rheumatic pains, exhaustion, hypothyroidism	Calcium storage and calcification in the soft tissues of the body, frequent thirst and urination, nausea, vomiting, weakness, loss of appetite	Cod liver oil, sunlight, egg yolk, fish; frequently added to dairy products	400 IU	400 IU (consider the possibility of overdose because of the addition of vitamin D to many dairy products)

VITAMINS, CONTINUED

	Symptoms of Deficiency	Symptoms of Toxicity	Found in	Recommended Daily Allowance (Adults)	Maximum Therapeutic Repair Dosage for Adults
E	Restlessness, fatigue, insomnia, menopause symptoms, muscle wasting, liver damage	High blood pressure may occur if high doses are taken at outset of use	Wheat germ, cold-pressed oils (sunflower, safflower), spinach, broccoli, sweet potatoes, almonds, walnuts	15 IU	400 to 800 IU
K	Bleeding disorders, hemorrhaging	Not toxic	Leafy green vegetables, tomatoes, pork, liver, carrots	None	500 mcg; antibiotics and sulfa drugs destroy K-containing intestinal bacteria; acidophilus culture 3 times daily replaces this friendly flora

How to Tell What You Need

Don't panic, thinking that discovering what your brain needs is a monumental task! When I started working with clients, I felt exactly that way, too. But over the years I devised many written screening tools that save a lot of wear and tear in discerning if certain lab tests are worth the expense. In the upcoming chapters are ways to screen yourself to determine if your symptoms cluster around certain biochemical imbalances. There are also detailed explanations as to which lab test will confirm absolutely that you are on the right track. After that, you will have the opportunity to use the very same formulas for your recovery that we use at our Center.

But let's back up a moment. What if we go through the above steps, but lab tests cannot seem to link your symptoms to a biochemical shortage or toxicity? This happens, of course, but it doesn't happen often. At that point, we can choose to do a blood test called a functional intracellular analysis (FIA) also called the comprehensive 3000 (see Appendix C for lab information). It measures the availability of many key vitamins and minerals and amino acids at the *cellular* level. Most tests measure what nutrients are present in your blood; the FIA gives you the real picture of how much actually gets taken up by your cells. All of us have some glitches in what we actually access, but most never find out these important facts. I'm a good example. I took B vitamins daily, so I knew I had those bases covered, yet my FIA showed low levels of B_1, B_6, and B_{12} *inside* my cells.

Many of you may also have some nutrient "dependencies," meaning diet alone can't supply enough of what your body uniquely requires. You will need to supplement, sometimes in megadoses, until those levels are sufficient for your needs. Then you will feel normal and stable.

So let's get on with our discoveries. In the next chapter, we'll tackle the anxiety and inner tension with which so many of you have learned to co-exist. But before we move on, use the following checklist to be sure you are making the initial changes we have discussed.

CHECKLIST

_____ You are on the diet that is right for you: low carbohydrate or moderate carbohydrate (read Chapter 3).

_____ You are taking your Balanced Emotions Basic Formula (read Chapter 2).

_____ You are choosing a physician to run lab tests, as you discover which ones are appropriate for you (see Appendix B if you need help with this).

Now let's add one more big item.

_____ You agree you will exercise regularly (minimum requirement here: a half-hour walk, four times a week).

PART THREE

Your Specific Emotional Needs

CHAPTER 5

When You Just Want to Hide in the Closet
Soothing the Anxious Brain

If you have battled anxiety all your life, you are not alone. In the 1980s, the National Institute of Mental Health conducted the largest study ever done on mental disorders. It found that anxiety disorders are the second most common mental health problem in the United States, second only to substance abuse. Surprisingly, medical intervention is rare, according to a second massive NIMH study. The results showed that *over three quarters of these people never received any treatment for anxiety, despite frequent visits to their doctors.*

As for those who do—these are some of the typical clients who arrive at the door of HRC, acutely anxious and seeking relief. Each had first sought help from a psychiatrist or family physician.

Ben, age twenty-four, came to HRC because of his anxiety attacks. He complained of living in a state of high inner tension since his teen years. Ben suffered from frequent bouts of nervous exhaustion. His eyes were sensitive to sunlight. He had acne and stretch marks on his skin. He said he tired easily but slept poorly, and had little dream recall except for nightmares. A psychiatrist had given him Xanax for his anxiety, and later went on to double his daily dose. By the time Ben came to us he needed even more to get relief from his symptoms. (Xanax is highly addictive yet requires escalation of the daily dose to reduce anxiety.) Ben could see he was on the road to addiction and he didn't want to add that to his problems. This was when he called Health Recovery Center. Lab testing pinpointed several underlying causes of his anxiety:

1. *an inherited but correctable biochemical mistake that causes anxiety, called pyroluria. (Pyroluria will be explained, in detail, later in this chapter.)*
2. *a heavy accumulation of copper in the brain, which can create anxiety. (Ben is a welder by trade.)*
3. *a sudden drop on his glucose test into a hypoglycemic state, accompanied by nervousness, anxiety, and worrying.*

These biochemical errors would only grow worse for Ben over time. How much Xanax would he finally need to relieve his symptoms? If Ben continued to use drugs, he would be a lifelong customer of his psychiatrist and a full-blown addict. And, as he observed, he was only partially helped by the drug. His symptoms were still there, as real as ever, just beneath the surface.

Marge, a thirty-five-year-old nurse, complained of anxiety, depression, and exhaustion. She had seen her doctor, who ordered some medical tests, but the causes were not found. When I looked at Marge's fingernails, I saw numerous white flecks and dots. She told me she gets frequent colds and often has headaches. She has been on antibiotics frequently over the years for urinary tract infections. She also said she is becoming more of a loner with each passing year. Her feelings of anxiousness and sadness go all the way back to childhood. On her first visit with me, she confided that the stresses of life were simply too much for her. Lab tests showed some major reasons for her struggle:

1. *Marge was pyroluric, so we realized she had always suffered from anxiety and fearfulness, although she covered it up well.*
2. *The many rounds of antibiotics had altered her immune system and allowed heavy colonization of candida yeast. This alone could account for her exhaustion, anxiety, and depression!*
3. *She had low levels of important minerals: potassium, calcium, magnesium, chromium, boron, iodine, and zinc.*

Such malabsorption often occurs as a result of candida yeast compromising the intestinal tract. Also, her low magnesium levels are significant, as this increases the lactate-to-pyruvate ratio in the body, which contributes to anxiety.

It was vital to address all of these imbalances. They were the real causes of Marge's unstable moods. Eventually Marge normalized with treatment.

Richard, a forty-five-year-old unmarried businessman, described himself as a loner who hadn't dated in years. He isolated himself except for his work. He told me he felt uncomfortable with strangers, and that he refused to be seated in the middle of the room in a restaurant; he wanted his back to the wall. He noticed that sometimes his face seemed swollen when he became stressed. His feet were usually cold, and he tired easily. Throughout his life he had gone to great lengths to hide his inner tension and fearfulness from others. A doctor recently put him on Prozac to lift his moods, but instead it gave him severe headaches. Richard is a vegetarian who believes protein doesn't agree with him. Lab evidence showed:

1. low thyroid functioning, which was keeping him tired and cold.
2. pyroluria, which was driving him more and more into isolation.
3. high candida antibodies, which indicated his immune system was at war with an overcolonization of Candida albicans yeast. (The candida yeast lined his intestinal tract, causing poor absorption of many nutrients.)
4. adrenal exhaustion, resulting in his having no buffer against stress.

Richard had lived with these conditions for many years. Fortunately, he finally decided to get some scientific answers. Within a month, his mood and energy had greatly improved. By our last session, he had met a young woman whom he was dating seriously. Life had finally brightened for him.

A New Way of Treating Anxiety

Anxiety that lingers across the months and years is almost always caused by an imbalance in your brain/body chemistry. Just because your doctor doesn't find these biochemical mistakes is no reason you should be told you need a psychiatrist to drug you, or a psychologist to try to talk away your imbalances. As we approach the twenty-first century, science has learned a *lot* about how the brain functions. Lab tests can now pinpoint abnormal levels of brain chemicals and body hormones, nutrient deficiencies, toxic chemical buildups, cerebral allergy reactions, and much more. It is no longer necessary to limp through life feeling unstable and trapped in a malfunctioning body. Unfortunately, it's still true that some medical doctors:

- don't give sufficient time to patients to ask the right questions and gather enough facts.
- don't order the lesser-known lab tests that help to solve the riddle of your symptoms.

And many HMO and preauthorized health plans may not pay for these lab tests because they may not consider it "customary." But all is not lost. My purpose for writing this book is to help you *recognize* groups of familiar symptoms and how your profile fits with biochemical errors known to cause such symptoms. These chapters show you how to gather the right facts. Thus armed, you only need to seek confirmation in lab tests. I will describe these tests in detail so you will understand clearly what to ask for, which tests will tell you about your health, and why they are recommended. Hopefully, your family physician will agree to order what is needed. If not, I will provide you with a list of national medical organizations that can put you in contact with doctors specializing in your area of need.

If you can't have the tests done at this time, but the clues fit you, I urge you to use the suggested repair formulas on an experimental basis. I say this because I know that these natural substances do not carry the risks that drugs do. Plus, any "negative" information is included with each formula for your protection. With or without testing, recovering your biochemical balance is your ultimate goal.

WHY NOT JUST USE ANTIANXIETY DRUGS?

No doubt about it: antianxiety drugs work fast! The benzodiazepine family of drugs—Valium, Librium, Xanax, and Ativan—artificially fire calming GABA neurotransmitters into the brain at a fast clip, continually damping down any ripple of anxiety.

At first, no one suspected the level of addiction they could induce. But it finally became apparent that our tolerance for these tranquilizers just grows and grows. And simultaneously, their ability to control symptoms weakens unless the dosage increases. For many unwary Americans (mostly women), tranquilizer addiction has turned their lives into nightmares. In their drugged state they act and feel like zombies, but when they try to reduce or quit taking the drugs, they suffer full-blown fearfulness, sweating, racing heartbeat, upset stomach, jitters, tenseness, even panic attacks. The *Physicians Desk Reference* (PDR) warns that these benzodiazepine drugs are only for short-term use, yet many people I have treated have been on them for years. Several years ago, our clinic came close to tragedy while trying to solve a heavy tranquilizer addiction in a strapping, thirty-year-old farmer, Andy. His doctor had loaded him with antianxiety drugs for several years until he had reached the zombie stage. Finally, his wife and children had walked away, seeing no future for them as a family. At that point, his parents brought him to our clinic.

Andy was a sweet-natured hulk of a man, and the staff became very attached to him. We began to lower his daily drug dose while reloading his near-empty GABA transmitters. And we ran lab tests to identify the biochemical causes of his lifelong anxiety. We were finding the answers we needed, but we cut back on his drugs too rapidly—and halfway through the program he attempted suicide. It certainly woke us up, and I learned a valuable lesson I'll never forget about how much time is really needed for reducing dependence on those wretched tranquilizers. It took eight weeks of a slow reduction before Andy went home—and even then, we continued lowering his dose. It was many more weeks before he was finally free and healthy again.

Through the years, doctors have continued to prescribe a succession of addictive drugs, especially for anxiety, in the mistaken belief that they will not cause dependence, or if they do that it was the patient's fault. For years morphine was used to treat opium addiction. Later, heroin was routinely used to try to break cocaine addiction. Barbiturates and benzodiazepines are still widely prescribed today for anxiety. After twenty-five years and a lot of patient anguish, the addictive nature of these drugs is finally being recognized.

As I mentioned, the PDR entries for Librium, Xanax, and Ativan all state that they are for "short-term relief of anxiety." In fact, the effectiveness of Ativan and Librium for long-term use—which is defined in the 1998 PDR as *more than four months*—"has never been assessed in systematic clinical studies."

About Xanax, the PDR says: "Even after relatively short-term use at doses recommended for treatment of transient anxiety (.75 to 4.0 mg daily) there is some risk of dependence. . . . Withdrawal of the drug *may cause a return of symptoms to a level substantially greater in frequency or more severe in intensity than those seen before active treatment was initiated.* . . . In any case, reduction of dose must be undertaken under close supervision . . . some patients may prove resistant *to all discontinuation regimens*" (emphasis added).

Describing Ativan, the *Physicians Desk Reference* warns that "withdrawal symptoms similar . . . to those noted in barbiturate and alcohol withdrawal: convulsions, tremors, abdominal and muscle cramps, vomiting, sweating have occurred following abrupt discontinuance."

These benzodiazepine drugs create a no-win situation. They provide temporary relief while they addict you.

You may be wondering about the new, nonaddicting antianxiety drug BuSpar. This antianxiety agent differs from the benzodiazepines in that it has no muscle relaxant or sedative effects. It is nonaddictive and so is not classified as a controlled substance. In vitro studies show that BuSpar has a high affinity for serotonin receptors, and may affect other neurotransmitter systems.

But this drug has never been tested for effectiveness beyond three to four weeks in controlled trials. Plus, the danger of BuSpar causing "acute and chronic change in dopamine-mediated neurological function" hasn't been resolved (according to the 1997 *Physicians Desk Reference*).

When BuSpar first made its appearance, the manufacturer marketed it heavily to alcohol treatment centers, because it is common knowledge how anxious and stressed the newly abstinent alcoholic is. Our HRC physician became enamored with it, prescribing it even though almost all of our clients either hated the side effects and stopped it immediately, or stopped taking it after their initial supply ran out. This went on for almost two years before it dawned on me that this drug was not delivering much of anything for its high cost (nearly $100 for an initial supply).

But rather than the cost of this drug, I am more concerned with the unknown damage BuSpar could cause from artificially stimulating important brain neurotransmitters. Recently, we all witnessed the cardiovascular damage caused by fenfluramine, a popular prescription diet pill that works by increasing the neurotransmitter serotonin—just as BuSpar does. Unfortunately, too much serotonin stockpiled in the body (not the brain) causes heart valve damage and even death. We don't know if BuSpar can inadvertently create a similar overabundance of body serotonin, so we should exercise caution.

Another class of drugs used for anxiety are the *beta-blockers*—Inderal, Atenolol, Tenormin—that suppress the brain's epinephrine, quieting a pounding heart and tremors. Michael Ormes, M.D., and Matthew Connolly, M.D., point out in the *PDR* that beta-blockers do not address the cause of anxiety and create such side effects as feelings of mental and physical slowness, cold hands and feet, aching muscles, and, occasionally, asthma. Still, such drugs remain popular with some public speakers—who probably would pass on them if they realized that beta-blockers slow their brain functioning.

By now I hope you are beginning to agree with me that utilizing the body's *natural* chemicals, rather than drugs, offers a far greater safety net against irreversible emotional and physical damage.

Do You Have an Anxiety Disorder?

It is time to discover if you fit the category of Generalized Anxiety Disorder, as defined in the American Psychiatric Association's *Diagnostic and Statistical Manual*, third edition, known widely as DSM III. The following questionnaire divides anxiety symptoms into four categories. If you are experiencing more than one symptom from three out of four categories listed, and if these symptoms have lasted *for at least one month of continual duration*, you can "officially" classify yourself as suffering from a generalized anxiety disorder.

Generalized Anxiety Disorder Symptoms

1. Motor Tension

____ Shakiness
____ Jitteriness
____ Jumpiness
____ Trembling
____ Tension
____ Fatigability

____ Inability to relax
____ Eyelid twitch
____ Fidgeting
____ Restlessness
____ Startle easily

2. Autonomic Hyperactivity

____ Sweating
____ Heart pounding or racing
____ Cold, clammy hands
____ Dry mouth
____ Dizziness
____ Upset stomach

____ Frequent urination
____ Diarrhea
____ Lump in throat
____ Flushing
____ High resting pulse
    & rate of respiration

3. Apprehensive Expectation

____ Anxiety
____ Worry
____ Fear

____ Rumination
____ Anticipation of misfortune to self or others

4. Vigilance & Scanning

    Hyperattentiveness resulting in:
____ Distractibility
____ Difficulty
    concentrating

____ Insomnia
____ Feeling on edge
____ Impatience
____ Irritability

Two other categories of anxiety disorders are *panic attacks* and *phobias*. In both, people suffer tidal waves of inexplicable fear. These "attacks" occur without any real danger being present. Major biochemical changes, however, are taking place within the body during each episode. The sudden outpouring of adrenal hormones in response to perceived danger or *in response to loading refined sugars*, will produce many common symptoms of anxiety: pounding heart, rapid breathing, racing pulse, rising blood pressure. Your body swings into fight-or-flight mode, flooding the brain with adrenaline to mobilize for action. Anxiety attacks are often one of the symptoms of low blood sugar levels. This is biochemically predictable: When glucose levels fall too low, the downward plunge must be stopped, or the result would be unconsciousness and, finally, death. The body breaks the fall by releasing a flood of adrenaline into the bloodstream. The adrenaline causes an outpouring of emergency sugar from the liver, refueling the brain and saving the day. Unfortunately, the effect of a surge of adrenaline coursing through your veins at a time when your brain has lost too much fuel to function normally can result in high anxiety or even panic disorder.

Phobias grow out of panic attacks. The association of extreme fear occurring in a particular setting sets the stage for irrational fears that recur when the situation is encountered again. Thus, some people fear being trapped away from home in a public setting (agoraphobics), while others fear heights, elevators, social situations, and so on. I remember getting my clothing caught in a moving escalator when I was a small child. After that frightening experience, I became convinced that the "monster" would suck me in and swallow me whole if given the chance. For years afterward I insisted on using only elevators. As a teenager, I finally taught myself to risk riding the escalator again.

The Hidden Biochemical Causes of Anxiety

People who live with the kinds of anxiety I've just described can't just talk themselves out of it. The symptoms may look and feel psychological, but they can't be reasoned away.

A majority of the thousands of people we have treated at HRC over the past two decades have complained of such anxiety problems. Over time, we have discovered many biochemical reasons for their suffering, and we found ways to scientifically measure our suspicions. We have seen many miracles happen as a result of correcting biochemical errors. Now I want to share all that we've learned, so that you, too, can recover your sense of well-being.

We will identify the following six probable biochemical causes of anxiety (and how to treat each of these conditions):

1. pyroluria
2. hypoglycemia
3. nutrient deficiency
4. elevated blood lactate

5. a high imbalance of excitatory neurotransmitters
6. food and chemical sensitivities

PYROLURIA AS A CAUSE OF ANXIETY

This disorder is connected to a genetic abnormal production of a group of body chemicals called *kryptopyrroles*. Kryptopyrroles, or pyrroles, are a worthless by-product of hemoglobin synthesis. Most people have very little, if any, pyrroles circulating in their bodies. (We know this through measuring levels of pyrroles excreted through urine.) Some of us, however, are not so fortunate. Pyrroles are abnormally high in about:

30 percent of schizophrenic persons
40 percent of persons with psychiatric problems
11 percent of the healthy population
25 percent of children with psychiatric problems
40 percent of alcoholics

Pyrroles do their damage by binding to aldehydes throughout the body, and causing their excretion along with the pyrroles. B_6 (pyridoxine), being an aldehyde, is, therefore, systematically removed from many sites to which it is vital, and a severe B_6 deficiency results. Equally damaging is the further scavengering done by the combination of B_6 and pyrroles. Together, this duo seeks out and attaches to zinc, and so both of these essential natural chemicals—B_6 and zinc—are promptly dumped into the urine.

The loss of B_6 and zinc is a psychiatric disaster. B_6 is the co-enzyme (meaning it is absolutely essential) in over *fifty* enzymatic brain reactions where amino groups are transformed or transferred. B_6 plays an important role in your nervous system's balance: It is required to utilize protein for energy. Brain depletion of dopamine and serotonin occur without B_6, creating ongoing anxiety and depression. B_6 slows the conversion of pyruvate to lactic acid; without B_6, there is an elevated level of lactic acid, creating anxiety.

Zinc deficiency also results in multiple disorders. The brain uses at least sixty zinc enzymes, so zinc deficiency has a marked effect on mood states. Anxiety and depression have been observed in patients who develop zinc deficiency as a result of intravenous feedings. These patients experienced prompt relief from their acquired depression after zinc was supplied.

Zinc plays a starring role in immune functioning and brain development and performance. A deficiency means poor growth, poor sexual development, and a raft of "emotional" problems—irritability, fatigue, apathy, amnesia, depression—as well as poor appetite and a poor sense of taste and smell. In the last decade, over fifty articles in professional journals established a link between anorexia nervosa and zinc unavailability. Zinc has the job of removing toxic metals from our brains, particularly copper, lead, mercury, and cadmium. Without zinc, high copper levels result in paranoia, violent behavior, mood swings, and schizoid behavior. High lead content leads to learning disabilities and behavioral disorders. Mercury toxicity results in anxiety, emotional lability, exaggerated responses, and insomnia. Elevated cadmium causes hyperactivity, hallucinations, and central nervous system toxicity.

Maintaining adequate levels of B_6 and zinc in our bodies is an absolute *must!* Their continual destruction can turn a healthy human being into an emotional cripple.

Our interest in pyroluria in this chapter is that it creates symptoms of inner tension and bouts of nervous exhaustion and fearfulness that can be traced back to childhood or the teen years. Without proper identification and treatment, pyrolurics slowly become loners in their attempts to avoid stressful situations. Their lives become an ongoing struggle to protect themselves from too much emotional and physical stress.

You have the opportunity now to investigate for yourself the possibility of pyroluria being the cause of your ongoing anxiety. If you score high on the test, take heart: *Pyroluria is correctable.* The important task is to identify it.

ARE YOU PYROLURIC?

The pyroluria screening test that follows will help you identify the physical and neurological symptoms that develop from losing large amounts of B_6 and zinc. The circulating levels of pyrroles in your body may be slightly elevated or profoundly abnormal, but in all cases, these levels rise even more when you are under stress. If you are B_6 and zinc deficient, you will easily identify with some of the following symptoms. If you score 15 or more, it will be worth your while to be tested for pyroluria—and to get on with the needed biochemical repair.

HRC PYROLURIA PRESCREENING TEST

Yes No

_____ _____ 1. When you were young, did you sunburn easily? Do you have fair or pale skin?

_____ _____ 2. Do you have a reduced amount of head hair, eyebrows, or eyelashes, or do you have prematurely gray hair?

_____ _____ 3. Do you have poor dream recall or nightmares?

_____ _____ 4. Are you becoming more of a loner as you age? Do you avoid outside stress because it upsets your emotional balance?

_____ _____ 5. Have you been anxious, fearful, or felt a lot of inner tension since childhood but mostly hide these inner feelings from others?

_____ _____ 6. Is it hard to clearly recall past events and people in your life?

_____ _____ 7. Do you have bouts of depression and/or nervous exhaustion?

_____ _____ 8. Do you have cluster headaches?

_____ _____ 9. Are your eyes sensitive to sunlight?

_____ _____ 10. Do you belong to an all-girl family, or have look-alike sisters?

_____ _____ 11. Do you get frequent colds or infections, or unexplained chills or fevers?

_____ _____ 12. Do you dislike eating protein? Have you ever been a vegetarian?

_____ _____ 13. Did you reach puberty later than normal?

_____ _____ 14. Are there white spots/flecks on your fingernails, or do you have opaquely white or paper-thin nails?

_____ _____ 15. Are you prone to acne, eczema, or psoriasis?

_____ _____ 16. Do you prefer the company of one or two close friends rather than a gathering of friends?

_____ _____ 17. Do you have stretch marks on your skin?

Yes No

_____ _____ 18. Have you noticed a sweet smell (fruity odor) to your breath or sweat when ill or stressed?

_____ _____ 19. Do you have—or did you have, before braces—crowded upper front teeth?

_____ _____ 20. Do you prefer not to eat breakfast, or even experience light nausea in the morning?

_____ _____ 21. Does your face sometimes look swollen while under a lot of stress?

_____ _____ 22. Do you have a poor appetite, or a poor sense of smell or taste?

_____ _____ 23. Do you have any upper abdominal, splenic pain? As a child, did you get a "stitch" in your side when you ran?

_____ _____ 24. Do you tend to focus internally (on yourself) rather than on the external world?

_____ _____ 25. Do you frequently experience fatigue?

_____ _____ 26. Do you feel uncomfortable with strangers?

_____ _____ 27. Do your knees crack or ache?

_____ _____ 28. Do you overreact to tranquilizers, barbiturates, alcohol, or other drugs—that is, does a little produce a powerful response?

_____ _____ 29. Does it bother you to be seated in a restaurant in the middle of the room?

_____ _____ 30. Are you anemic?

_____ _____ 31. Do you have cold hands and/or feet?

_____ _____ 32. Are you easily upset (internally) by criticism?

_____ _____ 33. Do you have a tendency toward morning constipation?

_____ _____ 34. Do you have tingling sensations or muscle spasms in your legs or arms?

_____ _____ 35. Do changes in your routine (traveling, new situations) provoke stress?

_____ _____ 36. Do you tend to become dependent on one person whom you build your life around?

Getting Medical Testing for Pyroluria

Your doctor can determine if you have elevated levels of pyrroles by submitting a urine sample to a lab for testing. Yet I have learned from experience that very few labs are proficient in doing this test.

Our initial experience with the accuracy of the results was excellent: The high symptoms matched high pyrrole readings. The lab that ran the tests was Dr. Carl Pfeiffer's Brain Bio Center in New Jersey. After six months of this good fortune, that lab became aware that their licensing disallowed interstate business, and we had to find a new lab. "No problem," I thought. "We'll find a lab closer to home." What happened then still haunts me. Some of the large labs never heard of the test and wouldn't run it. We finally located a well-established laboratory that claimed to have much expertise with this test. That year, almost every test result that came back *failed to match the symptoms*. I called many times to argue with the director. He insisted he was the expert, not me. Then I heard about a lab in Kansas that actually used the equipment designed by Dr. Pfeiffer to measure pyrroles. Dr. Pfeiffer had built several machines, and after his death, they were put into the hands of groups who continued his research. The Bio Center Lab in Wichita, Kansas, had Pfeiffer's own machine! We immediately flooded them with our tests, and voilà! All the lab results once again matched the screening symptoms. Gradually we found quite a few of our old clients who had been told they were not pyroluric, and retested them. They all showed high levels of pyrroles! A number of these people who were alcoholics had relapsed, returning to alcohol to relieve their stress and anxiousness. I couldn't fault them. They felt trapped between a rock and a hard place, and we had told them that we had done all we could. Thus I learned a huge lesson about relying on the truthfulness of lab tests even when symptoms are shouting in your face.

Have your doctor call the Bio Center Laboratory, 1-800-494-7785, to obtain the mailing kit and preparatory instructions. No fasting is required. Results are usually available within two weeks.

A Family Affair

Pyroluria runs in families, so if you're pyroluric, chances are the same anxiety and poor stress responses will occur in other family members. They may also suffer from fatigue, nausea, sensitivity, coldness, anemia, poor dream recall, and even suicidal depression.

Despite the burden of this inborn inner tension, most pyrolurics display a high degree of creativity. Pfeiffer cites two people who made great scientific and literary contributions but whose secluded lives reveal many of the red flags of pyroluria. Charles Darwin and Emily

Dickinson both possessed great creativity, but chose to isolate themselves from the world before they were thirty. When younger, they enjoyed friends and parties, but as the years went by, they became reclusive, choosing to maintain friendships by correspondence. Both developed "safe" environments for themselves and their work, avoiding any kind of outside stress. They shared a strong dependency on their families, both having the good fortune of protective fathers. Any change of routine or intrusion by someone outside the family provoked stress. Darwin suffered nausea and vomiting, as well as crippling fatigue and blinding headaches. Both shared bouts of depression, nervous exhaustion, crippling fatigue, and severe inner tension. Emily's eyes became so sensitive to daylight that she could no longer read. Their handwriting deteriorated markedly as the stresses of the years took their toll. I suspect that both Dickinson and Darwin would have tested dangerously deficient in B_6 and zinc.

Because of the clients we get at HRC, I can say that many pyrolurics today have not been forced into seclusion from the stress and tension of life. It is more likely that they hold down jobs and simply have become quite good at covering up their bouts of inner tension from others.

The Signs and Symptoms

I have observed that pyrolurics typically pick out strong, protective spouses. Often a pyroluric man will marry an older woman, more mother than wife. This preference changes as they recover their normal sense of well-being with biochemical repair.

Pyrolurics favor low-protein or vegetarian diets, being unable to tolerate protein well without B_6 and zinc. They have pale skin, with little B_6 and zinc to produce pigment coloring in both skin and hair. A Caucasian pyroluric may have a china doll complexion; an African-American pyroluric, the lightest skin in the family. Without a good immune system, they tend to be vulnerable to infection and may have unexplained chills and fever. Pyrolurics avoid eating breakfast, as they have no appetite for it, and may experience morning nausea. Motion sickness is common. Their upper dental arch is narrow, crowding the teeth. Zinc deficiency also causes poor tooth enamel. Pyorrhea from retracted gums is also a mark of too little zinc. Fingernails may be opaque or have white marks on them. The thinness of the nails, combined with the anxiety that is experienced, produces nail biters.

EXHAUSTED ADRENALS

A by-product of living with pyroluria is the gradual exhaustion of the adrenal glands. Over the years, the frequent outpouring of adrenaline in response to anxiety takes its toll and the adrenals no longer have the strength to respond properly. This condition, called hypoadrenocorticism, interferes with or destroys the ability of your adrenals to continue protecting you against stress, which adds more emotional instability.

A very accurate test, the adrenal cortex stress profile, has become available from Great Smokies Laboratories in North Carolina (see appendix C for information). The test involves collecting saliva samples four times over a twenty-four-hour period. Cost is much lower than the older adrenal tests, yet it effectively pinpoints current adrenal functioning. With this valuable information, adrenal steroids in the form of DHEA (dehydroepiandrosterone) and/or small amounts of cortisol can be prescribed to restore these important hormones.

Still, rebuilding your adrenals takes patience. Correcting your pyroluria, as well as ending your low blood sugar plunges (that set off the outpouring of adrenaline), will provide your adrenals with a chance to rest and heal. The raw materials your adrenals use to rebuild are vitamin C and pantothenic acid. Early Native Americans used to eat the adrenal organs of animals during winters to obtain vitamin C. In the pyroluria formula, you will find generous amounts of both vitamin C and pantothenic acid.

Important advice: *Decide now to completely stop using any form of caffeine.* Drinking caffeine to force your adrenals to pump out its meager supply of adrenaline only creates an illusion of energy. Your adrenals have great recuperative powers if you will just give them the chance to rest.

Without zinc, their skin tears rather than stretches, creating areas of stretch marks.

Depression is common, as is fatigue. If the lack of zinc allows brain copper to reach toxic levels, hyperactivity, paranoia, and even hallucinations may occur.

Living with high inner tension causes some pyrolurics to become easily irritated, and even violent when overstressed. Dream recall is usually rare until enough B_6 has been replaced in the brain. Tryptophan cannot break down into serotonin without B_6. Without adequate serotonin, there will be erratic sleep and ongoing irritability.

Treatment for Pyroluria

Pyroluria responds very quickly to nutritional treatment. Within one week there is noticeable relief, and often substantial recovery will occur within three to six months. The treatment regimen, however, is ongoing, to be maintained for a lifetime. The Health Recovery Center's pyroluria formula, which appears on page 154, contains the following essential nutrients, in addition to B_6 (pyridoxine) and zinc, to treat your pyroluria:

PYRIDOXAL 5 PHOSPHATE:

This is the metabolite that B_6 becomes. Sometimes that first step (from B_6 to P5P) is faulty, so it is wise to incorporate both forms of B_6. P5P also allows a higher intake of B_6 without reaching a toxic level (tingling or numb fingers and toes).

MANGANESE:

This is depleted in pyroluria and will be further reduced by taking zinc if not supplemented. Manganese is required for sugar protein metabolism and for cartilage and joint development. It plays a role in preventing depression and in delivering choline to the memory neurotransmitter acetylcholine.

WARNING: *In persons over forty, manganese may raise blood pressure. If this occurs, the dose should be stopped until blood pressure normalizes.*

MAGNESIUM:

A depletion of magnesium may be created by taking large amounts of B_6. Dr. Bernard Rimland, Ph.D., has found that adding magnesium to B_6 supplementation prevents such side effects as sound hypersensitivity, irritability, and involuntary urination, when taken at one half the dosage of B_6.

THE HRC FORMULA FOR ANXIETY (PYROLURIA)©

Nutrient	Dose	Directions
B$_6$* (Pyridoxine)	250 mg	1 capsule at breakfast 1 capsule at lunch (or until dream recall occurs)
Zinc picolinate†	25 mg	2 capsules at breakfast 1 capsule at lunch
Pyridoxal 5 phosphate*	50 mg	1 capsule at breakfast 1 capsule at lunch (equivalent to 500 mg B$_6$)
Manganese gluconate†	10 mg	1 capsule at lunch 1 capsule at supper
Magnesium	400 mg	1 capsule at breakfast
Niacinamide‡	500 mg	1 capsule at breakfast 1 capsule at supper
Pantothenic acid	500 mg	1 capsule at breakfast 1 capsule at lunch
Vitamin C	675 mg	1 capsule at breakfast 1 capsule at lunch

Note: If you are already taking any of the above nutrients, do not exceed the amounts for your total dosage (see chart page 56).

*Adjust B$_6$ dosage until you can recall your last dream before waking. DO NOT EXCEED 2,000 mg B$_6$/P5P combination doses.
†Zinc and manganese compete for absorption: DO NOT TAKE TOGETHER.
‡Take niacinamide cautiously if you are high histamine, as it raises histamine levels.

©Copyright 1999 Health Recovery Center. ™All Rights Reserved.

NIACINAMIDE (B$_6$):

Since the body must have enough B$_6$ to make niacin from tryptophan, a deficiency of niacin often occurs in pyroluria, causing pellegra-like symptoms. Abram Hoffer, Ph.D., M.D., a California researcher who has pioneered effective treatment for autism, has found niacin supplementation to be valuable in speeding the process of recovery. At HRC we use the niacinamide form; it is superior to niacin for relief of anxiety, since niacinamide penetrates the brain more easily.

PANTOTHENIC ACID AND VITAMIN C:

These antistress nutrients are needed to rebuild adrenal glands that are exhausted from living with the ongoing tension pyroluria creates. Without this repair, it is nearly impossible to lift the fatigue and weakness you experience.

The Impact of Stress on Pyroluria

If you have pyroluria, it is important to know that you can relapse into an episode of illness when you are severely stressed—from a car accident, the breakup of a marriage, the loss of a loved one, or any major anxiety-creating event. I have seen lab levels of kryptopyrroles *double* because of such unavoidable stress. But this knowledge can arm you ahead of time; be ready, if need be, to increase your nutrient levels (especially B_6 and zinc) and to cater to yourself in every way you can at times of stress, so as to blunt anxiety's effects on your hyperreactive chemistry. The formula I've given you will lower the elevated pyrroles, but in times of stress you'll want to work directly with your doctor to monitor your progress and adjust dosages as needed.

HYPOGLYCEMIA AS A CAUSE OF ANXIETY

If ever there was a recipe for anxious, unstable moods, the American junk-food diet is it! Do we seriously believe we can scavenge enough from fast foods, high-sugar foods, and foods in boxes and cans to function optimally? Most Americans keep their cars loaded with gas, but their brains are limping along, devoid of a steady supply of nutrients and glucose fuel. Blame the U.S. food industry; blame the carbohydrate craze that convinced us a fruit bar and cola is a sane breakfast; blame the food giants that entice children with their sugar-sweetened "play" food; blame today's lifestyle, which dictates "instant" meals out of boxes or from fast-food windows or pizza parlors. Blame the all-American custom of delivering "energy" through sugared colas or candy bars when our weary brains want fuel.

This *food lifestyle* guarantees a twofold disaster:

1. Tons of scientific studies prove that anxiety will occur when you wipe out certain vitamins, minerals, essential fatty acids, and amino acids from your body.

2. The more sugar and simple carbohydrates you eat, the more insulin is released, creating hypoglycemic episodes of low brain fuel (glucose). Anxiety attacks frequently accompany such brain deprivation. Don't believe that low blood sugar only causes hunger and fatigue. Take another look at Dr. Stephen Gyland's research on one thousand hypoglycemics. Commonly occurring symptoms are:

- nervousness, 94 percent
- cold sweats and tremors, 86 percent
- unprovoked anxiety and constant worrying, 62 percent
- rapid pulse and internal trembling, 57 percent
- pounding heart, 54 percent
- panic and shortness of breath, 37 percent

It's obvious that diet has a *huge* impact on the level of anxiety you're experiencing! If you see yourself participating in a sugar-laden lifestyle, double back to Chapter 3 and take another look at what you scored on the Hypoglycemic Symptometer, page 71. Then take a glucose tolerance test to find out once and for all if you have hypoglycemia. However, another, far less expensive, way to get the same information is to follow the appropriate diet in Chapter 3 (a real sugar addict will get faster results with the Low-Carbohydrate Diet). Expect your dietary transition to stable health and emotions to take from one to three weeks. Be patient; the rewards are enormous!

NUTRIENT DEFICIENCY AS A CAUSE OF ANXIETY

Certain B vitamins are crucial to reducing anxiety. In fact, the textbook description of anxiety neurosis matches exactly the symptoms of B_3 (niacin) deficiency: hyperactivity, nervousness, fatigue, depression, apprehension, and insomnia. Niacinamide is the preferred form of B_3 because it penetrates the brain far more easily than does niacin. In 1979, shortly after the original Valium patent expired, Hoffmann LaRoche, the drug company that made Valium, published an article entitled: "Nicotinamide is a brain-constituent with benzodiazepine-like actions." What that means is niacinamide (nicotinamide is the British name for niacinamide) acts like Valium and the entire group of benzodiazepines in the brain—with the difference, of course, that niacinamide is not addictive. The reason niacinamide is not widely used as a tranquilizer is simple: *it isn't patentable!* Drs. Abram Hoffer and Humphry Osmond, an orthomolecular psychiatrist who worked with Dr. Hoffer extensively, have found that a possible genetic deficiency exists in some people that requires them to need larger daily quantities of niacinamide to produce a normal state of calm. Since it is water-soluble, niacinamide is not stored long-term in the body. One to 3 grams in divided daily doses have been used successfully by many.

WARNING: *If you persistently experience nausea from taking niacinamide, it means your liver is unable to handle that amount of B_3. Immediately stop taking it for a while, and if you resume again, cut the dose in half.*

The B complex vitamins together play major roles in undoing anxiety:

- B_1 (thiamine) deficiency results in mental confusion, apathy, depression, fatigue, and a sensitivity to noise.
- B_2 (riboflavin) deficiency causes nervous system changes and an inability to convert foods into energy.
- B_5 (pantothenic acid) deficiency results in sleep disturbances and adrenal exhaustion, resulting in ongoing anxiousness.
- B_6 (pyridoxine) deficiency is the main culprit in pyroluria.
- B_{12} (cobalamin) deficiency causes mental confusion, neurological changes, and poor concentration.
- Folic acid deficiency causes deterioration of the nervous system, withdrawal, and irritability.

Another B vitamin, inositol, has kept a low profile for a long time. Researchers were not able to demonstrate deficiency symptoms until just recently. In the eighties, studies at the Princeton Brain Bio Center showed that inositol has quantitative brain wave effects similar to those of the tranquilizer Librium. At that time, Carl Pfeiffer knew inositol was interacting with powerful brain neurotransmitters, but he did not understand how loading inositol by supplementation might affect receptor function.

In 1996, Israeli researchers discovered that inositol converts into a substance that regulates the action of serotonin within nerve cells. This knowledge allowed them to treat obsessive-compulsive disorder (persistent intrusive thoughts and senseless repetitive behavior) successfully by giving 18 grams of powdered inositol three times a day. It worked as well and as quickly as the selective serotonin reuptake inhibitors (SSRIs) Prozac and Luvox, which are the accepted treatments for obsessive-compulsive disorder—and it accomplished this *without* drug side effects.

Inositol's ability to regulate serotonin, a calming neurotransmitter, has also been applied to treating panic disorder, and it has proven itself a powerful brain chemical in reducing anxiety. You will discover the right amount of B vitamins, including inositol, to take in our Anxiety Formula on page 161. But read the next two sections first. And the next time you indulge in a sugar "treat," remember that *you are using up your B vitamins to metabolize the sugar . . . a no-win trade off.* Your emotional stability depends on a *protein* snack and not a Twinkie!

ELEVATED BLOOD LACTATE AS A CAUSE OF ANXIETY

Also related to your intake of refined sugars is the level of lactic acid in your blood. The higher your sugar intake, the more elevated your blood lactate levels become. Lactic acid binds with calcium, and as a result, calcium isn't sufficiently available in the brain to control the spiraling of excitatory brain activity. Nor can it fulfill its role as a powerful central nervous system suppressant. Also, when low blood calcium symptoms are artificially created by an injection of sodium lactate, what results are symptoms of anxiety neurosis. Sugar, caffeine, and alcohol all increase the lactate to pyruvate* ratio in the body, resulting in anxiety. Luckily, certain nutrients work to raise your pyruvate levels, especially magnesium (to correct anxiety neurosis symptoms) and calcium and niacin (to enhance the conversion of lactate to pyruvate, thereby reducing abnormal levels of anxiousness).

You can also take pyruvate as a supplement to not only tip the anxiety scale back to balance but to influence weight loss and cell

*Pyruvate is the key metabolite that extracts the stored energy in glucose, and is involved in the biochemistry of our energy metabolism.

energy and endurance. In a clinical study, humans on diets with added pyruvate lost weight at a greater rate than a matched group eating the same number of calories but without added pyruvate. *The subjects lost about one third more weight due to a greater loss of body fat.* In another set of studies, the physical endurance of those taking pyruvate far outlasted that of those taking a placebo. *Pyruvate reduces fat without exercise, yet the accelerated fat loss does not cause the usual associated loss of muscle (body protein).* The optimal daily dose for weight loss is 5 grams. Taking more does not increase effectiveness.

A lab test can measure your lactate to pyruvate levels. For those who suffer from anxiety due, in some part, to elevated blood lactate levels, you should take the formula on page 161. But please read the next section first.

A HIGH IMBALANCE OF EXCITATORY BRAIN NEUROTRANSMITTERS AS A CAUSE OF ANXIETY

Certain brain chemicals are calming and relaxing, others are excitatory. A high imbalance of excitatory neurotransmitters helps to elicit stress and pinpoint adrenaline. Hearts pound and strong beta waves in the brain take over, creating a state of intense alertness. Our senses become more acute. All of these changes are a plus—if faced with a sudden, life-threatening situation. But some of us are "wired" to respond to far less threatening happenings with the same alarm system. Newly recovering alcoholics often seem to be a "bundle of nerves," as they have no more alcohol to soothe them. At HRC, we have always looked for natural ways to calm down such anxiety, and eventually we discovered the power of the inhibitory amino acids. The formula that we put together is named Bio-Alpha Waves, because those particular amino acids quiet the brain's intensive beta waves and increase the calming alpha waves. We've tested this combination on hundreds of clients and on most of our staff (who prefer to keep a bottle handy in their desk drawers!). It is composed of all of the following amino acids except tryptophan, which is available only through prescription:

TRYPTOPHAN
Tryptophan is the only substance in existence that makes serotonin, a powerful calming brain neurotransmitter. The many copycat anti-

depressant drugs now on the market confirm the popularity of flooding the brain with "mellowing" serotonin. Tryptophan's benefits in treating anxiety, panic, and obsessive-compulsive disorders have been well documented. (Remember, tryptophan is still available only by prescription in the United States.)

GAMMA-AMINOBUTYRIC ACID

Gamma-aminobutyric acid (GABA) is the most frequently occurring of all the calming neurotransmitters in our brains. Tranquilizers like Valium, Librium, Ativan, and Xanax work by stimulating GABA receptors. Treating individuals who develop drug addictions as a result of such prescriptions by reloading GABA has worked quite well, and many of these people continue to use GABA in place of their former drug to alleviate anxiety.

GLYCINE

This amino acid strengthens the calming alpha brain waves and reduces excitatory waves. It also works throughout the spinal column to relax and ease rigidity and tension.

TAURINE

This amino regulates the excitability of the nervous system. It is found in abundance around the heart muscle. In our brains, it's another inhibitory (calming) neurotransmitter.

Putting Together the Right Antianxiety Chemicals for You

The formula on page 161 addresses deficiencies in nutrients and aminos, and of pyruvate. Reloading these amino acids and B vitamins will quickly dampen an anxious state. The pyruvate will also give an added sense of calm. You do not need to worry about the safety of certain generous amounts; all of the B vitamins and vitamin C are water-soluble, so you *can't* overdose on them. And the aminos are also quite safe to take at these dosages. In fact, I have come to realize that taking too little can be sadly disappointing, in that nothing happens until the body obtains its needed levels, and required levels of certain B vitamins may be extraordinarily high in anxious persons.

Please remember this formula *is not for pyrolurics*. It is for the rest of us who want to turn off our hot-wired brains and mellow out.

| | THE HRC FORMULA | |
| | FOR ANXIETY (NON-PYROLURIA)© | |

Nutrient	Dose	Directions
Tryptophan*†	500 mg	1 capsule 3 times daily
GABA†	200 mg	1 capsule 3 times daily
Calcium/magnesium	250/125 mg	2 capsules at breakfast 2 capsules at supper
B complex	50 mg	2 capsules at breakfast 2 capsules at supper
Niacinamide	500 mg	1 capsule at breakfast 1 capsule at supper
Inositol (powder)‡		1½ teaspoon with each meal
Pyruvate	600 mg	1 capsule with each meal
Vitamin C (Ester C)	675 mg	3 capsules daily with meals
Alpha waves formula		2 capsules, 2 or 3 times daily

Note: If you are already taking any of the above nutrients, do not exceed the amounts for your total dosage (see chart page 56).

*Requires a doctor's prescription.
†Take this amino on an empty stomach between meals.
‡1½ tsp=4 g.

©Copyright 1999 Health Recovery Center.™ All Rights Reserved.

You will discover that, as you relax, your ability to focus on a task improves 100 percent.

FOOD AND CHEMICAL SENSITIVITIES
AS CAUSES OF ANXIETY

Mark, a young man in his early thirties, had been at the HRC center for less than a week when he claimed that his continual panic attacks had simply stopped. Now, such a fast turnaround might not sound plausible for someone who regularly frequented emergency centers in a state of high panic. But the clues to Mark's panic attacks had been obvious. He told me at our initial meeting that he had followed all my advice from my first book except that he could not give up wheat and dairy. In fact, every meal included some form of whole wheat and dairy products. He looked miserable when I asked him to stop using any form of dairy products and all breads, pasta, and cereals that were wheat-based. But his lab tests had demonstrated his inability to break down and digest these substances normally, and within a few days of being free of these troublemakers, Mark's panic attacks vanished.

Today, science is aware that peptides formed from digested proteins are *identical* to certain brain endorphins that are linked to panic attacks and other "mental" conditions. The first two discoveries in this area were peptides that came from poorly digested casein (milk protein) and gluten (wheat protein). These are the most common allergy foods in the United States today! Mark's lab tests confirmed a severe allergy response to wheat, gluten, and dairy. His panic attacks ceased for good when he stopped eating these foods. He says he is delighted with the trade-off.

I have seen some profound reactions from food and chemical intolerances, including crying, anger, loss of control, panic attacks, and even schizophrenic episodes. A tip-off to a food allergy is compulsive eating and a craving for certain foods. If you suspect you fall into this category, see Chapter 9.

Note: The medical doctors who specialize in the field of cerebral allergy are called clinical ecologists. To locate a physician in your area who can test and treat you, contact:

American Academy of Environmental Medicine
P.O. Box 1001-8001
New Hope, PA 18938
1-215-862-4544

Where Do You Fit In?

Now that you are familiar with the various biochemical problems that may underlie your anxiety, it's time to determine what you will do to satisfy your need(s). Look through these options and check all categories that apply to you:

____ Identify pyroluria with lab test (consult your physician).

____ Restore the missing natural chemicals that will correct pyroluria, if you have this condition (see the pyroluria formula on page 154).

____ Correct hypoglycemia and follow the diet that is right for you (review Chapter 3).

____ Restore key vitamins and minerals (review the recommended nutrients listed earlier in the chapter and take the nonpyroluria anxiety formula on page 161).

____ Increase pyruvate intake (consult physician to measure pyruvate-to-lactate ratio; take the non-pyroluria anxiety formula on page 161).

____ Increase your calming neurotransmitters (consult your physician for an amino acid assay and a tryptophan prescription; take the nonpyroluria anxiety formula on page 161).

____ Avoid food and chemicals responsible for cerebral allergy responses (see Chapter 9 and consult a physician for lab testing).

Even if you fit into several of these categories, you are now embarked on a program to restore your health. In some cases you'll need a physician's help. Where can you find one?

SPECIFIC DOCTORS FOR YOUR SPECIFIC PROBLEM

I urge you to seek medical advice from a doctor attuned to your special needs. Orthomolecular doctors are experts in both allopathic and nutritional medicine. They are able and willing to work with you on all of the lab tests I have just cited, and to monitor the restoration of neurotransmitter levels and vitamins, minerals, and other natural body chemicals. For a list of orthomolecular physicians and psychiatrists in Canada and the United States, contact:

Journal of Orthomolecular Medicine
16 Florence Avenue
Toronto, Ontario, Canada M2N-1E9
1-416-733-2117

CHAPTER 6

That Sadness Inside You
Dissolving Biochemical Depression

Who hasn't felt depression?
What's amazing is how many of us ignore it, don't recognize it, and just keep plodding along with no inkling of the sadness within ourselves.

I have talked to thousands of clients who showed classic signs of depression. Yet many (mostly male) denied any such problem. I can empathize with them. A few years after I buried my husband and my teenage son, I was watching a TV show on the subject of depression. All of the panelists remarked that they cried every day, and the "expert" psychiatrist then assured them that that was common to depression. This made me think, "I cry every day . . . does this mean I'm depressed?" Sometimes tears dripped from my eyes when I was simply relaxing and thinking of nothing! But I had refused to recognize my condition, feeling that it signified a "weakness" in me at a time when I was my family's sole provider as well as a full-time employee and student.

Over the next ten years, I grieved over even more losses: father and mother, best friend, a former fiancé, and my second husband. When I look back at these years, I believe I would have retreated to a dark closet to live were it not for what I was learning about orthomolecular medicine and how to restore the important brain chemicals that ongoing stress and sadness wipe out!

Many studies confirm that childhood abuse—physical, emotional, sexual—creates lifelong depression. Ongoing losses and heavy

stresses are also a setup for depression. Such life events, if prolonged, profoundly affect the brain's chemical balance. Remember
the description of the Japanese POW camp survivors in Chapter 1,
and how they finally came out of their post-traumatic states with
biochemical repair? Those "walking wounded" are not unlike those
of us who have existed through long periods of unrelenting stress.
Certainly therapy is a comforting release, but in these cases, talk
alone is not enough to undo the damage.

At HRC, we continually see clients whose presenting symptom
is depression despite their current use of one of the popular antidepressant drugs. Often their doctors have tried them on more than
one antidepressant but, oddly enough, have never assessed them for
the many other biochemical causes of depression before writing
that prescription.

Prescription antidepressants assume the problem is too little
serotonin or norepinephrine or dopamine—but neurotransmitter depletion is just *one* problem on this list. Your antidepressant drug may
well be inappropriate, even toxic, if your brain is forced to artificially elevate the neurotransmitters it doesn't need.

A 1992 study published in the *Archives of General Psychiatry*
tracked depressed patients who were being treated over an eighteen-
month period. They found only a 20 to 30 percent recovery rate after
this time, underscoring the surprisingly low benefits attained from
drugs and therapy. Similar conclusions were reached by researchers
Seymour Fisher, Ph.D., and Roger Greenberg, Ph.D., who spent years
reviewing studies of drug treatment for depression. They state that
the standard of "substantial improvement" can only be applied to a
meager 25 percent of patients. They cite sixteen controlled studies of
the newer antidepressants, which show that the majority of these
drugs (62 percent) show *no difference* in the percentage of patients
benefiting from an active drug as opposed to a placebo!

In February 1990, the *American Journal of Psychiatry* described several cases of major depression resulting in suicidal
behavior that followed the administration of antidepressants. Improvement occurred upon *cessation* of such drug use!

And, on February 28, 1991, Phil Donahue's TV talk show
featured former Prozac users who had become compulsively self-
destructive, and even murderous, after going on Prozac. Donahue's

telephone lines were flooded with calls across the nation reporting similar responses.

Happily, orthomolecular approaches have proven far more rewarding in treating depression. I've documented some of the experiences at HRC in treating depression with orthomolecular techniques as part of my dissertation research (published in the *International Journal of Medical and Biosocial Research*). The data was collected on one hundred Health Recovery Center clients in the last decade. It showed 61 percent were seriously depressed on entry to the center. Of these, *95 percent were depression-free within six weeks!* At the three-year follow-up, *74 percent* stated they continue to follow the regimen that took them out of depression and that they still felt stable.

Because of my son Rob's suicide, I have searched everywhere for the results of studies on depression. Many confirm the connections between brain biochemistry and depression and offer methods of emotional healing that have worked more reliably than drugs or talk therapy. Yet there is no *single* biochemical glitch—for example, not enough serotonin—that explains all forms of depression. In this chapter, you will learn about their fourteen different biochemical sources of depression. In addition—and perhaps most important— you will learn how to overcome *your* particular chemical problems. This may mean taking even more nutrients. It may require further changes in your diet. Or it may mean drug treatment to correct a medical condition that can precipitate depression. But first, of course, you have to confirm that you *are* depressed. Then you can evaluate the severity of your case.

How Do You Know You Are Depressed?

As many as one out of five Americans suffer from depression, and one in seven of those with major depression commit suicide. Another 15 percent are unsuccessful in their suicide attempts. (We'll talk more about suicide later in this chapter.) Yet the National Institute of Mental Health has said that as many as 70 percent of people suffering from depression fail to seek treatment.

Why do so many people fail to seek help? Many simply view themselves as being unable to handle stress well; others may be unwilling to assume the label of depression because of the social stigma often attached to the label. Whatever the reason, they—or you— need to get help. These are the common red flags of depression:

- Withdrawal from activity; isolating oneself
- Continual fatigue, lethargy
- Indecisiveness
- Lack of motivation, boredom, and loss of interest in life
- Feelings of helplessness, of being immobilized
- Sleeping too much; using sleep to escape reality
- Insomnia, particularly early morning insomnia (waking very early and being unable to get back to sleep)
- Lack of response to good news
- Loss of appetite or binge eating
- Ongoing anxiety
- Silent and unresponsive around people
- An "I don't care" attitude
- Easily upset or angered, lashing out at others
- Inability to concentrate
- Self-destructive behavior (including promiscuity)
- Lack of interest in sex
- Loss of interest in people and activities previously considered important
- Unusual impatience, hostility
- Suicidal thoughts or plans

How to Tell If Your Depression
Is Psychological or Biochemical in Origin

Biochemical depression has certain symptoms that distinguish it from depression stemming from negative life events. External changes such as loss of a relationship, a job, or a loved one may result in a self-limiting kind of depression. As life's events improve, this depression evaporates. In the interim, this kind of psychological setback will respond well to therapy. Group or individual counseling offers some necessary human empathy, and gradually new hopes replace the disappointments. You have reason to suspect that you are *biochemically* depressed if any of the following markers describe your depression:

- You have been depressed for a long time despite changes in your life.
- Talk therapy has little or no effect; in fact, psychological probing—questions like, Why do you hate your father?—leave you as confused as Alice at the Mad Hatter's tea party.
- You don't react to good news.
- You awaken very early in the morning and can't get back to sleep.
- You cannot trace the onset of your depression to any life event.
- Your mood may swing between depression and elation over a period of months in a regular rhythm (this suggests bipolar or manic-depressive disorder).
- Drinking alcohol worsens your depression the following day.

When Your Depression Is Severe

As important as identifying the cause of your depression is determining the depth of your feelings. If you have suicidal thoughts, *please* confide in your physician and a close friend or relative.

In the seventies, when I lost my son to suicide, the dominant belief about these deaths was dictated by psychological/sociological disciplines. Author C. J. Frederich, in writing about adolescent suicide, described the victims as coming from broken homes. They perceived themselves as helpless, rejected, and hopeless and were involved in drug and alcohol abuse. The high-risk person was seen to have such clinical features as:

- A depressive disorder
- The presence of anxiety and agitation
- Decreased feelings of physical well-being and multiple physical ailments
- Drug and alcohol abuse
- Taking prescribed medications like sleeping pills
- Presence of self-blame and guilt
- Loss of self-control (fits of anger and loss of temper)
- Lack of support system; no one to turn to, and no one dependent on the patient

---

DEPRESSION AND YOUR FAMILY TREE: IS YOUR DEPRESSION GENETIC?

There is a 67 percent chance of both identical twins being depressed if one of them suffers from depression. And this is true even if they are raised in completely separate environments! If your parent or brother or sister suffers from depression, you have a 25 percent chance of sharing this genetic trait. If *both* parents are depressed, the likelihood of the children becoming depressed soars to between 50 and 75 percent. Suicide also clusters in families.

Although such symptoms could be labeled "psychological," mounting research over the last twenty years now recognizes that they may also be caused by the biochemical malfunctioning of brain/body systems. In fact, such physiological changes are far more likely to provide the real explanation for the despairing brain that chooses to finally end its misery.

Today, the psychiatric profession has no trouble acknowledging the physical basis of depression. Where I believe their thinking is faulty is that SSRI (Prozac-type) drugs then become the blanket answer—and the consequences of not probing for the underlying physical causes of depression can be severe.

Recently, the daughter of a dear benefactor of our foundation called me in tears. She had sought her doctor's help for depression two months earlier and had been given Prozac. After a week there was brief relief, then nothing. The dose was promptly doubled and the same response occurred. Now her latest advice was to raise the dosage to four daily. Slowly her depression has become severe. She now feels suicidal!

I asked her a few questions—and a probable basis for her depression began to emerge:

- *Frequent yeast infections and sinus problems*
- *Cold hands and feet, chilled all the time*
- *Works full-time in a hair salon around chemicals*

This translates as: possible toxic levels of Candida albicans *yeast causing cerebral changes; possible Hashimoto's thyroiditis or autoimmune disease causing her immune system to mistakenly attack her thyroid gland; or possibly a cerebral (brain) allergy response to the strong chemicals she breathes at work. All can be proven or disproven through lab tests. There is a high likelihood that a candida infection, low thyroid, and chemical sensitivities are all contributing to her depression. If true, the high level of Prozac she was taking only served to toxify her liver and disrupt her serotonin receptor sites.*

Within two weeks lab tests confirmed our suspicions: She has begun the necessary repair program, and already is feeling improvement.

Dr. Carl Pfeiffer comments that in his clinical experience, he has found "the greatest factor in teenage suicide is pyroluria, the stress-induced deficiency in B_6 and zinc" (see Chapter 5). "With such a deficiency, the teenager is confused, anxious, depressed, and sleepless. The onset of this disorder is between 15 to 17 years." The pyroluric teenager is a good candidate for drug and alcohol use, which only worsens the stressful situation, making his or her depression continue on into and through the adult years.

According to Dr. Pfeiffer, a second biological cause of teen and adult suicide is the presence of too much histamine in the body. High histamine creates energetic, compulsive "doers"—the self-starters who ordinarily make the world better. But it also causes many to go through life in continuous depression, and this group has the drive and the impulsiveness to carry out suicidal impulses. (We'll talk about histadelia [high histamine] later in this chapter. I'll outline what lab tests will identify it, and how to correct this type of depression.)

As I describe both of these biochemical triggers for suicide, I strongly suspect that my own teenager had many of these symptoms. It is twenty years too late for Rob, but not for your teen or yourself or a family member who may be suicide-prone. If symptoms cluster on your written screening tests, take the results to your physician and ask him or her to order the confirming lab work.

The repair formulas in this book have been the acceptable methods of treatment at Health Recovery Center for over a decade. They usually do not include drugs. We have continued to use natural

replacement chemicals with our clients because of the astonishing turnaround they produce. I encourage you to share this book
with your physician if he or she is unfamiliar with this orthomolecular approach.

Distinguishing Between Depression Types

There are two types of depression, and both—bipolar (manic depressive) and unipolar (depressed)—involve miserable, depressing
moods. However, their underlying biochemical causes are different,
as are their respective symptoms. At HRC, we have uncovered repair formulas that have proved invaluable in rebalancing both kinds
of errant chemistry, but first you need to recognize the depression
type that fits your condition.

MANIC DEPRESSION (BIPOLAR DISORDER)

This category of mood disorder alternates a depressed mood with
sudden shifts into a high-energy, euphoric, manic state. The identifying characteristic of these mood swing disorders is that they occur
and reoccur in cycles that may be predictable. (*Note:* I am not describing mood swings that recur over a twenty-four hour period. The
basis for that phenomenon is hypoglycemia [see Chapter 2]).

Manic episodes can be exhausting, yet there is no way to slow
them down without biochemical intervention. In these states, there
is usually little sleeping and little appetite. Some manics may be ob-
sessed with spending money, extramarital affairs, heavy drinking,
and gambling; others are just overexpansive to everyone. Although
bipolar disorder is twice as common in women as in men, I watched
a male friend who was bipolar, and on no medication, go through
black times where he could not get out of bed and function for
weeks at a time. But as soon as his mood shifted upward, he was
wildly gregarious and entertaining.

Some bipolar people may see their manic episodes take another
form. These individuals are overly suspicious and paranoid. In mania, their persecutory paranoia becomes grandiosity, and they are
angry and irritable with everyone who (they think) stands in the way
of the many wonderful achievements they feel they offer society. In
this elation phase their excessive self-confidence, disturbed sense of

judgment, and inappropriate social behaviors may well disrupt their careers and relationships.

The Biochemical Bases of Bipolar Depression

Many studies pinpoint biochemical abnormalities in bipolar moods, among them acetylcholine sensitivity, body clock arrhythmias, and vanadium toxicity. However, there is no unified theory as to why these abnormalities exist.

ACETYLCHOLINE SENSITIVITY AS A CAUSE OF MANIC DEPRESSION

Research at the National Institute of Mental Health suggests that bipolar people are hypersensitive to acetylcholine, a chemical that carries memory messages in the brain. They found that cholinergic receptors (the chemical hitching posts on cells that receive acetylcholine) are far more numerous in the brains of manic depressives.

One substance that blocks acetylcholine is lithium, a natural salt that everyone has in low levels. It is the current drug of choice for treating bipolar depression. But is it the best treatment? At high levels, lithium has been shown to seriously interfere with acetylcholine and other receptors that create our moods, emotions, and memory. The *Archives of General Psychiatry* reported the effects of lithium on healthy volunteers as a "general dulling and blunting of personality functions." I myself have heard lithium-using clients describe their emotional state of mind as feeling like they are in "a dial tone" world, with no highs or lows.

Psychiatric News outlined the widespread difficulties that lithium causes in a 1986 article titled "Lithium and Memory Loss." Besides causing memory loss, the high doses of lithium needed to stop manic moods are often toxic to the nervous system, causing tremors in many users. And at high levels lithium suppresses thyroid function and can cause hypothyroidism and mental confusion, according to the *Journal of Clinical Psychiatry*.

There needs to be a better alternative for treating manic depression than high dosages of lithium. Orthomolecular research has shown that B complex deficiencies commonly occur in 80 percent of manic depressives. Also, many bipolars are anemic, with low levels of B_{12} and folic acid, and show a lower uptake of inositol when compared to a control group. So orthomolecular physicians have now paired the use of lithium with the intake of daily B complex vitamins, which work synergistically with lithium. In this way, high lithium doses can be substantially reduced, thus eliminating many devastating side effects.

Another exciting, safe substance that has a lithium-like effect on the brain is the amino acid taurine, which is a calming, inhibitory neurotransmitter that naturally blocks the effects of excitatory transmitters like acetylcholine. Manic depressives have very low taurine levels when measured in the lab. A taurine deficiency causes far greater symptoms in women than men (hypothyroid, lethargy, and depression), and bipolar disorder is *twice as common* in women. Science also documents hereditary depression in taurine-deficient persons. Taurine has been successfully substituted for lithium (500 mg three times daily) and, unlike lithium, has *no* side effects.

BODY CLOCK ARRYTHMIAS
AS A CAUSE OF MANIC DEPRESSION

If you are manic depressive, another abnormality may show up as disturbed body rhythms. Just as you show mood swings, you also have measurable disturbances in your daily rhythmic cycling or body clock. One study showed that four out of seven manic depressives could quickly end their depressions by starting their day at one A.M. rather than at seven.

Interestingly, the drug lithium is known to change and alter periods of rhythmic cycling. There is a form of *natural* lithium (nonprescription) derived from vegetable concentrates (lithomin) that was very effective in treating bipolar disorder. All participants in a study with patients who had a bipolar diagnosis showed tremendous improvement after taking lithomin. Six weeks later, when they were taken off the natural lithium, they *all* regressed to their former state of depression within *three days*. When the natural lithium was resupplied, they again recovered from their depression. This study strongly suggests the high lithium doses prescribed by most M.D.s that leave people toxic and physically trembling are not at all appropriate for everyone. Lithomin is an over-the-counter form of lithium with no adverse side effects. At Health Recovery Center, we use a 50 microgram product (taken with meals) called Lithinase (to obtain it, call us at 1-800-247-6237).

VANADIUM TOXICITY AS A CAUSE OF MANIC DEPRESSION

One more natural mineral level to check if you are bipolar is vanadium. Four separate studies report manic depressives have significantly higher amounts of this in their blood, and an excessive body load of vanadium has been known to trigger mania. Vanadium toxicity has also been associated with depression and melancholia.

Loading ascorbate (vitamin C) reduces the damage from excessive vanadium in the body. Studies in *Lancet* and the *British Journal of Psychiatry* show levels of vitamin C in bipolar patients are so low as to indicate borderline or actual scurvy. *Replacement of vitamin C is critical for these people.*

These studies make a strong case for the value of nutritional repair for bipolar depression, and it may even be a better alternative than drug therapy. It is certainly less toxic and offers far less or no side effects.

Here are the formulas you should take if you are suffering from manic depression.

A NATURAL FORMULA FOR BIPOLAR DISORDER© TO BE USED BY THOSE WHO ARE *NOT* TAKING PRESCRIBED LITHIUM		
Nutrient	**Dose**	**Directions**
Vitamin B complex	50 mg	2 capsules 3 times daily with food
Vitamin C (Ester C)	675 mg	2 capsules 3 times daily with food
Taurine	500 mg	1 capsule 3 times daily on an empty stomach
Lithomin	50 mg	1 capsule 3 times daily with food
Note: If you are already taking any of the above nutrients, do not exceed the amounts for your total dosage (see page 56).		

UNIPOLAR DEPRESSION

Unlike the roller-coaster emotional swings that bipolar patients endure, unipolar depression signals an ongoing dismal mood that does not lift. This inner sadness pervades daily life, sapping future

**A NATURAL FORMULA FOR BIPOLAR DISORDER© TO BE USED BY
THOSE WHO ARE TAKING PRESCRIBED LITHIUM**

If you are presently taking prescribed lithium, it is depleting your stores of:
- Folic acid
- Calcium
- Thyroid
- Vitamin C

1) Be sure to get your thyroid checked by your M.D.
2) Also begin adding the following formula to your daily regimen:

Nutrient	Dose	Directions
B complex	50 mg	2 capsules daily at mealtime
Ester C	675 mg	4 capsules daily at mealtime
Cal/Mag	25/75 mg	6 capsules daily at mealtime

Note: If you are already taking any of the above nutrients, do not exceed the amounts for your total dosage (see page 56).

© Copyright 1999 Health Recovery Center.™ All Rights Reserved.

dreams and ambitions. Living your life devoid of any joy leads to hopelessness and despair. It is absolutely essential to find the biochemical cause(s) that keep you a prisoner in your own body, and that is what we are about to do. You may be surprised at the number of promising avenues for us to investigate together.

The Biochemical Causes of Unipolar Depression

A few years ago many of us didn't expect our doctors to nail down the causes of our illnesses; we only asked that they make the symptoms go away. Now it has finally dawned on us that if we don't discover the cause and eliminate it, we may have to relive the same misery in the future. Fixing symptoms offers only a short-term solution.

Over the last eighteen years I have seen a parade of people with different causes for their unipolar depression. The following represents the most common categories:

Neurotransmitter depletion of serotonin or norephinephrine
Essential fatty acid deficiencies in the brain
Vitamin and mineral deficiencies or dependencies
Hypothyroidism (including Hashimoto's thyroiditis)

Hypoglycemia, or excessive sugar and caffeine use

Brain allergy reactions to foods and cerebral sensitivities to airborne chemicals

Systemic buildup of fungal molds and candida yeast

Histadelia (abnormally elevated histamine)

Buildup of heavy metals in the brain (e.g., cadmium, lead, copper)

Brain damage from alcohol or drugs, prescribed or otherwise

NEUROTRANSMITTER DEPLETION OF SEROTONIN OR NOREPINEPHRINE AS A CAUSE OF DEPRESSION

We've talked in earlier chapters about the natural chemicals that make possible all communication between brain cells and the immune system, endocrine system, and, in fact, the entire body. They are the substances that govern our emotions, memory, moods, behavior, sleep, and learning abilities. These brain neurotransmitters are manufactured from the amino acids we extract from food, and our supply is entirely dependent on the presence in our bodies of these amino acid precursors.

The two major neurotransmitters involved in preventing depression are serotonin (converted from the amino acid tryptophan) and norepinephrine (converted from the amino acids L-phenylalanine and L-tyrosine). The new antidepressant drugs are based on firing one or both of these neurotransmitters into the brain. The drugs Prozac, Zoloft, and Paxil all claim to reverse depression, as well as a host of other behavioral and emotional problems, simply by blocking the uptake of serotonin back into the neurotransmitters, thus artificially elevating the levels of serotonin.

On first reading this, this mass-marketing of antidepressant drugs sounds wonderful, but the avalanche of media reports and lawsuits from adverse reactions have made us take a second look.

WHY PROZAC, ZOLOFT, AND PAXIL COULD CAUSE IRREVERSIBLE DAMAGE

It is possible that using these selective serotonin reuptake inhibitors (SSRI drugs) will, over time, cause serious biochemical changes in the brain receptors for serotonin, and that these changes may be permanent. For example, in *Talking Back to*

Prozac, Dr. Peter Breggin reports: "The brain develops an ominous reaction [from taking Prozac] that continues to increase over time. The mechanism—called down-regulation—causes receptors for serotonin literally to disappear from the brain. In many areas in the brains of experimental animals, the receptors drastically diminish in number, sometimes with losses as high as 60% in regions of the brain involved in mental functioning."

The human body consistently takes this tack when it senses an overload of a natural substance. For example, if you continually take large amounts of cortisone, a synthetic adrenal hormone, your own production of natural adrenaline will stop and your adrenals will gradually atrophy. Likewise, taking thyroid will shut down your own natural thyroid production. Thus it stands to reason when you flood your brain with inordinate amounts of serotonin, the same sensing mechanism will begin to shut down some of your serotonin receptors (as happened in animal trials) in an attempt to control the overload. We don't know if serotonin receptors will ever reactivate—it is bewildering that the FDA has not required studies—although we do know from studies that organs like the thyroid and adrenals do have serious difficulty restoring themselves to normal levels. And the drug companies do not carry out the easy and inexpensive tests about serotonin receptor sites on humans; perhaps they fear that a finding of irreversible receptor loss would result in lawsuits against them.

Most of us have believed that Prozac's approval by the FDA came after thousands of patients were observed long-term. It may surprise you to know that the FDA trials were only four to six weeks in length, and the grand total of Prozac-taking patients in those studies amounted to 286 (read *Talking Back to Prozac* for more information). None of these participants included hospitalized psychiatric patients, suicidal individuals, children, or the elderly. Although the study outcomes were never made public, Dr. Breggin obtained the actual results through the Freedom of Information Act. In its "Summary of Basis of Approval," the FDA states that fourteen protocols involving controlled studies were submitted by Eli Lilly. Four of them compared Prozac to a placebo, and of these, the FDA used only three as evidence of some beneficial effect. Of the remaining ten studies, two were positive about Prozac, and eight showed an older antidepressant, imipramine, to be more effective. The FDA selected only the five "positive" studies and discarded the other nine! Dr. Peter Breggin's books—*Talking Back to Prozac* and *Toxic Psychiatry*—are replete with the above facts and references. I recommend them to you for the sake of your own mental health.

Effexor, the newest antidepressant drug, blocks the reuptake of not just serotonin but norepinephine as well. Effexor was described in *Psychiatric News*, on February 4, 1994, as "Prozac with a Punch"—but Dr. Breggin notes that cocaine and amphetamines also block serotonin and norepinephine. In addition, he reminds us that they block the reuptake of dopamine, so cocaine and amphetamines could well be marketed simply as "Prozac with a Double Punch!" In other words: There is a close similarity between such street drugs and these prescribed drugs. Why is it we only hear about cocaine and amphetamine addiction?

SmithKline once touted the amphetamine/sedative combination Dexamyl as a miracle drug for depression. It took time before the dangerous effects of amphetamines were understood, and now they are classified as "controlled substances," along with narcotics and cocaine! So I advise you to be wary about taking any drugs such as Prozac, Zoloft, and Paxil, when the studies have only been short-term and certainly not exhaustive.

Instead of using drugs to "restock" your brain's supply of vital neurotransmitters such as serotonin and norepinephrine, and end the depression their absence causes, you can take amino acid capsules daily. In doing this, you reload these neurotransmitters so that their firing mechanism has a continuous full load to deliver to your brain. In contrast, the artificial SSRI drugs do not raise neurotransmitter levels. Instead, they trap what little you have and keep using it over and over in the brain, blocking it from dissipating.

Taking amino acids instead of drugs

- is much less expensive.
- is much safer (no side effects).
- is more natural, and
- accomplishes the same outcome in most cases.

So how do you know whether you need tryptophan, phenylalanine, or tyrosine? Your depression symptoms will be quite different, depending on which neurotransmitter is depleted. Look at the following to recognize what you are missing:

SYMPTOMS INDICATING TRYPTOPHAN IS NEEDED TO
INCREASE SEROTONIN LEVELS
- sleeplessness
- anxiety
- irritability
- nervous depression

SYMPTOMS INDICATING TYROSINE OR L-PHENYLALANINE IS
NEEDED TO INCREASE NOREPINEPHINE LEVELS
- lethargy
- fatigue
- sleeping too much
- feelings of immobility

HOW TRYPTOPHAN WORKS:

The essential amino acid tryptophan is the *only* substance able to "manufacture" serotonin, the neurotransmitter that controls moods, sleep, sex drive, appetite, and pain threshold. Eating disorders and violent behavior have been traced to serotonin depletion. Replacing needed serotonin can quickly lift your depression and end your insomnia.

In one notable study, a Dutch medical researcher demonstrated that the combination of tryptophan (2 g nightly) and vitamin B_6 (125 mg three times daily) could restore patients with anxiety-type depression to a normal mood state in four weeks. (The type of depression that is accompanied by anxiety and sleep disturbances is most likely to respond to tryptophan—serotonin's precursor.)

Research conducted in 1997 at McGill University in Montreal has found that men produce 52 percent *more* serotonin than do women. This would explain why more women than men appear to experience a shortage of this chemical critical to mood regulation, and why more are likely to suffer from depression and/or eating disorders.

USING TRYPTOPHAN TO MAKE SEROTONIN:

Tryptophan has had the misfortune of acquiring a bad reputation due to a single event in 1989. At that time, its largest manufacturer, Showa Denka in Japan, accidentally contaminated its product. Until then, we had used tryptophan at HRC for nine years with great success and no ill effects. However, that contaminated batch was enough for the U.S. Food and Drug Administration to prohibit all future sales of tryptophan in the United States—this despite the fact that the rest of the world, including Canada, continued and continues to have access to this irreplaceable amino acid.

U.S. scientists were able to prove that the deaths and illnesses that resulted from the bad batch of tryptophan were not caused by the amino acid itself but by its contamination. It has been several years since the *New England Journal of Medicine* reported the evidence that confirmed this, yet the FDA continues to block over-the-counter sales of tryptophan (other than 5HTP, which I believe is not safe—see page 27). Today, tryptophan has finally been restored to baby food in the United States. It has also been made available—but by prescription only. Most U.S. citizens and their physicians are unaware this has happened, and only certain pharmacies dispense it. Two pharmacies (and their 1-800 numbers) that HRC physicians use to order tryptophan are listed on page 45. Even though this natural substance is available, your doctor may still be resistant to writing a prescription for tryptophan rather than Prozac, as he may be unfamiliar with its benefits. And now that the FDA has classified this amino acid as a drug, its price has quadrupled!

Tryptophan is not a drug. It is an essential amino acid much needed to support life and sanity. In an interesting coincidence, Prozac made its first appearance within days of the ban on tryptophan. Now a whole family of serotonin-stimulating drugs has been made available, too—but none of them can *create* an iota of serotonin (unlike tryptophan). As they block the natural reuptake into the neurotransmitters, *our levels of serotonin are slowly becoming even more depleted.* Almost all of our clients at HRC have taken a serotonin-firing antidepressant—Zoloft, Paxil, Desyrel, Prozac, Serzone—before coming to us. Typically, our physician switches them to the natural serotonin precursor, tryptophan, which promptly restores their serotonin levels. Usually, the situation was that their firing mechanisms worked fine, but there was very little serotonin available to fire.

GUIDELINES FOR TAKING TRYPTOPHAN:

- Like all natural substances, tryptophan needs help to convert to serotonin. These co-enzymes are B_6 and vitamin C (see the formula on page 182).
- Tryptophan converts to niacin before finally becoming serotonin. If your body is deficient in niacin, the tryptophan you take will supply you with niacin, not serotonin. For this reason, it is a good idea to take a B complex vitamin daily. It will give you both B_6 and niacin and allow your tryptophan to make more serotonin.
- It is good to take tryptophan with the B vitamin inositol, which changes into a substance that regulates serotonin's effectiveness within nerve cells. A double-blind study reported in 1995 confirms inositol's effectiveness with depression. Inositol powder is sweet and good-tasting. One and a half teaspoonful three times daily is the researched dosage according to the *American Journal of Psychiatry*.
- Of all the amino acids, tryptophan is least able to cross the blood-brain barrier. It must pass this biological hurdle in order to be converted to serotonin. You can give it the right "nudge" by taking it with fruit juice. The carbohydrate will trigger insulin release, which will assist the tryptophan across the blood-brain barrier. Always take tryptophan on an empty stomach.

IS TRYPTOPHAN SAFE FOR EVERYONE?

Tryptophan has been widely used by orthomolecular physicians, clinics like Health Recovery Center, and the general population in doses of 1 to 6 grams daily. Since it is not stored in the body, you cannot accumulate toxic levels. However, taking high doses of tryptophan can produce side effects. Among them are:

- feeling drowsy the next morning.
- bizarre or strange dreams (although this is rare).
- increased blood pressure in persons over sixty who already have high blood pressure.
- aggressiveness (this rare side effect can occur in the absence of sufficient co-nutrients needed for the normal conversion of tryptophan to serotonin).

THE HRC FORMULA FOR DEPRESSION DUE TO SEROTONIN DEPLETION©		
Nutrient	**Dose**	**Directions**
Tryptophan*	500 mg	2 to 8 capsules per day in directed doses: • 1 or 2 midmorning • 1 or 2 midafternoon, • 2 or 4 at bedtime *Take all dosages on an empty stomach with fruit juice.*
Vitamin B complex	50 mg	2 capsules at breakfast 2 capsules at supper
Ester C	675 mg	2 capsules daily
Inositol	12 g powder	1½ teaspoons of powder 3 times daily (1½ teaspoons = 4 g)

Note: If you are already taking any of the above nutrients, do not exceed the amounts for your total dosage (see chart page 56).

*Tryptophan is available only by prescription in the United States and Canada. Your doctor can order it only from certain pharmacies. Two that we use are: The Hopewell Pharmacy, 1-800-792-6670, and College Pharmacy, 1-800-888-9358.

© Copyright 1999 Health Recovery Center.™ All Rights Reserved.

Also, there *are* certain individuals who must avoid tryptophan or use it carefully. These are:

- anyone who takes an MAO (monoamine oxidase) inhibitor for depression. If so, do not take tryptophan until ten days after your last dose of MAO inhibitors.
- anyone with severe liver disease. (A damaged liver cannot properly metabolize tryptophan or certain other amino acids.)
- pregnant women. (You may be able to take 500 to 1,000 mg of tryptophan, but only with the approval and supervision of your physician.)
- anyone taking an antidepressant.

A commonly asked question at HRC is: Can I combine tryptophan with an SSRI antidepressant? Combining SSRI drugs and tryptophan

THE EFFECTIVENESS OF ST. JOHN'S WORT (HYPERICUM)

Before leaving the subject of serotonin enhancement, you may want to consider another natural substance that can do just that in a way similar to SSRI drugs. Seventy percent of German physicians prefer St. John's wort to treat depression and anxiety. A meta-analysis of its effectiveness was published in the *British Medical Journal* in 1996. Twenty-three double-blind studies involving 1,757 patients were analyzed. St. John's wort proved significantly superior to placebos, and as effective as Prozac and other standard antidepressant drugs. The big advantage of using hypericum instead of antidepressants is its safety and lack of side effects. St. John's wort works by inhibiting serotonin reuptake, just like the many new antidepressant drugs, but without the loss of libido or any violent outbursts, nausea, anxiety, or nervousness.

The standard dose is 300 milligrams, three times daily, between meals.

WARNING: Do not use St. John's wort if you are currently taking an antidepressant drug prescription. First see your doctor about discontinuing your drug.

WARNING: Do not combine the HRC formula for depression due to serotonin depletion with St. John's wort.

Consider St. John's wort as an *alternative* solution if, after you have reloaded your serotonin neurotransmitters, you are still depressed. Give yourself two weeks on the HRC formula before you switch to St. John's wort; the herb will help block the serotonin from recycling back to the neurotransmitter. (The effect is to create a lot of extra serotonin in your brain.) If, after three weeks on St. John's wort, you still do not get relief, it's time to pursue another biochemical cause of your depression rather than serotonin depletion.

is inviting a deluge of serotonin into the brain. It's dangerous to do and in most cases not recommended. We do have some clients who are taking a very small dose (5 mg) of Prozac in conjunction with daily tryptophan, and the result has been exactly right *for them*. But: *Do not play with this or any other combination of tryptophan and antidepressant drugs. Your doctor MUST supervise such an experiment.*

THE HRC FORMULA FOR DEPRESSION DUE TO NOREPINEPHRINE DEPLETION©		
Nutrient	**Dose**	**Directions**
L-phenylalanine*	500 mg	1 to 3 capsules per day in divided doses on an empty stomach
OR		
L-tyrosine*	500 mg	4 to 10 capsules per day in 2 or 3 equal doses on an empty stomach
Vitamin B$_6$	50 mg	1 capsule 3 times daily with food
Ester C	675 mg	2 capsules daily

Note: If you are already taking any of the above nutrients, do not exceed these amounts for your total dosage (see chart page 56).

* Start with the lowest dosage and slowly increase over two weeks. Cut back on dosage if symptoms occur.

© Copyright 1999 Health Recovery Center.™ All Rights Reserved.

USING TYROSINE OR L-PHENYLALANINE TO MAKE NOREPINEPHRINE:
Tyrosine is another essential amino acid needed for the formation of the neurotransmitters known as catecholamines, which include dopamine, norepinephrine, and epinephrine. It is also a constituent of brain hormones such as thyroid and estrogen. This amino, found largely in meats and cheeses, has an amazing effect on depression. A number of studies appearing in *Lancet* and the *American Journal of Psychiatry* have found that tyrosine can succeed where antidepressants fail.

Inside your brain, tyrosine is converted into the neurotransmitter norepinephrine, which has been described as the brain's version of adrenaline. The high that cocaine produces comes from its ability to activate norepinephrine while inhibiting serotonin. This chemical reaction causes the brain to race until its supply of norepinephrine is depleted. The crash leaves addicts exhausted, depressed, extremely irritable, and craving more cocaine. Large doses of tyrosine can reduce withdrawal symptoms and prevent serious depression among cocaine addicts.

We have used tyrosine at the Health Recovery Center for over ten years with no adverse effects. The usual dose is 3 to 6 grams per day, taken on an empty stomach. You must also take B_6 and vitamin C to guarantee conversion of tyrosine to norpinephrine.

Important: As an alternative to tyrosine, you may take the amino acid L-phenylalanine, which also makes norepinephrine in the brain. Many studies confirm L-phenylalanine's amazing antidepressant effects. In one, this potent amino acid was found as effective an antidepressant as the popular drug imipramine (Tofranil).

L-phenylalanine has one important advantage over tyrosine in treating depression: It can be converted to a substance called 2 phenylethylamine, or 2-PEA. Low brain levels of 2-PEA are responsible for certain depressions, and only phenylalanine corrects it. If you are affected, tyrosine will not be successful for you. The only way to find out is by trial and error.

I recommend you *start by using L-phenylalanine*. If it makes your thoughts rush (an effect often described as "brain racing"), you don't need 2-PEA and should switch to tyrosine.

IS TAKING TYROSINE OR L-PHENYLALANINE SAFE FOR EVERYONE?

Besides the effect of brain racing, another disadvantage to taking phenylalanine is its slight potential for raising blood pressure. And there is some evidence that excess L-phenylalanine can cause headaches, insomnia, and irritability. For these reasons, it is important to begin with a low dose.

L-phenylalanine doses range from 500 to 1,500 milligrams daily taken on an empty stomach. Symptoms of an overdose are: headache, insomnia, irritability, and brain racing.

Some individuals should *not* take tyrosine or L-phenylalanine.

- Anyone with high blood pressure should avoid phenylalanine or take very low doses (100 mg) at first and monitor blood pressure as dosage is increased.

- No one taking an MAO inhibitor for depression should take *either* tyrosine or L-phenylalanine.
- No one with severe liver damage should take either of these amino acids.
- Pregnant women should not take these amino acids unless they are approved and supervised by her physician.
- No one with phenylketonuria (PKU) should use L-phenylalanine.
- No one with schizophrenia should take either amino acid (except with the approval and supervision of a physician).
- No one with an overactive thyroid or malignant melanoma should take either amino acid.
- If you are being treated for any serious illness, consult your doctor before taking these amino acids.

ESSENTIAL FATTY ACID DEFICIENCIES IN THE BRAIN AS A CAUSE OF DEPRESSION

We know that both serotonin and norepinephrine need to fire appropriately to prevent depression and to create normal moods. But without adequate essential fatty acids to create this communication, these important neurotransmitters cannot send their signals properly. The result is ongoing depression.

Patrick, a longtime AA member, was proud of his two decades of sobriety. However, most of those years were spent in therapy for his bleak depression. He had tried a variety of antidepressant medications, but none proved effective. Hoping to lighten his oppressive mood, Patrick had even given up caffeine, and, finally, his three-pack-a-day cigarette habit! Nothing worked! At our first session, he told me life seemed entirely hopeless. I was not surprised to learn that his father had been depressed all his life and often talked of suicide, and his maternal grandfather and two uncles also suffered ongoing depression. Patrick's lab tests gave us all the clues we needed: His tryglycerides and cholesterol were both twice as high as the normal range, and his essential fatty acid analysis showed low levels of these important substances.

Patrick had been given drugs to lower his cholesterol and triglycerides, but he chose not to use them. Instead, with our help, he *changed his diet to include large quantities of cold-water fish and EPA capsules to reload the omega-3 essential fatty acids. He also took gamma-linolenic acid to supply his brain with adequate prostaglandin E_1 (an omega-6 metabolite that I will describe later in this chapter). Within five weeks, his lifelong depression was gone, and he had lost fifteen unwanted pounds. When last tested, his triglycerides had fallen from 391 to 113, and his cholesterol was down from 301 to 160.*

Because the brain is over 60 percent fat, brain tissue is heavily dependent on fatty acids to control moods and behavior. Patrick's brain was "running on empty," and the elevated cholesterol and try-glycerides in his body were red flags that certain blood fats were "clumping," thickening the blood and interfering with the delivery of oxygen and nutrients to his brain.

In a 1993 study, researcher/physician Charles Glueck found that high cholesterol and elevated triglycerides were the sole cause of depression in patients with hyperlipidemia. He reports in *Biological Psychiatry*, "We have shown that, in patients with high triglycerides who were in a depressive state, the more you lower the triglycerides the more you alleviate their depression."

I am willing to bet that most of you have been brainwashed into thinking that all fats are a dangerous addition to your diet, to be avoided at all costs. *Don't believe it!* The low-fat and no-fat chant of the American Heart Association and the national media simply do not fit the research of the nineties. They are not telling you the whole story. The only truly dangerous fats in today's diets are the *artificial* fats that have been altered by long periods of heating (deep-frying) or hydrogenation processing for a longer shelf life. These "partially hy-drogenated" fats or "trans-fatty acids" have no nutritional value. They are high-risk substances that cause coronary heart disease and im-pair the brain's ability to make its essential brain fats.

High amounts of trans-fatty acids are found in, among others:

- candy, cookies, and bakery goods.
- corn, potato chips, and tortilla chips.
- shortening and mayonnaise.
- salad dressing (except olive oil) and margarine
- french fries, mushrooms, cheese puffs, chicken nuggets, and other deep-fried items.

Read labels and be aware of the words *may contain partially hydrogenated oil*. This indicates the presence of the *real* killer fats, not the omega-3 and omega-6 EFAs we need for normal brain functioning.

Fatty acids make up most of the brain's nerve membranes. All of the brain's branching networks are dependent on fatty acids. Most important, the firing and receiving of messages in the brain—synapses, where the real business of nerve communication and brain activity takes place—are critically dependent on brain fats (EFAs). And we are entirely dependent on our nutritional intake for them, as our bodies do not manufacture most fats. Without enough essential fatty acids, neurons fire poorly, even die off.

Both of the brain's two essential fatty acid groups—omega 3 and omega 6—contribute to correcting depression. One is not more important than the other, but the intake ratio of omega 3 to omega 6 is. Americans today have a much higher intake of the wrong fatty acids. Deficiencies in either group can cause problems, and should be addressed by changes in your diet.

OMEGA-3 DEFICIENCY:

A few years ago I heard Donald Rudin, M.D., author of *The Omega-3 Phenomenon*, explain that the intake of omega-3 fatty acids has declined by *80 percent* over the past seventy-five years. This has come about by:

- decreased fish consumption.
- increased use of omega-3-deficient oils like corn and sunflower oils.
- elimination of cereal germ in milling practices (cereal germ contains the fatty acids).
- hydrogenation of oils commercially.
- a *2,500 percent* increase in the use of trans-fatty acids (which interfere with the uptake of essential fatty acids).
- a *250 percent* increase in the use of sugar (which interferes with the enzymes needed for fatty acid synthesis).

To find out if you are deficient in omega-3 EFAs, see how many symptoms in the following chart pertain to you:

BODY CLUES TO LOW OMEGA-3 EFA AVAILABILITY©

The following symptoms are red flags that you have inadequate stores of omega-3 essential fatty acids.

Eight or more symptoms indicate a problem

____ Dry skin
____ Dandruff
____ Frequent urination
____ Irritability
____ Depression
____ Attention deficit
____ Soft nails
____ Allergies
____ Lowered immunity
____ Weakness
____ Fatigue, lethargy
____ Dry, unmanageable hair
____ Excessive thirst
____ Brittle, easily frayed nails
____ Hyperactivity
____ "Chicken skin" on back of arms
____ Dry eyes
____ Learning problems
____ Poor wound healing
____ Frequent infections
____ Patches of pale skin on cheeks
____ Cracked skin on heels or fingertips
____ Aggressiveness

This list is partly drawn from Dr. Michael Schmidt's book *Smart Fats.*

Changes are needed in your diet to reverse this life-threatening omega-3 deficiency situation. Here is my best advice:

- Add fish (especially cold-water fish like salmon and tuna) to your diet several times weekly. Eggs and chicken are also good sources of omega 3.
- Trade your southern oils for flaxseed oil and borage seed oil (not for cooking). Coconut oils and butter are better for cooking.
- Buy only whole-grain breads (they still contain the germ of the grain).
- Read food labels carefully to avoid "hydrogenated oils" and "trans-fatty acids."
- Eliminate refined sugars from your diet.
- Take daily capsules of cold-water marine fish oil.

MEASURING ESSENTIAL FATTY ACID LEVELS

Your red blood cells can be analyzed for their fatty acid content. This lab test quickly reveals whether sufficient omega-3 and -6 EFAs are present in your body—and the answers could dramatically change your quality of life and longevity. One lab doing this testing is:

Great Smokies Diagnostic Laboratories
63 Zillicoa Street
Asheville, NC 28001-0621
1-828-253-0621

OMEGA-6 DEFICIENCY:

A moment ago I mentioned that Americans get far more omega-6 than omega-3 fatty acids. Even so, most of the omega-6 oils that you ingest have been altered by hydrogenation processing. This interferes with their uptake into the brain. Although scientists know the danger of hydrogenation, the industry insists on making a profit on cheap, low-quality oils and altering them to avoid rancidity.

Over a decade ago, I was introduced to Dr. David Horrobin's work with GLA (gamma-linolenic acid), an omega-6 EFA. When we began to supply clients with GLA, we were amazed to see suicidally depressed persons turn around within ten days—even though they had lived a lifetime with depression! Certain ethnic groups have proven to be more susceptible to a genetic inability to manufacture enough of a crucial antidepressant brain metabolite made from GLA, called prostaglandin E_1 (PGE1). These ethnicities are the Irish, Scottish, Welsh, Scandinavian, and Native Americans. Further research may very well widen the scope of susceptibility to other ethnicities. At HRC, we have seen PGE1 deficiency in other northern European descendants.

In his book *Essential Fatty Acids and Immunity in Mental Health*, Charles Bates, Ph.D., provides a list of factors that suggest an omega-6 essential fatty acid deficiency. Use the following chart to determine your own susceptibility.

OMEGA-6 EFA DEFICIENCY DEPRESSION SCREEN

_____ 1. Depression among close relatives.

_____ 2. A family history of suicide, schizophrenia, or other mental illness; alcoholics or fanatic teetotalers in your family tree, or any religious fanaticism among family members.

_____ 3. Depression since childhood or teens that temporarily abates if you drink alcohol.

_____ 4. A personal or family history of Crohn's disease, hepatic cirrhosis, cystic fibrosis, Sjögren-Larsen syndrome, or atopic eczema.

_____ 5. A personal or family history of ulcerative colitis, irritable bowel syndrome, premenstrual syndrome, scleroderma, diabetes, or benign breast disease.

_____ 6. Experiencing an emotional lift from certain foods or vitamins.

_____ 7. Winter depression that lightens in the spring.

_____ 8. A tendency to abuse alcohol, or feel it affects you differently than others, or noticing that your depression worsens after drinking alcohol. Trouble with alcohol in your teen years.

_____ 9. Ancestry that is one quarter or more Celtic Irish, Native American, Welsh, Scottish, or Scandinavian.

_____10. Pyroluria, which creates a lack of zinc and B_6, the co-enzymes necessary to convert GLA into PGE1.

If you have 4 or more of the above symptoms, you will benefit from supplementation.

Based on material from Essential Fatty Acids and Immunity in Mental Health *by Charles Bates, Ph.D. (Tacoma, Wash.:* Life Sciences Press, 1987).

The key nutrient that is missing, gamma-linolenic acid (GLA), has only recently achieved proper recognition. Most of us make adequate amounts of GLA in our bodies, provided the conversion is not blocked by trans-fatty acids. But in the typical American diet that is exactly what happens, and we wind up with no GLA to make the powerful brain antidepressant metabolite PGE1, or prostaglandin E1.

A good example of PGE1 deficiency depression is Barbara, who came to the Health Recovery Center straight from another clinic, where she had been treated for depression. She was taking 60 milligrams of Prozac but was still feeling hopeless. She had been away from home for several months in her quest for help, and now she desperately missed her husband and children. Three things stood out about her chemistry: (1) her depression went back to childhood; (2) tests showed she was severely pyroluric, which means she had no B_6 and zinc to convert GLA into the antidepressant brain metabolite, PGE1; and (3) in her Scandinavian family, there was a history of diabetes, alcoholism, and depression.

With the addition of the omega-6 essential fatty acids, and

THE HRC FORMULA FOR DEPRESSION DUE TO EFA DEFICIENCIES©

Nutrient	Dose	Directions
Gamma-linolenic acid (GLA, omega-6 EFA)	300 mg	1 capsule with each meal (900 mg total per day)
Omega-3 fatty acids (Cold-water fish [EPA])	360 mg	1 capsule with breakfast 1 capsule with supper
Vitamin B$_6$	250 mg	1 capsule daily with meal
Vitamin C (Ester C)	675 mg	1 capsule daily with meal
Niacinamide	500 mg	1 capsule daily with meal
Magnesium	400 mg	1 capsule daily with meal
Antioxidant complex		2 capsules daily with meal

CONTAINING

Beta-carotene	10,000 IU
Vitamin E (*D-alphatocopheryl acetate*)	75 IU
N,N Dimethylglycine	100 mg
Vitamin C (*calcium ascorbate*)	100 mg
L-cysteine	100 mg
Silymarin (*milk thistle extract*)	100 mg
Glutathione	60 mg
Methionine	50 mg
B$_6$ (*pyridoxal-5 phosphate*)	10 mg
Zinc picolinate	10 mg
Selenium methionine	75 mcg
Co-enzyme Q10	10 mg

Note: If you are already taking any of the above nutrients, do not exceed these amounts for your total dosage (see chart page 56).

their necessary co-enzymes, as well as treatment to correct her py-roluria, Barbara's depression lifted within two weeks. She went home committed to taking a formula like the one on this page. She knows if she stays with these nutrients, continues a healthy diet high in EFAs, and avoids refined sugars, she will never again be a victim of her genetic depression. Her children, too, will reap the benefits of what she has learned about their family genetics.

The formula just provided contains all the necessary ingredients to lift your EFA-deficient depression. I've found you can expect marked changes for the better after only *one week*!

VITAMIN AND MINERAL DEFICIENCIES
OR DEPENDENCIES AS A CAUSE OF DEPRESSION

Among the consequences in the brain of nutritional deficiencies are depression, anger, listlessness, and paranoia. Unfortunately, the connection between depression and vitamin or mineral deficiencies is often missed.

Marty was a young man of twenty-five who had lived on the street and in shelters since age seventeen. He was severely depressed and regularly erupted into violent, in-your-face shouting episodes.

Marty's brother had recently died. His father, wanting to help the only child he had left, went in search of Marty, but when he finally found his son, his plans to open his home to him unraveled because of Marty's unstable behavior. When we talked on the phone, Marty's dad felt the situation was hopeless. Having lost my own son to suicide, I, of course, refused to give up. I suggested the obvious: that eight years of malnourishment and semi-starvation from living on the streets had taken their toll on Marty's mental and physical health. I pleaded for the chance to help him.

But before Marty's first week at Health Recovery Center had ended, every staff member had visited my office to tell me to send Marty away because of his wild mood swings. His anger would escalate to intense rage and then dissolve into uncontrollable crying and despair. I wondered if I had made a terrible misjudgment, but stubbornly took a wait-and-see attitude. Finally, Marty's lab results arrived. His tests showed extensive nutrient depletion across the board. We loaded him with nutrients by intravenous infusions and B complex injections, as well as by mouth. Slowly, his tears and rages dried up and an endearing, humorous young man emerged. Many lifestyle changes also contributed to his recovery, but one of the most important was the replacement of key natural substances that relieved his severe depression. When Marty headed home a few weeks later, his depression was gone and his rages had mellowed into a lot of natural energy for life!

From Marty's example, and from the examples of countless others we've treated at HRC, it seems evident that adequate intake of brain nutrients is essential for combating depression. Let's now look at exactly which of these natural substances make the most difference.

DEPLETION OF B COMPLEX VITAMINS:
B complex vitamins are essential to mental and emotional well-being. They cannot be stored in our bodies, so we depend entirely on our daily diet to supply them. B vitamins are destroyed by the intake of refined sugars, nicotine, caffeine, and alcohol.

Here's a quick rundown of the recent findings about the relationship of B complex vitamins to depression:

- **B_1** (thiamine) deficiencies trigger depression and irritability and can cause neurological and cardiac disorders.
- **B_2** (riboflavin) deficiencies were found in *all* of 172 successive patients admitted to a British psychiatric hospital for treatment of depression (reported in the *British Journal of Psychiatry*).
- **B_3** (niacin) depletion causes depression, anxiety, apprehension, and fatigue.
- **B_5** (pantothenic acid) deficiencies result in depression, fatigue, and chronic stress. B_5 is needed for hormone formation, the uptake of amino acids, and the brain chemical acetylcholine, which combine to prevent certain types of depression.
- **B_6** (pyridoxine) deficiency can disrupt formation of the antidepressant neurotransmitters. Vitamin B_6 is the co-enzyme needed for the conversion of tryptophan to serotonin, and phenylalanine and tyrosine to norepinephrine. (*Note*: The relationships of these neurotransmitters to depression is discussed earlier in this chapter.)
- **B_{12}** (cobalamin) deficiency is a common cause of depression.
- **Folic acid** deficiency is a common cause of depression.

HOW SAFE ARE VITAMIN SUPPLEMENTS?
All of the B complex vitamins just discussed are water-soluble. This means they cannot accumulate in your body or be stored for future use. Amounts beyond your nutritional needs are dumped into your urine. As a result, there is no danger of overdose.

MINERAL DEFICIENCIES CAUSING DEPRESSION:

The following minerals are essential to mental and emotional well-being:

- **Magnesium:** Deficiency results in depression. This cause-and-effect relationship was first reported in the *Journal of the American Medical Association* in 1973.
- **Calcium:** Depletion affects the central nervous system, causing nervousness, depression, irritability, and apprehension. Hyperparathyroidism causing hypercalcemia also causes depression, social withdrawal, and loss of interest.
- **Zinc:** Depletion results in apathy and lethargy. When zinc is low, copper levels in the brain may rise to a toxic stage, resulting in fearfulness and paranoia.
- **Iron:** Depression is often a symptom of chronic iron deficiency. Other symptoms include general weakness, listlessness, exhaustion, lack of appetite, and headaches.
- **Manganese:** This metal is needed for proper use of the B complex vitamins and vitamin C. Since it also plays a role in amino acid formation, a deficiency may contribute to depression that stems from low levels of the antidepressant neurotransmitters (serotonin and norepinephrine). Manganese also helps stabilize blood sugars, preventing hypoglycemic mood swings.
- **Potassium:** Depletion is frequently associated with depression, fearfulness, weakness, and fatigue. A 1981 study found depressed patients more likely than the control subjects to have decreased intracellular potassium. Decreased brain levels of potassium were also found during autopsies of suicides.

HOW SAFE ARE MINERAL SUPPLEMENTS?

Unlike water-soluble vitamins, minerals *can* be stored in your tissues. Refer to the charts on pages 122–132 for the RDAs and therapeutic treatment levels. *Do not exceed the recommended therapeutic doses unless under a physician's care*, since the accumulation of minerals in your body could be dangerous.

HYPOTHYROIDISM (INCLUDING HAIT) AS A CAUSE OF DEPRESSION

Hypothyroidism causes depression because there is an insufficient supply of oxygen to the brain. With low thyroid function, oxygen cannot be used efficiently. Linus Pauling contends that all depression could be eliminated if brain cells received sufficient oxygen. A deficiency in thyroid hormones can be caused by either Hashimoto's Autoimmune Thyroiditis (HAIT) or by an underproduction of the thyroid hormone.

HASHIMOTO'S AUTOIMMUNE THYROIDITIS (HAIT):

The stress showed on Michael's face as he described how empty his life had become. For years he had been in therapy and had taken a variety of antidepressant drugs, to no avail. His job in middle management seemed secure, and he didn't have an unstable romantic relationship going on. But depression had been a part of his life for many years, and it was slowly wearing him down. He confided that a few days earlier he had bought a gun, which he planned to use to kill himself if we could not help him. Needless to say, he got my immediate attention.

Our physician ran a lot of tests that seemed promising, but after two weeks we came up empty. Michael seemed more depressed than ever, and I was beginning to worry. Finally I asked him to keep track of his body temperatures upon waking. A week of readings revealed consistently subnormal temperatures. Even though the standard thyroid test results were within range, our doctor treated him with a trial run of Armour thyroid—and waited for the results from a thyroid-antibody blood test.

Michael's response to thyroid seemed nothing short of a miracle. He perked up even before we had lab evidence that he was hypothyroid. His type of thyroid problem is called Hashimoto's Thyroiditis, where his own immune system mistakenly produces thyroid antibodies.

Hashimoto's Autoimmune Thyroiditis (HAIT) is becoming a far more common diagnosis than it was in the past, occurring in 2 out of 100 today as compared to 6 out of 100,000 in the 1930s. The classic symptoms of HAIT are:

1. severe fatigue combined with a low level of energy that lasts for only a short time.
2. anxiousness, ranging from constant inner tension to panic attacks, that can lead to seeking relief in addictive tranquilizers.
3. depression resulting from ongoing exhaustion and a bone-weariness that prevents one from leading a normal life. May even lead to suicidal thoughts.
4. heart palpitations, and irregularities in heartbeats.
5. joint and muscle aches.
6. poor short-term memory.
7. tendency to sleep poorly.
8. low libido (sex drive).
9. food and chemical sensitivities.
10. swelling or lumps in throat, making swallowing difficult.

If any of these symptoms fit you, ask your physician to check further. But beware: *The usual laboratory tests for thyroid (T3, T4, and TSH) do not always tell the whole story.* Often the production of thyroid is normal. But a new test, the fluorescence activated microsphere assay (FAMA), measures the presence of thyroid antibodies that your immune system is sending out to attack and kill off your thyroid hormones. This test is available from a number of labs. We use:

Immuno Diagnostic Laboratories
10930 Bigge Street
San Leandro, CA 94577
1-800-888-1113

What causes the autoimmune response that results in HAIT is still unclear. Dr. Langer, drawing from his own clinical experience, speculates that HAIT is caused by viral infections such as chronic Epstein-Barr virus or systemic candidiasis. Both weaken and confuse the immune system into triggering the body's autoimmune response. Whatever the cause, the result is the same as having little or no thyroid hormone.

HYPOTHYROIDISM CAUSED BY UNDERPRODUCTION OF THYROID HORMONE:
Allison was only twenty-eight but she had repeatedly tried suicide from age seventeen on. In high school, she had been hospitalized

because of her severe depression and anxiety. She suffered from intense postpartum depression after delivering her only child. Over the last ten years, Allison had many psychiatric interventions but no one had considered testing her thyroid.

Yet her appearance fairly shouted "thyroid dysfunction!" Her voice had a hoarseness to it, and her skin was rough and dry. Her hair was thinning, her fingers and ankles were retaining fluid, and she was puffy and swollen around the eyelids. Despite the warm temperatures she was bundled up in a heavy sweater. Because her concentration was poor and her energy nonexistent, she could barely care for her child and hold down her part-time job.

Fortunately, her lab work held every answer we needed: All of her thyroid results were completely out of range—completely below normal. She also was making antithyroid antibodies to knock out the last ghost of any remaining thyroid hormone. In addition, she had tested severely pyroluric. I finally understood why she kept trying to commit suicide: The emotional pain must have been unbearable.

Our physician assured her that her physical problems had a name and they were all fixable. A prescription of Armour thyroid (a natural extract of bovine thyroid) brought back her energy and concentration. Her hair grew thicker, her skin became dewy, and her swollen face, fingers, and ankles lost all their puffiness. Gradually, her depression faded away.

While other factors contributed to Allison's spectacular turnaround—she started dealing with her hypoglycemia and pyroluria simultaneously—the amazing change in her personality—the light in her eyes, the bounce in her walk, and the smile on her face—were the result of thyroid hormone replacement. Allison will need to take these magical, natural chemicals all her life.

The following hypothyroidism checklist was developed by Keith Sehnert, M.D., a medical consultant at Health Recovery Center and a well-known medical writer.

HYPOTHYROIDISM CHECKLIST

Yes No

___ ___ 1. Do you have a hoarseness to your voice that has not always been there?

___ ___ 2. Do you have any swelling of the face?

___ ___ 3. Do you have dry, scaly skin?

___ ___ 4. Do you have decreased sweating?

___ ___ 5. Has your hair become drier and more coarse?

___ ___ 6. Do you have a decrease in your eyebrows toward the side of your face?

___ ___ 7. Have you had a decrease in the amount of scalp hair?

___ ___ 8. Have you noticed a "dirty" or thickened skin appearance of your elbows and knees?

___ ___ 9. Do you get tired easier than you used to?

___ ___10. Have you ever been told you had an enlarged heart?

___ ___11. Do your ankles swell or do you otherwise notice evidence of body-fluid retention?

___ ___12. Do you have less-than-normal energy?

___ ___13. Have any of your blood relatives had thyroid disease?

___ ___14. Does cold temperature bother you in the sense that you like the room temperature higher than other people or you wear more clothing or need more bedcovers than others?

___ ___15. Do you have difficulty pronouncing words?

___ ___16. Have you had an unexplained increase in weight recently?

___ ___17. Do you have rough skin or brittle nails that have not always been this way?

___ ___18. Do you have difficulty concentrating?

___ ___19. Are you unusually forgetful?

___ ___20. Do you feel that you are emotionally unstable but that this has been only in recent weeks or months?

___ ___21. Do you feel tired after a usual night of sleep or has your sleep or rest requirement increased?

___ ___22. Do you have times when you have difficulty breathing?

___ ___23. Do you have constipation or delay of or difficult bowel function?

___ ___24. Have you had problems conceiving children?

___ ___25. Is there any problem with your sex drive?

___ ___26. Do you have irregular menstrual flow?

If you have ten or more positive symptoms, it is worth pursuing hypothyroidism as a cause of your depression.

LAB TESTING OF YOUR THYROID:

To assess thyroid function, the standard blood tests measure two components of thyroid hormone: tri-iodothyronine (T3) and total thyroxine (T4). A test for thyroid-stimulating hormone (TSH) done on the same blood sample helps determine if thyroid function is normal. Almost all labs will run the T3, T4, and TSH. However, some lab tests may prove unreliable. Thyroid expert Broda Barnes, Ph.D.,

M.D., who has published more than a hundred papers and several books on the role of the thyroid gland in human health, comments on the diagnostic flaws in the present thyroid tests T3 and T4:

> The efforts ... to measure thyroid activity by determining the amount of hormone stored in the gland or, alternatively, the amount present in the bloodstream fail to do what really counts: provide an indication of the amount of thyroid hormone available and being used within cells throughout the body. They are somewhat akin to trying to get an idea of a thrifty man's spending habits from the amounts in his wallet or his bank account. The tests for the amount of hormone in the gland or bloodstream tell us nothing about how much is being spent.

So cautiously consider the results of these lab tests, and make sure to use the other diagnostic methods available.

The FAMA test can reveal the presence of antibodies formed against the thyroid. It also can identify changes that precede full-blown hypothyroidism by seven or eight years. Availability: Only certain labs offer the FAMA (see Appendix C for names and addresses).

HOME TESTING OF YOUR THYROID:

To self-test for hypothyroidism, you can use the procedure first described in the *Journal of the American Medical Association* by Dr. Barnes. The test could not be simpler! People with low thyroid function have lower than normal body temperatures because they are not burning up as much food as they should. All you have to do for this test is determine whether your body temperature is lower than normal. Use a basal thermometer, not a fever thermometer. (The basal type is commonly used for women trying to get pregnant—or trying to avoid pregnancy—to determine, on the basis of an increase in body temperature, when ovulation occurs. Basal thermometers are available in most drugstores.)

Upon waking, place the thermometer snugly under your armpit for ten minutes. If it registers below 97.8 degrees, and if you have ten or more of the symptoms of hypothyroidism, you probably need to take thyroid hormone.

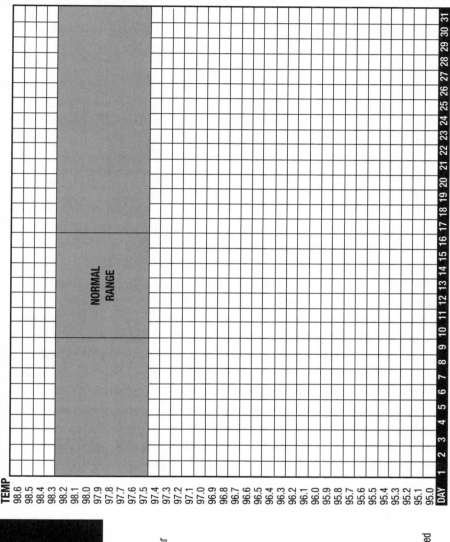

THE HRC THYROID TEMPERATURE CHART©

Directions:

1. Shake down your basal thermometer and put it on a night stand or on a chair near your bed.

2. When you wake up in the morning, immediately place the thermometer snug in your armpit.

3. After resting still for ten minutes, remove the thermometer and record the temperature on the chart on the appropriate day.

4. For women of menstrual age, the second, third, and fourth days of their period are valuable to record.

5. Do not use an electric blanket, heating pad, or heated water bed on test days.

TEMP																														
98.6																														
98.5																														
98.4																														
98.3																														
98.2																														
98.1																														
98.0																														
97.9																														
97.8																														
97.7																														
97.6																														
97.5																														
97.4																														
97.3																														
97.2																														
97.1																														
97.0																														
96.9																														
96.8																														
96.7																														
96.6																														
96.5																														
96.4																														
96.3																														
96.2																														
96.1																														
96.0																														
95.9																														
95.8																														
95.7																														
95.6																														
95.5																														
95.4																														
95.3																														
95.2																														
95.1																														
95.0																														
DAY	1	2	3	4	5	6	7	8	9	10	11	12	13	14	15	16	17	18	19	20	21	22	23	24	25	26	27	28	29	30	31

NORMAL RANGE

Use the chart on page 201 as a graph for tracking your temperature. A pattern should emerge within two weeks. If your home test shows a temperature consistently under 97.8 degrees, see your physician to discuss treatment. If your doctor wants more information on your testing method, refer him or her to Dr. Barnes's book *Hypothyroidism: The Unsuspected Illness.*

Dr. Barnes treats thyroid disorders with natural desiccated thyroid (bovine or pork) rather than synthetic thyroid preparations. The *New England Journal of Medicine* just published a study that now cites T3 and T4 (found only in natural desiccated thyroid) as having much more effectiveness in improving mood and neuropsychological functioning for hypothyroid patients than the drug version thyroxine (which contains T4 only).

HYPOGLYCEMIA, OR EXCESSIVE SUGAR AND CAFFEINE USE, AS A CAUSE OF DEPRESSION

You'll recall that hypoglycemia means having too little glucose available to fuel your brain adequately. (Glucose is the brain's *only* fuel.) This condition occurs from pumping too much insulin as a result of junk-food diets high in refined sugars, caffeine, and nicotine. In his studies of twelve hundred hypoglycemic patients, Stephen Gyland, M.D., found that *86 percent* were suffering from depression as well. That's an amazing percentage! More recently, positron-emission tomography (PET) scans have verified that glucose metabolism is often reduced in the brains of patients who are depressed. The list on page 203, which is based on Dr. Gyland's work, compares the symptoms attributed to hypoglycemia with those common to depression. *If you suspect that hypoglycemia underlies your depression, reread Chapter 3 carefully; you should experience noticeable relief of your symptoms once you adopt the hypoglycemia diet recommended there.*

BRAIN ALLERGY REACTIONS TO FOOD, AND CEREBRAL SENSITIVITIES TO AIRBORNE CHEMICALS, AS CAUSES OF DEPRESSION

The connection between food allergies and depression was a revelation to me. Early on at HRC, I became aware of bizarre mood swings in some of our clients, even though they were closely following a hy-

SYMPTOMS OF HYPOGLYCEMIA AND DEPRESSION	
Hypoglycemia	**Depression**
Nervousness	Nervousness
Irritability	Irritability
Exhaustion	Exhaustion
Depression	Depression
Drowsiness	Drowsiness
Insomnia	Insomnia
Constant worrying	Constant worrying
Mental confusion	Mental confusion
Rapid pulse	Rapid pulse
Internal trembling	Internal trembling
Forgetfulness	Forgetfulness
Headache	Headache
Unprovoked anxieties	Unprovoked anxieties
Digestive disturbances	
Faintness	
Cold sweats	

poglycemia diet. Luckily, I met George Kroker, M.D., about that time. He is a brilliant allergist and chemical ecologist who taught me that sensitive brains can react to chemicals and to foods with an allergic response, even as other body organs do (i.e., your skin may react allergically, with hives).

I first saw this phenomenon in alcoholics who were supersensitive to the alcoholic grains they drank. Wheat usually topped the list. Once they were abstinent, they chose to replace their alcohol intake with lots of pastas, breads, cereals, and other wheat products—and then they continued to complain about depression and fatigue!

One of our early clients, Mary, showed such a Jekyll-and-Hyde change in her behavior, I could hardly believe a food was responsible for this. Our protocol at that time was to clear the brain of allergy substances through a modified five-day fast and then test for susceptible foods. At the end of Mary's fast, her constant depression was gone and she was elated. But her newfound stability lasted only until she tested wheat. Within two hours she crashed! Crying over the phone, she told me the program didn't work and that she would not be back. The next day she had recovered enough to talk about what happened. She recognized her abnormal brain response to wheat and began to see that she craved wheat in her diet to take her out of withdrawal and make her feel better temporarily. It provided her with a short high before a corresponding low. Mary had never associated the downside—her depression—with her wheat "binges." Proof was easily established by avoidance for several days and then by consuming a meal of the suspected substance.

Still, Mary's resolve to avoid wheat lasted only a few days. Then she succumbed to temptation and ate an entire pizza for lunch. An hour later she arrived for her therapy group and began sobbing inconsolably, while the others groped for emotional explanations for her behavior. After her wheat reaction wore off, her depression once again lifted.

Of course, wheat is not the only substance capable of triggering a maladaptive reaction in the brains and nervous systems of sensitive people. Many of us have found that the foods we choose to binge on (bingeing offers a *big* clue as to what we're allergic to) and the many chemicals we breathe (e.g., gasoline, paint odors, formaldehydes) cause reactions in us.

I personally know how affected my brain used to get from heavy colognes and perfumes. In just over an hour's time, my thinking slowed and I felt spacey. I was tested in a clinical ecology lab for ethanol (almost all perfumes are ethanol-based) and became uncontrollably sleepy. I leaned my head on the shoulder of the person beside me and dozed off. When I came to a few minutes later, I was embarrassed and bewildered at being so completely taken over by a few mysterious drops under my tongue. (I didn't know what was being tested.) Today my immune system is far stronger, but I still get mildly light-headed around ethanol products. Others may react to chemicals with anger or by feeling low. Some alcoholics react by craving another kind of ethanol: alcohol. In fact, many house painters and garage mechanics have a low state of intoxification as a result of breathing these fumes all day. It is not by chance that they head straight for a bar after work!

Food addictions keep you coming back for more of certain foods because you love the initial highs they provide as they lift you out of your withdrawal state. You don't understand that the downside of your addiction(s) may be depression, anxiety, or confusion from the inevitable withdrawal.

If you suspect you are food-addicted or chemically sensitive to substances that affect your brain and cause depression, be sure to read Chapters 8 and 9 carefully to learn about identifying and eliminating these culprits.

SYSTEMIC BUILDUP OF FUNGAL MOLDS AND CANDIDA YEAST AS CAUSES OF DEPRESSION

During the past fifteen years, we at HRC have seen a long line of clients who are fighting an internal war with overgrowth of the common intestinal yeast *Candida albicans*. I can usually tell during the first interview who is a probable candidate for treatment of candida-related complex (CRC). People suffering from this problem appear depressed, tired, anxious, and so spacey that they often can't follow what I'm saying. They tell me they crave sugar, and they have telltale signs of yeast invasion throughout their bodies. Their immune systems are depressed, and many foods cause bloating and produce allergic/addictive responses.

If you suffer from CRC, your depression won't lift until these yeast colonizers are attacked and eliminated. In Chapter 9 you will find a full discussion of yeast-related disorders and their symptoms, as well as an explanation as to why some of you are particularly susceptible to yeast overgrowth. There are also instructions for testing and treatment of candida-related complex.

HISTADELIA (ABNORMALLY ELEVATED HISTAMINE LEVELS) AS A CAUSE OF DEPRESSION

Histamine is a chemical that is found everywhere in the body. Inside your brain, it can cause emotional havoc if levels sink too low or rise too high. High histamine persons (histadelics) tend to be compulsive, obsessive, driven, high-energy types who often suffer from ongoing depression. Because of their inborn energy and impulsivity, they are at high risk for suicide if they cannot alleviate their depression. In the next chapter I describe the other emotional states that abnormal levels of histamine can cause.

It is important to recognize that the depression high levels of histamine triggers does not respond to the usual drug therapies or to electric shock. But lowering the histamine levels does bring about the needed relief. This is done by blocking and detoxifying histamine. A natural amino acid, methionine, does this safely. Dilantin, the antiepilepsy drug, has sometimes been used because it destroys the folic acid that is needed to make histamine. Yet I have not liked the side effects, such as abrupt personality changes, our HRC clients have experienced from blocking histamine with Dilantin. Usually, a regimen of methionine, calcium, zinc, and manganese has proved sufficient to stabilize a high histamine person.

If you suspect this familial disorder fits you, complete the histadelic screen in the next chapter (on page 219) to check your symptoms. If you score high, you will want to confirm your histamine status with a laboratory blood test. Recommended labs and the HRC formula for histadelics are in Chapter 7.

BUILDUP OF HEAVY METALS AS A CAUSE OF DEPRESSION

A buildup of heavy metals such as cadmium, lead, and copper can result in severe brain alterations and seeming "personality changes" of confusion, mind racing, paranoia, violence, and hallucinations. Specifically, excessive mercury in the brain causes depression.

The greatest mercury exposure the public faces is from dental amalgams, pesticides, cosmetics (read the labels), and inland lake fish whose waters have become chemical dumping grounds. Mercury toxicity symptoms include fatigue, depression, weakness, tremors, memory loss, nervousness, uncoordination, numbness and tingling of the lips and feet, and emotional instability. Luckily, selenium binds mercury and protects against its toxic effects.

A hair analysis will measure your mercury exposure, whether recently or long ago. Using hair analysis instead of blood is preferred, as blood analysis can only show recent mercury exposure. Mercury can be successfully removed from the body through vitamin C intravenous chelation therapy. Consult your physician or refer to the "Alternative Medicine Resources" in Appendix B for a referral to a doctor in your area who can do chelation therapy.

One last word about mercury poisoning: Mercury-silver amalgams are being phased out worldwide. In Sweden, Japan, and Germany, mercury fillings are outlawed in women of childbearing age. In the United States today, our "silver" dental amalgams typically contain 48 to 60 percent mercury, 15 to 37 percent silver, 12 to 18 percent tin, and up to 26 percent copper. With each additional silver dental filling, our mercury levels increase. Dentists and their assistants are particularly subject to exposure to high mercury concentrations daily—and dentists now lead all other professions in suicides!

BRAIN DAMAGE FROM ALCOHOL OR DRUGS, PRESCRIBED OR OTHERWISE, AS A CAUSE OF DEPRESSION

Alcohol, street drugs, and prescription drugs all have one thing in common: They deplete your body and brain of essential natural chemicals, many of which keep you emotionally stable. They fire off excessive amounts of your brain's neurotransmitters and endorphins, leaving near-empty sites in the brain. In fact, many substance abusers may have only marginal stores of natural chemicals in their brains even *before* using their drug of choice. The ability of drugs to deliver a quick "feel better" fix strongly appeals to these individuals with molecularly unstable brains and nervous systems, and this unavailability of normal amounts of essential brain chemicals is the most likely reason that most drug experimenters embrace ongoing drug use.

ALCOHOL AND OTHER STREET DRUGS:

Alcohol- and drug-addicted persons who stop their use still experience cravings, depression, anxiety, and unstable moods. Without the buffer of drugs, they feel the full brunt of brain and nervous system changes that their heavy use has caused. Without embarking on a program of physical repair, feeling good is not just around the corner, and uncomfortable symptoms linger for years. According to a Johns Hopkins University study, researchers found the following ongoing symptoms in 4,312 *abstinent* former alcoholics over a ten-year period:

- depression
- hostility
- anxiety
- paranoia
- psychosis
- phobia
- inadequate and inferior feelings

The study also showed a painfully slow reduction in symptom intensity, with levels dropping slowly over a long period of time.

So, suicide remains prevalent even among *treated* alcoholics— one in four deaths is from suicide and it usually occurs within the first year after treatment (*Archives of General Psychiatry*, 1984).

The disease of alcoholism assaults one's sanity by depleting key stabilizing chemicals in the brain. Counseling cannot correct such damage. *Physical* repair is essential.

In my book *Seven Weeks to Sobriety*, I laid out a self-treatment alcoholism program very similar to our successful model at the Health Recovery Center, where our recovery rate is about 75 percent. The table on page 209 is the same basic HRC detox formula (see the book for additional formulas). It is a combination of amino acids, vitamins, minerals, and other nutrients that eliminate cravings and reduce withdrawal symptoms. This formula does the critical work of replacing the natural chemicals that alcoholism has destroyed and repairing the damage. It is based on the work of researchers worldwide. The doses have been tested and fine-tuned over eighteen years of use. We have also devised formulas for recovering from cocaine, narcotics, marijuana, and other drugs. Those of you who have gotten yourselves hooked on a drug that now owns you, trust me: There is a better way to feel good! Just call the center at 1-800-24-SOBER. Tell us the drug to which you are addicted and we will individualize the right formula to get you drug-free and stable.

PRESCRIPTION MEDICATIONS:
Throughout this book, I repeatedly preach about avoiding all prescribed medications whenever possible. They are toxic and cause many worrisome side effects. Certain prescription drugs are well known for causing depression. According to a 1993 *British Medical Journal* article, the following prescription drugs cause depression:

> heart medications
> blood pressure medications (i.e., diuretics and calcium channel
>   blockers)*
> estrogen replacement therapies
> sleeping pills
> benozodiazepines

It is imperative that you examine the dates of your prescription medication(s) in conjunction with your onset of depression symptoms. If you trace your depression back to embarking on a prescrip-

---

*New research shows a *500 percent increase in suicide* in calcium channel blocker users (*British Medical Journal* 316:741–745, 1993).

THE HRC DETOX FORMULA©

Nutrient	Dose	Directions
Glutamine	500 mg	2 capsules 3 times daily, ½ hour before meals
Free-form aminos*	750 mg	2 capsules 3 times daily, ½ hour before meals
Tyrosine*	800 mg	1 capsule 3 times daily, ½ hour before meals
Tryptophan†	500 mg	2 capsules ½ hour before bedtime
Vitamin C (Ester C)	675 mg	2 capsules 3 times daily with meals
Multivitamin/mineral complex		2 capsules 3 times daily with meals
Calcium/magnesium	300 mg (150 mg per capsule)	2 capsules 3 times daily with meals
Gamma-linolenic acid (GLA)	300 mg	1 capsule 2 times daily with meals
Pancreatic enzymes	2,000 mg pancreatin	2 capsules 3 times daily with meals
Omega-3 fatty acids (Cold-water fish [EPA])	360 mg	1 capsule with breakfast, 1 capsule with supper
Melatonin (for sleep)	3 mg	1 or 2 capsules ½ hour before bedtime

Note: If you are already taking any of the above nutrients, do not exceed the amounts for your total dosage (see chart page 56).

Do not take these amino acids if you have liver damage.

†*Tryptophan is available only by prescription in the United States and Canada. Your doctor can order it only from certain pharmacies. The two that we use are: Hopewell Pharmacy, 1-800-792-6670, and College Pharmacy, 1-800-888-9358.*

Read instructions for this formula in Seven Weeks to Sobriety *or call: 1-800-247-6237.*

© *Copyright 1999 Health Recovery Center.™ All Rights Reserved.*

tion drug, you will want to find a more natural solution for your problem. Make an appointment with a naturopathic physician for such help. At the very least, ask your doctor to choose an alternative drug for you.

Where Do You Fit In?

Now that you are familiar with the various biochemical problems that can underlie depression, it's time to determine what to do about the one(s) responsible for your bleak mental state. Here are your options. Check all the categories and means of repair that apply to you:

_____ Identify and treat vanadium toxicity that can cause bipolar disorder (page 174).

_____ Raise taurine and natural lithium levels through the Natural Formula for Bipolar Disorder (page 175).

_____ Restore levels of folic acid, vitamin C, calcium, and thyroid if presently taking lithium (see formula for those on prescribed lithium, page 175).

_____ Restore the neurotransmitters serotonin and/or norepinephrine (through the formulas on pages 182 and 184).

_____ Replace the omega-3 and omega-6 essential fatty acids (through the formula on page 192).

_____ Restore key vitamins and minerals (review the list of essential vitamins and minerals earlier on pages 194–195).

_____ Treat hypothyroidism (consult your physician).

_____ Correct hypoglycemia (review Chapter 3).

_____ Avoid foods/chemicals responsible for cerebral allergy reactions (see Chapters 8 and 9).

_____ Treat candida-related complex (see Chapter 9).

_____ Identify and treat histadelia, or high brain levels of histamine (see Chapter 7 for more information).

_____ Identify and remove any toxic stores of mercury. (A hair analysis will measure toxic metal buildup. If present, consult your physician about removal.)

_____ Eliminate alcohol and other drugs, prescribed or not, that cause depression. (For alcoholism, detoxify with the formula on page 209. For those recovering from addiction to cocaine, narcotics, marijuana, and other street drugs, call 1-800-24-SOBER for specific help. For prescription drugs, consult with your physician for alternative choices that do not induce depression in you.)

SPECIFIC DOCTORS FOR YOUR SPECIAL BIOCHEMICAL PROBLEM

I urge you to seek medical advice when dealing with depression, especially if it is severe. I also urge you to choose a doctor attuned to your special needs. Orthomolecular physicians have expertise in both allopathic and nutritional medicine. They are willing to treat physical disorders with an array of biological weapons, a combination of both drugs and powerful nondrugs from our natural pharmacy. These physicians can help you with:

Restoration of neurotransmitter levels
Hypoglycemia testing and treatment
Vitamin, mineral, and essential fatty acid testing and restoration
Histamine testing
Hair analysis
Thyroid testing and treatment

For a list of orthomolecular physicians in your area, within Canada and the United States, contact:
Journal of Orthomolecular Medicine
16 Florence Avenue
Toronto, Ontario, Canada M2N 1E9
1-416-733-2117

A clinical ecologist will be able to test you for food and chemical allergies and candida-related complex. For a list of such physicians in your area, contact:

American Academy of Environmental Medicine
Box CN 1001-8001
New Hope, PA 18938
1-215-862-4544

If you need help getting free of alcohol or street drugs, call me at

Health Recovery Center
3255 Hennepin Avenue South
Minneapolis, MN 55408
1-612-827-7800
or at
BIO-RECOVERY: 1-800-24-SOBER

CHAPTER 7

When You're Living with Paranoia or Compulsive Perfectionism
The Two Extremes of Histamine Imbalance

There is a single substance in our brains that causes incredible chaos when it rises to abnormal highs or falls dangerously low. Histamine causes our tears to flow, and determines our pain sensitivity and sexual libido. The paranoid soul who lives with sweaty palms, a racing mind, and a growing sense of grandiosity is existing on an ever-dwindling supply of brain histamine. On the other side of the spectrum is the compulsive and obsessive, sleep-deprived go-getter: He or she has a brain that is bathed in super-normal amounts of this neurotransmitter. How unfair that both are living out their days as prisoners of unbalanced chemistry! Today, solutions exist. But that wasn't the case during my early years at Health Recovery Center, when I found myself completely frustrated by the high histamine levels of clients who swept into my office, in high arousal about life in general.

Being compulsive, obsessive people, these clients had come to HRC for an instant fix. Many of them had extremely successful careers, fueled by their remarkable drive and energy, but they were crumbling internally from continual tension and depression. Usually they were seriously depressed, and may even have had suicide attempts in their own or in their family history. They told me they didn't sleep much or well. They cried at the drop of a hat and were terribly impulsive. Those of them who had tried drugs tended to get hooked on heroin or other narcotics and sometimes alcohol. (That's because all of these substances block histamine and improve symptoms only temporarily.) And the pattern repeated itself in these kinds of clients: Their enthusiasm ran unrealistically high the first few days, but there was no staying power. Often, before the first week was over, these clients lost interest and abandoned the program in order to return to drugs, or they found some new project to take them off down another road. When I finally recognized the similar characteristics of these dropouts, I realized their profiles fit perfectly with Dr. Carl Pfeiffer's description of high-histamine persons! I then knew we must intervene *immediately* if we hoped to hold their attention. We began using Dr. Pfeiffer's instructions for lowering histamine that appear later in this chapter. These natural histamine blockers turned the tide, and made enough difference early on to thwart the impulsiveness of these people.

Now we rarely lose such clients, and once they are well they are some of the most vocal supporters of these methods.

It will be invaluable for you to be able to identify your own signs of abnormal histamine levels, because they are *100 percent correctable*. You will no longer be a lifelong prisoner of your brain chemistry, and you will finally be feeling good for years to come. This chapter will alert you to the profiles of the paranoid as well as the obsessive perfectionist, and point you to the natural corrective formulas that treat these histamine imbalances and help you to heal emotionally.

How Histamine Works in the Brain

Inside the brain, histamine plays an important role in all sorts of reactions. In the hypothalamus, histamine stimulates the release of the important neurotransmitters serotonin, dopamine, and norepinephrine. Another role of brain histamine is to counterbalance dopamine in that area of the brain that filters incoming sensory information. With too little histamine, dopamine levels are elevated. The result of having *too little* histamine can be thought disorders like paranoia, or hallucinations that feel as if your mind is playing tricks on you. You may see or hear things abnormally, and your ears may ring. You will probably make grandiose plans but never have the energy to carry them out.

Other psychiatric symptoms develop when *too much* histamine heightens and distorts the release of the key neurotransmitters. When histamine levels are abnormally high, there is a tendency to hyperactivity, depression, aggressiveness, compulsive behavior, and a racing brain. You may grow obsessive about sex, cry easily, have abnormal fears, and contemplate suicide.

Such consequences of histamine imbalance in the brain were first discovered at the New Jersey Psychiatric Institute in 1966. Dr. Carl Pfeiffer and his colleagues devised a method for accurately assaying the histamine content of tissue, followed by the discovery that the blood (and therefore, presumably, the brain) of most schizophrenics contained abnormal levels of histamine.

They watched seventy-two chronic schizophrenics with abnormally low histamine gradually improve as levels were restored to normal. Another group of their patients showed highly elevated histamine. These patients experienced a marked reduction of such symptoms as depression, obsessions, compulsions, and need to engage in ritual as their histamine levels were brought down to the normal range.

It is now well established that over two thirds of schizophrenics have abnormal histamine readings. However, many of the people we treat at Health Recovery Center also have marked histamine abnormalities and almost all are *not* schizophrenic.

Let's look closely at the examples of abnormal histamine symptoms, and then figure out how to correct this errant chemistry.

ALL ABOUT LOW HISTAMINE

Low histamine (histapenic) people share certain characteristics. These are a direct result of diminished neurotransmitter firing, excessive blood copper, and ongoing deficiencies of zinc, vitamin C, folic acid, and niacin (B_3), which continue to deplete histamine stores and elevate copper levels. The resulting mental overstimulation often produces racing thoughts and grandiose ideas. There may be sensory dysperceptions—that is, hallucinations—or distortions in the perception of time and how they see their bodies. Paranoia and suspicion is usually a common identifying symptom. Use of alcohol or recreational drugs tends to occur in binges, and contributes to increasing their paranoia. Since such people are easily fatigued and frustrated, none of their many grandiose plans ever come to completion. Ongoing irritability makes them difficult people with whom to coexist. Physically, any excess weight is unevenly distributed

THE LOW-HISTAMINE CHILD

In his book *Orthomolecular Psychiatry*, Dr. Linus Pauling gives a composite case history of a low-histamine child.

> The patient is a hyperactive male child who is unnaturally healthy. For example, the rest of the family may get head colds, but this low histamine child misses the cold, or the virus infection fails to produce a rhinitis. He is hypoallergic ... he may show no signs of pain even when seriously bruised or when a venous blood sample is obtained. Corporal punishment is relatively useless because a slap causes little pain. The child is constantly active and sleeps poorly. His attention span is short, so learning is poor. Although his ability in some areas may be high when tested, a high degree of disperception may be present ... such as sensory, time, body, self, and perception of others.

on hips and thighs (e.g., pear-shaped). They have many dental fillings because of a lack of saliva. Their body hair is always plentiful. They have far fewer colds, airborne allergies, and headaches than persons who are not histapenic, but they do tend to have food allergies and to be chemically sensitive. They may even suffer from stuttering and from ringing ears. Commonly, libido is low and there is difficulty achieving orgasm due to low body secretions. An unusual characteristic of histapenics is their high pain threshold, allowing them to tolerate a great deal more pain than most people. Now let's focus on how to treat low levels of histamine.

Diet and Low Histamine

Diet plays a critical role in abnormal levels of histamine, as my own experience at HRC shows.

Seth's parents had come to HRC and begged us to test him for imbalances, as he was "unmanageable" at age four. A chubby, fair-skinned youngster, Seth was phenomenally healthy: no colds, earaches, or infections. He seemed continually agitated and frus-

trated, sometimes exploding into temper tantrums. In one of these rages, Seth crushed a lightbulb in his hand but showed no pain. His mother said discipline had proved relatively useless, as Seth did not react to any punishment for his antics. His parents were at their wits' ends to manage him.

Seth's lab tests showed histamine levels that were abnormally low. We also checked for food and environmental allergies, accumulation of heavy metals in the brain, and nutrient deficiencies. Treatment centered on raising his histamine into the normal range using a formula similar to the one on page 221, and by adding other nutrients that Seth lacked. Diet especially played an important role. A high-protein diet worked best, as it provided the needed amino acid histidine, which easily converts to histamine. Refined carbohydrates—sugar, white flour, and junk foods—were prohibited. Seth had been living on white flour in the form of white bread sandwiches, crackers, potato chips, and pasta. He loved cookies and sweets. The family loved colas and kept a ready supply on hand. Seth's special diet needs meant no more junk food in the house.

Within a few weeks the tantrums stopped and a calmer, more alert youngster emerged.

Seth was fortunate to be able to correct his chemistry at such a young age. I often see adults in midlife who have wrestled with too little histamine all their lives. They don't know what's wrong with them, although they may instinctively feel the cause is biochemical. Diet can play an important role in fixing what's broken—but it's also extremely critical that copper levels be measured.

Copper and Low Histamine

Brett, a recent client, was living on two antidepressant drugs, Wellbutrin and Effixor, but he still felt anxious and depressed and had bouts of crying. Brett complained that he had lost his sex drive, tired easily, and felt irritable and frustrated most of the time. A growing sense of paranoia had affected his job relationships. Lab testing showed not only low histamine levels but also abnormally high hair copper: eight times the normal level!

The toxic effect of copper stems from its properties as a nervous stimulant. Excess copper creates histapenia (low histamine) by decreasing histamine in the brain. It also contains the enzymes that regulate histamine, so too much copper allows histamine degradation to take place. The lowered histamine levels, in turn, allow more copper to accumulate. High levels of copper in the brain can cause a state of restlessness, insomnia, violence, depression, irritability, paranoia, and high blood pressure. The gradual accumulation of copper in the brains of aging people also contribute both to hearing loss and paranoia.

Brett's blood was Type A, and such people are far more prone to sequestering copper. Among hospitalized schizophrenics, there is a disproportionate number with Type-A blood—and 50 percent of schizophrenics are histapenic! A young Type-A woman with histamine levels of 22 (the norm is 40 to 60 mg/ml) told me that after four months of raising her low histamine levels, her inner "voices" had stopped!

The formula on page 221 includes generous amounts of zinc, manganese, niacin (B₃), and vitamin C—all of which work to lower copper. It is also imperative to *avoid all multivitamins that contain copper*.

THE PARANOID PROFILE

Paranoid low-histamine individuals live with a variety of mental aberrations, all due to copper intoxication. They are unduly suspicious; experience disorientation, depression, clouded consciousness, and self-destructive tendencies; and may develop unusual religious preoccupations. They are sensitive to tiny inconsistencies, adversities, or criticisms in life situations that no one else notices; these get blown out of proportion in their minds and overemphasized. Many paranoiacs become night owls, both to avoid social contacts and to cut down on the stress and noise that is prevalent during the day. Dr. Pfeiffer points out that the sun's geomagnetic forces, which have been shown to influence schizophrenia, are lessened at night. Yet going without sleep for several nights contributes to paranoia. And certain drugs like cocaine, amphetamines, or acid (LSD) will produce paranoia by interfering with normal sleep patterns. In fact, as Dr. Pfeiffer tells us, "Alcohol, barbiturates, and sleeping pills can unmask latent paranoia."

Note: Be aware that two more common prescriptions can cause the problems of paranoia. An antiepileptic, Dilantin, destroys the body's intake of folic acid. Over several years of use this will cause severe paranoia and a state of low histamine. Birth control pills also raise

COPPER AND POSTPARTUM PSYCHOSIS

Postpartum psychosis also has, as a likely cause, greatly elevated copper and ceruloplasmin due to increased estrogen levels during pregnancy. Symptoms of this psychosis are disorientation, depression, sleep disturbances, self-destructive tendencies, and paranoia. The mother may biochemically be so distraught that she rejects her new baby. The low histamine formula (on page 221) may be used to reduce copper levels in the new mother. *Note:* If no treatment is given, the copper will gradually drop to normal over several months, finally providing a total remission of her psychosis.

copper levels, and so can cause similar problems. Physically, excess copper can cause restlessness, insomnia, and high blood pressure. It also tends to foster right-brain dominance. The prevalence of deafness is as high as 30 percent among younger paranoiacs. Copper's stimulative effect in the central nervous system is similar to that of the drug dexedrine.

So if you have low histamine levels, it is important to get sufficient nightly sleep, and to avoid both recreational and prescription drugs that induce paranoia. But most important is correcting the high tissue copper level. The imagined enemy simply dissolves with biochemical rebalancing.

DO YOU HAVE LOW HISTAMINE?

The following screen will reveal a strong indication of low histamine. (A lab test will then be a good investment for confirmation.)

THE HISTAPENIC PERSON (LOW HISTAMINE)

Yes No

____ ____ 1. Do you get canker sores?

____ ____ 2. Do you have slow sexual responsiveness or a low libido?

____ ____ 3. Do you have tension headaches or seldom have headaches?

____ ____ 4. Do you have heavy growth of body hair?

____ ____ 5. Do you tend to carry any excess fat in your lower extremities rather than evenly distributed around your body (a pear-shaped figure)?

____ ____ 6. Do you have a lot of dental fillings?

____ ____ 7. Do you have a head full of grand plans but are easily frustrated?

____ ____ 8. Are you suspicious of people or do you feel paranoid?

____ ____ 9. Have you ever heard voices inside your head?

____ ____ 10. Are you able to stand pain well?

____ ____ 11. Do you have ringing in your ears?

____ ____ 12. Do you get few or no colds?

____ ____ 13. Do you have low tolerance for medications or drugs?

____ ____ 14. Do you tire easily?

____ ____ 15. Do you need at least eight hours of sleep, and are you a slow riser in the morning?

____ ____ 16. Is your mouth usually dry?

____ ____ 17. Do you have a tendency to despair, or have bouts of crying?

____ ____ 18. Do you experience frequent irritability?

____ ____ TOTAL SCORE

Note: Don't expect to have all of these symptoms. But having ten or more suggests that a lab test for blood histamine is in order.

To get tested for histamine levels, you can take a blood test that measures the level of histamine available in the brain/body. Health Recovery Center's preferred lab for such a test (because of consistently accurate results that match client symptoms) is:

Bio Center Laboratory
3100 North Hillside
Wichita, KS 67219
1-800-494-7785

Results are usually available within two weeks.

How to Treat Low Histamine (Histapenia)

The substances in the low histamine formula on page 221 interact to raise histamine to normal levels in your body. The amino acid trypto-

THE HRC FORMULA FOR LOW HISTAMINE©		
Nutrient	**Dose**	**Directions**
Tryptophan*	500 mg	2–4 capsules at bedtime
Histadine	500 mg	1 capsule 3 times daily ½ hour before meals
Vitamin C (Ester C)	675 mg	1 capsule 3 times daily with meals
GLA	300 mg	1–2 capsules per day
Omega-3 fatty acids (Cold-water fish [EPA])	360 mg	1 capsule with breakfast 1 capsule with supper
Niacin (B$_3$)† (nontimed released	500 mg	1 capsule 2 times daily with meals
B$_{12}$ dots	500 mcg	2 dots per day
Folic acid	800 mcg	1 capsule 3 times daily with meals
Manganese gluconate	10 mg	1 capsule daily with meals
Zinc picolinate	25 mg	1 capsule 2 times daily with meals
Quercetin	300 mg	1 capsule 3 times daily with meals

Note: If you are already taking any of the above nutrients, do not exceed the amounts for your total dosage (see chart page 56).

Tryptophan is available only by prescription in the United States and Canada. Your doctor can order it from certain pharmacies. Two options are: Hopewell Pharmacy 1-800-792-6670 and College Pharmacy 1-800-888-9358.
† Do not take niacin if you have liver damage.

phan, taken with fruit juice, easily reloads serotonin, a calming neurotransmitter that reduces agitation and corrects sleep disturbances. The amino histidine elevates histamine levels, but it is important to remember that histidine also binds with zinc, making it unavailable, and this zinc deficiency then results in the inability to store histamine. For this reason, our formula calls for generous amounts of zinc. (Pyrolurics need to pay particular attention to providing themselves with adequate zinc; otherwise, there will be a prompt return of symptoms rather than a permanent solution.) Zinc, vitamin C, and manganese have the ability to excrete copper or inhibit its absorption in your body. They also protect against copper harming your brain tissue for oxidation. The B vitamins niacin (B_3), folic acid, and B_{12} produce and raise histamine. But for the B vitamins to act effectively there must be a substrate of omega-3 essential fatty acids present in the brain. Cold-water fish is a rich source, and it is equally important to combine omega-3 with omega-6 EFAs (like GLA) to protect against unbalancing these two powerful brain chemicals. Quercetin helps the body build up histamine stores. These nutrients have a synergistic action that will guarantee you noticeable improvement in a very short time. It is much easier to raise histamine than to lower it.

Once you embark on the low-histamine formula, you can expect relief from some symptoms in about one week.

THE TIMETABLE FOR RELIEF OF SYMPTOMS IN HISTAPENIA*
- Drippy palms
    - Mind racing
        - Insomnia
            - Hypomania
                - Hallucinations
                    - Obesity
                                        - Paranoia

| One Week | One Month | One Year |

HIGH HISTAMINE: A FORMULA FOR SUCCESS—OR TRAGEDY

High histamine (histadelia) runs in families. This can well account for successful "dynasties," as such families, like the Kennedys, are endowed with the kind of energy and drive that most of us only dream about. Individuals with histadelia are aggressive, productive, Type-A people who drive themselves obsessively toward success. The large histamine pools they possess cause their brain neurotransmitters to overfuel and fire excessively. The following conditions may result.

*Taken from Dr. Carl Pfeiffer, *The Schizophrenias: Ours to Conquer.*

• Histadelics are often overstimulated, almost manic. Their compulsive drives may lead them to alcohol in an effort to break their inner tension and find some peace.

• Sleeping is problematic. People with histadelia are light sleepers, usually needing seven or less hours. Yet insomnia can be severe.

• If histamine levels are too high, phobias, compulsions, and disappearing thoughts and words develop. These people are the perfectionists and the "doers" who never seem to know how to relax. Histamine increases their cellular metabolism so their body temperature may be above normal and they burn up their food quickly. Thus, typically, histadelics have no problem with weight gain. If there is a weight problem, it is coming from food and chemical allergies that set off hunger or bingeing. Upon identification and avoidance of these allergic triggers, histadelics will slowly lose unwanted body weight (this process may take a full year) and recover the natural high-energy levels that their allergies were masking.

• Because of their elevated metabolic rate and higher body temperature, histadelics have bodies that develop anatomically to help dissipate the extra heat; their ears, nose, hands, and feet may be enlarged. Fingers and toes are usually long. I often ask clients to show me their second toe. In a histadelic, it is frequently longer than the big toe. They also have very little facial and chest hair, which again help to promote the more rapid loss of extra body heat.

• Suicidal depression puts these people at high risk because they have the energy to carry out a suicide plan and the impulsiveness to act quickly, without thinking it over. But not all histadelics are depressed. It is not known why some are depressed and others are not.

• Since histamine produces an abundant production of fluid secretions, histadelics have an overproduction of saliva that keeps their teeth free of cavities. (Sometimes, saliva is literally dripping from the corners of the mouth.) Let's look more closely now at the common behavioral tendencies many people with histadelia engage in. Achieving sexual orgasm is easy because of their increased mucus. This mucus also assists the smaller, faster male sperm in winning the race to fertilize the egg, so high histamine families produce mostly male children.

• Most histadelics have a very low pain threshold and will overreact to pain. Headaches and respiratory allergies are common.

THE HIGH-HISTAMINE CHILD

Most histadelic children are very self-motivated and achievement-oriented. Some, however, are so self-directed that they resent giving up control to a parent or teacher. They can't stand being told what to do by adults. These youngsters become disruptive within their families and classrooms, and physical discipline only causes their behavior to intensify. They may not easily make friends with their peers, preferring much younger children or adults. If counseling is pushed upon them, it typically will fail. A diagnosis of "oppositional defiant disorder" often results. Histadelic children tend to get obsessively hooked on activities. This can be advantageous to the child who pursues learning or sports, but will present problems if the focus is on negative activities, such as playing video games excessively.

Drug use among histadelic (high-histamine) teens is five times as likely as with histapenic (low-histamine) young people. These drugs steadily worsen their nervous system imbalances. If they start smoking cigarettes, they may become chain-smokers. It is important to channel the child's obsessive-compulsive tendencies into more productive activities.

If you suspect your child fits the category of high histamine, a blood test will be able to pinpoint the level. Drugs are not usually required to lower histamine, as you will see from the formula on page 229. To have histamine levels just on the high side of normal is a real blessing. The natural energy and drive to succeed in life gives this child a competitive edge. The danger lies in letting histamine rise to such high levels that there is suicidal depression, impulsive sexual addiction, or uncontrollable obsessions.

Drugs and Alcohol Attract Many Histadelics

For years I wondered why obsessive, driven people wanted to pump tons of caffeine and sugar, and even cocaine, crack, and amphetamines, into their systems to further stimulate them. I finally realized that many are attempting to lift a chronic black depression that does not respond well to antidepressants.

Many histadelics have discovered that opiates (heroin, morphine, opium, codeine) are strong histamine reducers. Alcohol also has some histamine-reducing action. When the histamine is lowered, the depression often fades. Unfortunately, each of the above drugs has a dark side. By the time such histadelics arrive at Health Recovery Center, their drug use has driven them right to the edge.

Carla, a young professional woman who was using both cocaine and alcohol in large amounts to control her black depression, drove from the East Coast to Minneapolis seeking help from Health Recovery Center. She then spent three more days cruising around the center, "checking us out." I finally had the opportunity to talk to her and ease her mind. I could tell she was histadelic as she recited her history. Despite much success in a high-powered sales position, Carla felt suicidal and exhausted. Still she kept pushing herself. She had many physical complaints: joint pain, headaches, hay fever, and stomachaches. Carla had a mouthful of gorgeous white teeth, and long fingers and toes. She was thin and attractive, yet she said she ate every hour because of hunger! Her life story included a suicide attempt. She had been doing a chemical balancing act of using alcohol to quiet her obsessive drive—she could handle a quart without a hangover—and relieving her depression with cocaine. But this was killing her. Carla had been to a standard type of chemical dependency treatment program the prior year, where she spent thirty days telling a group of strangers the intimate details of her life. The experience did nothing to control the pools of histamine that fed her suicidal depression and inner tension. She said she feared I was about to sign her into the same kind of treatment.

Only when I began to describe to Carla all the earmarks of her chemistry and what had to be done biochemically to finally bring relief did she begin to trust me.

It's been over a year since Carla completed the Health Recovery Center program. Her recent letter told me she is still on a strict diet and taking her regimen of natural chemicals, and that she is still sober and free of depression. She described her recent activities: She had applied for and had been offered three new sales positions. (She settled on the best one.) She sold her house and bought a new one in the last month, works out at the gym three days a week, and takes skating classes four times a week. Obviously, Carla is still a high-histamine person, but now her strict controls allow her the joy of accomplishing without the pain of depression or the inner tension of being driven to perform. That balance had to happen biochemically. Talk therapy had changed nothing for her.

Suicidal Depression and High Histamine

Out-of-control histamine levels lead to serious depression in about one half of histadelics, according to a study of Dr. Carl Pfeiffer. He offers both Judy Garland and Marilyn Monroe as examples of probable histadelics who suffered a suicidal death.

Most histadelics have several suicides in their family history. The depression that plagues them does not respond well to antidepressants and not at all to shock therapy. An early diagnosis of excessive histamine is important as it safeguards them—or you—against impulsively deciding to deal with continual inner tensions and suicidal ideations by ending their lives. Ordinary brochures about suicide fail to warn that the most likely candidates are compulsive, depressed kids and adults.

I cannot help but think of the suicide of my own son, which seemed to happen without warning. Rob had many histadelic characteristics. He was full of overabundant energy and was always active, yet his room was unbelievably neat and orderly (compulsiveness). He ate continually but was lean and lanky (rapid metabolism). His teeth were in excellent shape (high saliva production). In many ways he was a perfectionist and very creative. His decision to take his life came without warning to anyone. Rob even had a wild love life, unbeknownst to me. At his wake, girls I had never seen before described to me how they had climbed in and out his window late at night. His casket became a repository of love notes. High sexual libido, indeed, is a sign of high histamine level.

Sexual Addiction and High Histamine

The high libidos of histadelics seem to set them up for trouble. Being loyal to one partner is a big order for someone who is addicted to the joys of sex. I have had clients who describe their compulsion to pick up a prostitute or cruise porno bookstores and peep shows as being a part of their regular activities. They claim this addiction is not unlike that with alcohol or drugs; it seems to build up the longer they try to abstain, until, finally, there is a period of binge-ing on these activities. Other clients simply engage in multiple affairs without trying to resist them. Also, the employee who is sexually harassing co-workers through inappropriate touching or sexual language may be suffering from a sexual addiction. Therapy is certainly needed, but also important is modifying the out-of-control histadelic libido by lowering the histamine levels. And that can be achieved through adhering to the formula on page 229.

DO YOU HAVE HIGH HISTAMINE?

The following screen is used at Health Recovery Center to determine the likelihood of excessive blood histamine.

THE HISTADELIC PERSON (HIGH HISTAMINE)

Yes   No

____ ____ Do you tend to sneeze in bright sunlight?

____ ____ Were you a shy and oversensitive teenager?

____ ____ Can you make tears easily, and are never bothered by a lack of saliva or a dry mouth?

____ ____ Do you hear your pulse in your head on the pillow at night?

____ ____ Do you have frequent muscle cramps?

____ ____ Do you have a high sensitivity to pain?

____ ____ Do you find it easy to have orgasms with sex, and do you have a high libido?

____ ____ Do you get headaches regularly?

____ ____ Does your mind go blank at times?

____ ____ Do you have seasonal allergies, such as hay fever?

____ ____ Do you tend to be a light sleeper?

____ ____ Do you need only five to seven hours of sleep each night?

____ ____ Do you burn up foods rapidly?

____ ____ Have you thought seriously of suicide?

____ ____ Can you tolerate high doses of medication or drugs?

____ ____ Do you have large ears and long fingers or toes? (Is your second toe as long as or longer than your big toe?)

____ ____ Are you addicted to drugs, alcohol, or sugar?

_____ _____ Are you a perfectionist or an obsessive, Type-A personality who feels driven?

_____ _____ Are you impulsive?

_____ _____ Do boys predominate among your siblings?

Note: Don't expect to have all of these symptoms. Ten or more will suggest that a lab test for blood histamine is in order. See the advice earlier in this chapter about the test (page 220).

How to Treat High Histamine (Histadelia)

Histamine levels will decrease and symptoms lessen in response to daily doses of methionine, an amino acid that significantly detoxifies histamine by methylating the ring structure forming N-methylhistamine in the brain. Calcium, taken morning and evening, releases additional histamine stores and lowers levels in the body. With magnesium, it acts as a natural tranquilizer.

If your histamine level is extremely high, your physician may prescribe the drug Dilantin (phenytoin), which works rapidly to interfere with histamine and bring levels back to normal. I have not liked the side effects—insomnia, severe headaches, mental confusion, hyperexcitability, and more—that I've seen with Dilantin, so its use should be reserved for difficult cases only.

Avoid a high-protein diet, as most proteins contain histidine, the amino acid from which you will synthesize even more histamine. A preferable diet is one high in vegetables and fruits.

The HRC formula on page 229 offers other substances to specifically address compulsivity and obsessiveness. A 1977 study by J. Yaryura-Tobias, M.D., established that tryptophan and its co-enzymes vitamins C and B_6 stabilized obsessive-compulsive patients within six months by using tryptophan to increase serotonin, the brain's calming neurotransmitter. Often a dose of 500 milligrams, combined with a *small* amount of Prozac (5 mg per day), seems to work amazingly well in difficult cases. An Israeli study recently appearing in the *American Journal of Psychiatry* reports that the B vitamin inositol effectively eliminates symptoms of obsessive-compulsive disorder over a six-week period, and unlike current drug treatments, it has absolutely no side effects! Inositol works by regulating the action of serotonin within the nerve cells; it has a soothing effect on spinal

THE HRC FORMULA FOR HIGH
HISTAMINE AND COMPULSIVE/OBSESSIVENESS©

Nutrient	Dose	Directions
Tryptophan*	500 mg	1 capsule, 2 or 3 times daily, ½ hour before meals
Methionine	500 mg	1 capsule, 4 times daily, ½ hour before meals
Vitamin C (Ester C)	675 mg	1 capsule, 2 times daily, with meals
Calcium/magnesium	150 mg 75 mg	2 capsules, 3 times daily, with meals
B_6	250 mg	1 capsule daily, with meals
Inositol (18 g total)		1½ tsp. 3 times daily, with meals
Phosphatidylcholine powder 55% conversion to acetylcholine		2 heaping Tbs daily, with meals

Note: If you are already taking any of the above nutrients, do not exceed the amounts for your total dosage (see chart page 56).

Tryptophan is available only by prescription in the United States and Canada. Your doctor can order it only from certain pharmacies. The two that we use are: Hopewell Pharmacy, 1-800-792-6670 and College Pharmacy, 1-800-888-9358.

© Copyright 1999 Health Recovery Center.™ All Rights Reserved.

cord nerves, the brain, and cerebrospinal fluid, and produces antianxiety effects similar to the drug Librium.

Histadelics also benefit from raising depleted levels of acetylcholine in their brains. This can be done by taking the precursor phosphatidylcholine. Phosphatidylcholine is found in lecithin, but also elsewhere. Acetylcholine stabilizes brain membranes, greatly improves mood, and restores short-term memory. We use a granular powder form of phosphatidylcholine that has a 55 percent conversion rate—the highest available today. It can be mixed with milk or applesauce.

Note: Avoid taking multivitamins or B complex vitamins that contain folic acid and B_{12}, both of which increase body stores of histamine. But you will want to take the other B vitamins I've mentioned, as they play a huge role in stabilizing your nervous system.

THE TIMETABLE FOR
RELIEF OF SYMPTOMS OF HISTADELIA*
• Depression
  • Blank mind
    • Obsessions
      • Compulsions
        • Rituals
          • Phobias

| One Week | One Month | One Year |

A Word About Getting Your Doctor's Cooperation

If you fit the profile of too high or low histamine, you deserve to know with scientific accuracy what the real picture is. As you try to schedule the tests, you may discover that not all doctors have even heard of this relatively new research.

I urge you not to be dissuaded from ordering the confirming lab tests. If your doctor is unwilling to cooperate, it is time to find a physician who cares. Refusing you this needed information doesn't affect your doctor at all, but he may be condemning you to a lifetime of struggling with an out-of-balance brain. Appendix B has a list of medical organizations that will provide you with the names of physicians in your area who will work with you. It is very important that you consult with the appropriate physician regarding your own particular case and course of treatment.

WHERE DO YOU FIT IN?

We've now covered more possibilities that may cause unstable emotions. If you recognize that you feel paranoid, continually plan big projects but lack the energy to carry them out, or that you put on weight that is distributed in a pear-shaped fashion, you have some strong clues to follow.

* Taken from Carl Pfeiffer, M.D., Ph.D., *The Schizophrenias: Ours to Conquer.*

Or, if you have the markers of a driven, compulsive person with a high sex drive and/or are depressed and suicidal, I encourage you to press on in finding the relief you deserve. Here are your options:

_____ Find an orthomolecular or holistic physician to work with you (see Appendix B for referrals).

_____ Have the lab test that measures your serum histamine (see Appendix C for lab references).

_____ Correct any abnormal histamine levels by using the appropriate formula (page 221 and 229) provided in this chapter.

Please remember that the formulas for treating high and low histamine levels that are found in this chapter are easily obtainable. The same high-quality nutrients we use at Health Recovery Center are available from Bio-Recovery at 1-800-247-6237. You will be able to get your questions answered at this 800 number, as well as having your orders sent to you overnight.

CHAPTER 8

From Zero to Spontaneous Combustion in Seconds
Controlling Irritability, Anger, and Sudden Violence

By now your repair program should be picking up speed. You've altered your diet to include mostly fresh, whole foods and tossed out the sugary junk food and all that caffeine. You are remembering to feed yourself quality snacks that keep your blood sugar up. These changes are slowly paying off. We've looked at a number of problems traditionally categorized as "psychological" (anxiety, depression, paranoia, and compulsiveness) that may really be due to the depletion or overabundance of certain brain chemicals, and you now have the insight to identify and correct these biochemical mistakes.

On the following pages I'll discuss ongoing irritability, angry outbursts, and aggressive behavior that can lead to violence. The debate still rages as to whether the basic causes of violence are psychological, sociological, or biological in origin, but new research on this subject may surprise you. Can these emotional states have a physical basis? Yes. There is mounting research indicating that people who act out in this way are not just the product of too much poverty, too little nurturing, and other social/psychological problems. There are biochemical triggers in some of us that make outbursts of anger and violence predictable. Let's take a look at the evidence.

What's Causing Our Anger and Violence?

Matt had a hard time keeping a job because of his short fuse and aggressive behavior. As a child, he had been diagnosed as having attention-deficit disorder, and had grown up on Ritalin. Now his

*psychiatrist had put him on three different antidepressants simulta-
neously in an attempt to calm him down. When I met Matt, he was
feeling miserable because his wife had recently filed divorce papers.
He seemed not to be hearing most of what I said to him. He was restless and made several double entendre sexual remarks that irked me.
That first week at the Center, he became so angry that he put his
hands tightly around the neck of a female staff worker as though to
choke her. I hoped we could tolerate his behavior until his lab results
came back and gave us a reason to work with him. When the results
were in, it was a relief to see that Matt was loaded with high levels of
copper, cadmium, and lead. To add to his distress, his histamine
was severely elevated, and he was hypoglycemic. All of these physical
abnormalities made him appear emotionally out of control.*

*The toxic metals had to go, and his histamine level had to come
down before the sudden anger and wild outbursts would quiet
down. Gradually, Matt's aggressiveness faded and I became quite
fond of him. After almost a year, we heard from Matt again. He
was doing well and taking college courses with the intent of working with kids with attention-deficit disorder. (With his experien-
tial knowledge, he should prove invaluable in his new field.)*

*Tom, another client with a hair-trigger temper, came to us from
New Mexico. He was severely hypoglycemic. During his glucose
tolerance test, he released an extremely high amount of adrenaline
to raise his blood sugar. That outpouring of adrenaline, when the
brain is too low on fuel to function normally, often triggers aggressive behavior. We were able to control Tom's wild outpouring of
adrenaline by correcting his hypoglycemia. But his story was a lot
more complicated.*

*Tom had built his home in an area of the country that is high
in uranium. The water he drinks is coming through carcinogenic
granite. The body's uranium level should be under .2; Tom's was
819! He was actually radioactive! Tom's copper levels were also
quite elevated, probably because of his occupation as a plumber. The
cumulative effect of all these toxins were depression, fatigue, and
severe irritability.We used zinc to chelate out his excess copper, but
no one was able to advise us on how to remove uranium. We were
told that calcium chelation may be of some value. The eventual improvement in Tom's energy level and temperament probably came*

about because of his strict diet and his regimen of chelating nutri-ents. (*Note:* Certain states are at risk for uranium radioactivity: Vermont, Colorado, New Mexico, and California.)

Today, anger and violence are all around us, from drive-by and freeway shootings to the explosive tempers and hostile "drop dead!" expressions on the faces of salespeople, office workers, neighbors, and even children. *What is making Americans so angry?*

Our last half century has produced a cascade of changes in the lifestyles of most of us. We call it progress, but our bodies are not yet twenty-first-century models. The brain, central nervous system, and immune system simply can't adapt fast enough to the abrupt rise in the intake of substances that alter us:

1. Poor diets: The foods and drinks we consume are laden with additives and dyes, and are highly sugared; many are processed and refined until all nutrition is gone. Such diets create hypoglycemia.
2. Chemical sensitivities: We live with daily exposures to synthetic chemicals in the air we breathe, the sprayed produce we eat, and the drugs we ingest.
3. Toxicity of trace metals: Increasing stores of toxic metals and toxic trace elements accumulate and alter our brain chemistry.
4. Vaccinations: We inject several dozen live viruses into our children over and over for immunization purposes.

These are the most common reasons for Americans living in high arousal most of the time. We are unable to feel and act normally because of the toxic condition of our brains and bodies, and so we explode into anger, irritability, and even violence.

But there *are* things we can choose to do to reduce the risk of these conditions. Let's find out what they are.

DIET AND VIOLENCE: HOW ADEQUATE
BRAIN FUEL (GLUCOSE) STEMS VIOLENCE AND ANGER

A tribe of Central American Indians, the Quolla, were studied by American anthropologists back in the 1970s. These Indians have a reputation for violence dating back to the sixteenth century, unpremeditated murder being common among them. The researchers discovered that Quolla diets were very poor: high in refined sugars and alcohol, and short on basic nutrition. In fact, *every tribesman tested turned out to be hypoglycemic.* What's more, the most violent of the Indians had spectacular surges of adrenaline when their glucose levels fell too low!

By now, you should know enough about hypoglycemia to understand what can happen under these circumstances: by the time the adrenaline is released, the "reasoning" brain is turned off, leaving the "animal" brain in charge. At best, this situation can erupt into verbal anger. At worst, it can bring on physical aggression that can have tragic consequences.

Consider this depressing scenario: An abusive individual leaves a party in a hypoglycemic state that was brought on by an evening of drinking and junk-food snacks. He or she arrives home about the time the adrenaline hits the bloodstream. At this point, anyone unfortunate enough to cross his or her path may be subjected to uncontrollable anger, even physical abuse. Counseling has little to offer these people; our prisons today are full of violent hypoglycemics who are paying a high price for uncontrolled behavior. Thus, maintaining constant adequate glucose levels should be one of the most important functions of our biochemical being. *Our brains need glucose so that we can think clearly.*

Luckily, some very exciting research exists on how diet changes can control violent behavior in boys. In 1980, an East Coast juvenile detention home compared the behavior of boys who ate their "normal" menu (high in sugar and processed foods) with a second group of their boys whose sugar intake was secretly reduced: no more soft drinks, no more table sugar or highly sugared breakfast cereals, jellies, or sweets. Researcher Stephen Schoenthaler, Ph.D., found the results astonishing: The two dozen boys on the low sugar diet had a 45 percent lower incidence of reported disciplinary actions than the first group!

Dr. Schoenthaler has since expanded the study to include 276 juveniles at that center. He has found that those who were arrested for violent crimes showed the greatest behavioral improvement on a "no sugar" menu—a 77 percent reduction in disciplinary incident reports.

Dr. Carolyn Brown, Ph.D., is the director of a similar institution in Berkeley, California. She treats violent and delinquent juveniles with biochemical repair as well as therapy. Special attention is paid to possible hypoglycemia, allergies, and brain toxicity. She

A WORD TO PARENTS OF UNRULY TEENS

How ironic that I am now handing out advice on this subject, after having put up with countless out-of-control behaviors from my own teenager, Rob, without a clue as to how to stop it. Looking back now, it really hits me in the face! Rob seldom ate with us. He drank several colas daily and loved candy and fast food. His mood swings were incredible. My formerly well-mannered "A" student was even arrested for taking a swing at a plainclothes policeman and breaking the man's glasses! I had no idea until only months before he took his life how hypoglycemic Rob was. He would have been a perfect model for the roller-coaster confusion and irritability that a hypoglycemic brain endures.

If you have teenager(s) who never eat with the family and are subsisting on the great American junk-food diet, sit them down and teach them about the high price they are paying for starving and abusing their delicate brains. They are old enough to prove it to themselves. Make a deal with them to drastically clean up their diet and limit all sugars for one month. The rewards by then will be obvious: a clear brain, sustained energy, and feelings of stability and calm. Regaining access to a healthy, curious brain that wants to learn and succeed in life will change their whole future. How I wish someone had given me this advice for Rob!

described her nutritional approach to correcting behavior to the 1977 U.S. Senate Select Committee on Nutrition and Human Needs: "We have seen incredible results in the last two years. The most noticeable one is related to blood sugar. If we give these children protein every two hours, their behavior is kept in much better control. . . . The difference is amazing. They are learning to read . . . [they] have truly moved ahead. [These kids] probably would have been the kind of children [who] would never have [attended] school again."

If you see your children, partner, or even yourself shifting moods every few hours, and failing to control sudden flare-ups of anger or irritability, the most likely explanation is fluctuating blood sugar. You should reread Chapter 3 on the hypoglycemia diet. If you want absolute scientific proof, call your doctor to schedule a five-hour glucose tolerance test (see page 72).

The Need for Omega-3 Oils in Our Diet

Violent behavior has also been escalating worldwide, wherever the American diet has been adopted. Despite dire warnings from omega-3 EFA research pioneers like Donald Rudin, many cultures have replaced the omega-3 oils found in their native diets with the high omega-6 fatty acids (vegetable oils) found in ours. Only recently have Japanese researchers begun piecing together what has been happening to their population, which began Westernizing their culture after World War II. Dr. Harumi Okuyama and his colleagues noted in 1992 that "increased dietary linoleic acid (Omega 6) and relative Omega-3 essential fatty acid deficiency are major risk factors for *western-type cancers, cardiovascular and cerebrovascular diseases*, and also for *allergic hyperreactivity*. We also raise the possibility that a relative Omega-3 EFA deficiency may be affecting the *behavioral patterns* of a proportion of the young generation in industrialized countries" (emphasis added).

Japanese youth today have very low plasma omega-3 fatty acids, which is directly due to their being the biggest consumers of modern commercial foods that are soaked in high omega-6 (linoleic acid) vegetable oils. The increased ratio of omega 6 to omega 3 over the last decades was a result of following the mistaken Western advice that reducing animal fat by replacing it with omega-6 linoleic acid (corn, safflower, sunflower, and soybean oils) will lower cholesterol, thus preventing heart attacks. But statistics now correlate a very high incidence of death through violence, including suicide, in this population, so a drop in mortality has never been achieved.

In 1996, Dr. T. Hamazaki and his colleagues did a double-blind study with Japanese university students where they monitored their "aggression against others" responses during an entire school year. During this time, one of the two groups was supplemented with DHA, the highly polyunsaturated omega-3 oil that is needed in the brain and eyes for proper visual and central nervous system functioning. This group showed no change from normal behavior. The control group, however, which received no DHA, showed a big increase in aggressive behavior! What all this means to you and me is that to achieve a sense of calmness and control, we should be eating a lot of salmon and cold-water fish, or taking a couple of tablespoons of flax powder or flax oil or capsules of cold-water fish oil every day—besides, of course, eating the proper diet (see Chapter 3).

CHEMICAL SENSITIVITIES AND ANGER

A few years ago, a counselor from another clinic came to see me. Roger was having trouble controlling his emotions and feared his explosive anger was about to cost him his job. Worse, he recognized he was having suicidal thoughts. He was very frightened. At our initial interview I discovered that Roger was drinking twenty-five cups of coffee and a six-pack of cola every day! Correcting his hypoglycemia calmed the mood swings, but his behavior was still unpredictable. Not until he told me about his hobby, taxidermy, did I begin to suspect the culprit. In his off-hours, Roger was inhaling solvents, glues, and thinners that just might explain the symptoms that continued to trouble him. To find out, I sent him to a clinical ecologist (a new breed of medical allergist) for tests. Roger's test results showed a dramatic reaction to ethanol and formaldehyde. Upon exposure in the lab, Roger became quite paranoid and angry. The tests also revealed sensitivities to wheat and dairy products that brought on delayed reactions of severe irritability and fatigue.

Roger recovered by giving up caffeine, nicotine, refined sugars, and wheat and dairy products and minimizing his exposure to ethanol and formaldehyde.

Over the years I've met many house painters, garage mechanics, hair salon workers, printers, and others who continually inhale chemical fumes on the job. Many are severely reactive to these toxins. Their altered brains create drastically altered behavior. Sudden anger, irritability, and even violence have been linked to brain allergies.

The late, distinguished allergist, Theron Randolph, M.D., first proposed over fifty years ago that many physical and emotional disorders may be related to exposure to environmental chemicals. He discovered that susceptible people first experience a pleasing, addictive high followed eventually by withdrawal symptoms. The chart on page 239, adapted from Randolph's book, *An Alternative*

THE UPS AND DOWNS OF ADDICTION

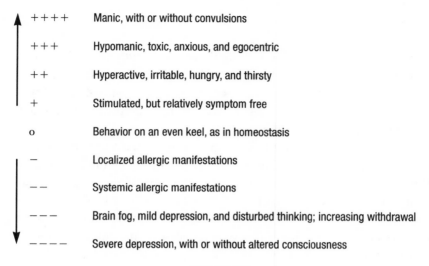

INCREASING
STIMULATION

++++	Manic, with or without convulsions
+++	Hypomanic, toxic, anxious, and egocentric
++	Hyperactive, irritable, hungry, and thirsty
+	Stimulated, but relatively symptom free
o	Behavior on an even keel, as in homeostasis
−	Localized allergic manifestations
− −	Systemic allergic manifestations
− − −	Brain fog, mild depression, and disturbed thinking; increasing withdrawal
− − − −	Severe depression, with or without altered consciousness

INCREASING
WITHDRAWAL

Note: The plus signs indicate increased brain stimulation, as a reaction to ingesting allergic or addictive substances. The minus signs mean decreased brain functioning following withdrawal of the allergic or addictive substances.

Approach to Allergies, will give you an idea of the range of these symptoms, from the initial "up" to the subsequent withdrawal or "down." The more stimulated (intoxicated) by the chemical you are, the more severe your withdrawal will be.

A Health Recovery Center study published in 1987 in the *International Journal of Biosocial and Medical Research* showed that 56 percent of our alcoholic clients were sensitive to chemicals in the environment. The most common offender was ethanol, which is contained in a wide range of products:

- natural gas
- gasoline
- some paints
- automobile exhaust
- alcohol

- soft plastics (new car odors)
- certain hand lotions and perfumes
- disinfectant cleaners
- tobacco smoke
- hydrocarbons

The most common allergic reactions were fatigue, exhaustion, spaciness, irritability, mental confusion, and depression. The magnitude and severity of these responses was startling, and included sudden intense anger, tears and sobbing, falling asleep, and the sudden inability to think or speak coherently.

All of these symptoms can be readily produced and extinguished in an allergy testing lab. The procedure involves placing a sample of the suspect chemical under the tongue (sublingual testing). If a reaction occurs, it can be turned off by placing a much more minute (neutralizing) dose of the same substance under the tongue, using a homeopathic technique. These test results provide convincing evidence for skeptical clients and those who suspect that their symptoms are all in their minds.

Plus, certain physical conditions can compromise the blood-brain barrier, so that neurotoxic substances in our blood can penetrate into the brain. When we are ill, depressed, or overstressed, or if there is physical damage to the body, this can occur. Then, potentially harmful substances like heavy metals (e.g., lead, cadmium), *Candida albicans* yeast, inflammation-producing kinins, and/or other allergens and their reacting antibodies can enter the brain. Immune reactions within the brain can cause swelling, damage nerve structures, and reduce access to oxygen (energy), and may unbalance neurotransmitter production—all of which radically affects our thinking and behavior.

Are You Chemically Sensitive?

Chemically sensitive persons often fight a losing battle to feel stable because their brains are continually "under attack" in our modern-day society. The following describes the life we lead as humans upon entering the twenty-first century (you'll recognize that much of the description applies to your own life):

Most of us spend our nights sleeping on polyester sheets and pillowcases. Usually, these have been saturated with formaldehyde in our dryers to make them smell and feel good. Our clothing is often synthetic and laced with no-iron and drip-dry chemicals. Our shower water reeks of chlorine, "a poisonous element with a suffocating odor" according to many dictionaries. Perfumes in our soaps, lotions, and shampoos come from ethanol, as do most cosmetic aromas.

The foods we eat are a hodge-podge of chemicals. Our fruits and vegetables have been grown and sprayed continually with synthetic pesticides. Our meats are full of synthetic hormones and antibiotics. Breads are loaded with artificial flavoring, additives, and dyes. Most foods come wrapped in polyethylene.

Our new houses and office buildings are built so tightly that their synthetic fibers and materials (i.e., plywood and carpeting) can't gas out, leaving sensitive persons with ongoing headaches and low-grade illnesses. Today, there is often no such thing as throwing open a window at work for some much needed fresh air!

Thus many chemically sensitive persons fight a losing battle to feel stable.

The chemical screening test (page 242) is based on a questionnaire originally developed by Dr. Theron Randolph, the "father of clinical ecology." If after taking this test, you believe you are chemically allergic (sensitive), you should consult a clinical ecologist/allergist for further testing and treatment (see Appendix B for medical referrals). I myself was tested several years ago by Dr. George Kroker in La Crosse, Wisconsin. The result was a real eye-opener. Before exposure, I had completed a short exercise that required me to match symbols. After the mysterious dose, I was asked to match another page of symbols. I was so sleepy and muddled that I simply could not perform at a normal pace. I felt as though my IQ had suddenly dropped fifty points. Then, with a neutralizing dose under my tongue, I brightened up. The substance responsible for my confusion and fatigue was ethanol, the base of most perfumes and aftershave lotions. This test result explained why I had been having trouble concentrating when clients wore a lot of cologne or after-shave.

GATHERING MORE EVIDENCE

Besides the provocative challenge testing I just described, it is often helpful to look at two more tests that may prove invaluable:

HEALTH RECOVERY CENTER CHEMICAL SCREENING TEST

Does exposure to any of the following substances tend to provoke a response, from strong dislike to noticeable symptoms?

	Yes	No
1. Newspaper print		
2. Soft plastics (i.e., vinyl, acrylic)		
3. Tobacco smoke		
4. Fabric store odors		
5. Diesel or auto exhaust		
6. Cooking gas		
7. Pesticide sprays		
8. Insecticide strips		
9. Mothballs or crystals		
10. Fabric softeners (i.e., Bounce)		
11. Detergents		
12. Ammonias		
13. Bleaches		
14. Scented cosmetics		
15. Scented perfumes or aftershaves		
16. Scented deodorants, antiperspirants		
17. Oven cleaner		
18. Furniture polish		
19. Floor wax		
20. New carpets		
21. New car odors		

	Yes	No
22. House paints		
23. Turpentines		
24. Foam rubber pillows		
25. Copier machines		

Answer yes or no to the following questions.	Yes	No
1. Do you live near heavy traffic?		
2. Do you live near factory pollution?		
3. Do you live near crop spraying?		
4. Do you have a gas clothes dryer?		
5. Do you have a gas water heater?		
6. Do you have a gas kitchen stove?		
7. Do you have a gas fireplace?		
8. Do you have a gas space heater?		
9. Do you feel worse in the winter when your home is more closed up?		
10. Are you aware of smelling any odors upon entering your house • Musty, moldy smells? • New house smells? • Plastic smells? • Leaky gas?		
11. Is your sense of smell below average?		
12. Have you been bothered by chemicals that you encounter on the job?		
13. Have you been exposed to chemicals at work, either now or in past jobs?		
14. Do you have hobbies that involve working with glues, solvents, paints, or other chemicals?		
15. Do you get severe hangovers from alcohol?		
TOTAL YOUR ANSWERS HERE		

Scoring: If you have fifteen or more yes answers, it is highly likely that you are chemically sensitive.

- A *hair analysis* is the best indicator we have of heavy metal buildup in the brain. (I'll talk more about this simple test later in this chapter.)
- A test for *candida yeast* may uncover what is suppressing your immune system and muddling your brain (more on candida in the next chapter).

TURNING OFF YOUR CHEMICAL REACTIONS

Once you have nailed down (through lab tests) the substances that play tricks with your brain, desensitization to the chemical culprit(s) can occur through a three-step procedure.

First: A chemical ecologist can prepare a neutralizing dose containing minute amounts of the chemical to which you are sensitive. When this is placed under your tongue, the chemical sensitivity fades within minutes. At the same time, your immune system's ability to handle that chemical is strengthened. You may get a prescription of "drops" to take home and use daily until your immune system can handle the exposure normally.

Second: Your doctor will recommend you take sodium and potassium bicarbonate in the form of Alka-Seltzer Gold or give you a prescription for alkali salts. These salts effectively neutralize the excess acidity that develops in the body during allergic reactions. Two tablets of Alka-Seltzer Gold help reduce the symptoms that occur from chemical exposure. The adult dose is two tablets every four hours, not to exceed eight tablets in a twenty-four-hour period.

Third: It is essential to avoid as much as possible the chemicals to which you are sensitive. Also avoid or eliminate chemicals in your home that could potentially cause problems, including:

- gas appliances
- cigarette smoke
- perfumed cosmetics and perfumed hair spray
- soft vinyl and acrylic items
- spray cleaners for ovens, baths, and kitchens
- air fresheners

You can further reduce chemical intake by drinking only deep-well water or bottled spring water. Avoid chlorinated tap water and foods

that have been heavily sprayed with chemicals. Switch to organically grown products. Room and car air filters also help minimize
exposure to chemical fumes. If you must work around chemicals,
consider wearing a portable charcoal mask.

FINDING THE RIGHT DOCTOR

In the United States, we have the American Academy of Environmental Medicine, which can refer you to a clinical ecologist in your
area who can test and treat you for chemical sensitivities (see Appendix B for details).

There are also a number of excellent books on chemical hypersensitivity (see Appendix D), which can give you more information
on this common problem. Meanwhile, begin taking several capsules
of antioxidants daily (see the formula on page 50). These will help
protect your brain from oxidation damage and heighten your immune system functioning.

TRACE METAL SENSITIVITIES AND VIOLENCE

I found myself seated next to the main speaker at a state conference
on brain disorders a few years ago. Dr. William Walsh, Ph.D., spoke
about being able to identify violent people through their trace metal
chemistry. His story is fascinating. In 1975, he and other researchers
at Argonne National Laboratories decided to get involved with helping just-released prisoners from a nearby penitentiary that he described as a "dumping ground for the hopelessly violent and
incorrigible." The researchers began their work believing that these
men were products of their environment and poor nurturing. So
when a prisoner was released, the scientists met him at the gates
with new clothes, a job interview, a place to live, and so on. It took
two years of watching the high recidivism of these violent offenders
before realizing something was very wrong. Once Dr. Walsh's team
faced the fact that psychological or sociological changes made no
difference, they turned to exploring whether this population could
be *physiologically* different from the rest of us.

Their search began with lab tests of blood and urine. But they
could not find any significant clues to a violent predisposition in the
results. About this time they met Dr. Carl Pfeiffer, who advised them

to focus on trace metal buildup (such as lead, copper, zinc, and manganese). New studies were showing lead and cadmium are predominant *only* in violent people! The scientists therefore began testing hundreds of violent prisoners, looking at the hair levels of trace minerals and metals—and the results were just as Pfeiffer had predicted! Moreover, they could fit most of the violent subjects into two categories from the results of their hair analysis: Type-A people were episodically violent but felt remorse following an "explosion"; Type-B individuals, with a different configuration of trace metals, were, according to relatives and teachers, mean and nasty continually. Type B's felt no remorse for their acts of violence, and had been antisocial since childhood.

The first study published by Walsh's group, the Health Research Institute, was an eye-opener, too. They had studied pairs of brothers, one of whom had many violent incidents and the other (living in the same house) who was a well-behaved kid and doing very well in school. In every instance, the violent boys had abnormal trace metal levels that fell into either Type A or Type B of the four classifications of disordered chemistry that they put together from their research.

These four divisions are:

Type A: severe episodic violence
Type B: sociopath/severely assaultive
Type C: intermediate episodic violence
Type D: mild episodic violence

After publishing their research, the Institute was challenged by UCLA researchers to prove their findings by matching two hundred blind hair samples, half from violent prisoners and half from students and businesspeople. The accuracy of identification was almost 100 percent, except for a mistaken identification of a couple of prison guards as belonging to the violent group.

What follows are the four biotypes identified by the Health Research Institute. (Their research base included more than 150,000 people!) Early identification of these violent types and effective treatment through rebalancing their errant chemistry is the best hope we have of reducing the incidents of violence in this country.

Four Types of (Violent) Behavior Disorder
(As identified by the Health Research Institute, Naperville, Illinois)

Type A
(Includes 40% of all behavior-disoriented chemistries)

COMMONLY OBSERVED CHARACTERISTICS

Episodic violence, followed by remorse for behavior

Jekyll-Hyde behavior, common in men

Poor stress control

Attention deficit disorder

Academic underachiever

Tantrums and physical fighting common in males

Resistive behavior, promiscuity, mood swings, and nonviolent delinquency, common in women

Acne

Blood histamine either abnormally high or low

Sunburns easily

Allergies

Behavior changes triggered by chocolate

HAIR ELEMENT TEST LEVELS

Elevated copper

Depressed zinc

Elevated lead, cadmium, and other toxic metals

Elevated iron

Depressed sodium, potassium, manganese, and calcium (*Note:* The magnesium is either very elevated or very depressed.)

OTHER BIOCHEMICAL ABNORMALITIES

40 percent are pyroluric

30 percent are hypoglycemic

30 percent are malabsorbers

All histamines levels are in the abnormal range (too high or too low)

Treatment for Type A's involves correcting abnormal levels of minerals and toxic metals, and testing for pyroluria, hypoglycemia, abnormal histamine levels, and malabsorption. Type A children improve substantially (85%) within twenty-five days of treatment.

Type B
(Rare—only 0.3% of the population)

COMMONLY OBSERVED CHARACTERISTICS
Frequently assaultive
Total lack of conscience or remorse
Pathological liars
Cruelty to animals and people
Antisocial/sociopath behavior
Sleeps only three to four hours nightly
Could be serial killer/mass murderer
Fascination with fire
Strongly aggressive
High pain threshold
Obsessive compulsive

HAIR ELEMENT TEST LEVELS
Elevated calcium
Elevated magnesium
Depressed manganese
Elevated sodium
Severely depressed copper
Depressed zinc
Elevated iron
Elevated lead and/or other toxic metals

OTHER BIOCHEMICAL ABNORMALITIES
Elevated histamine levels
Elevated kryptopyrroles (pyroluric)

Treatment for Type B's involves restoring normal levels of mineral and histamines and removing toxic metals. Pyroluria must also be corrected.

Type C
COMMONLY OBSERVED CHARACTERISTICS
Malabsorber (50% need hydrochloric acid [stomach acid]; others have an intestinal problem)
Underachiever
Delinquent

Argues, but does not hurt others
Slender
Shoplifter
Seldom maintains a driver's license
Impulsive
Mildly aggressive
Low amino acid levels in blood testing
Irritable
Can't hold job, shows poor work performance

HAIR ELEMENT TEST LEVELS
Depressed calcium
Depressed magnesium
Depressed copper
Depressed zinc
Depressed manganese
May have elevated levels of lead, cadmium, mercury, nickel, aluminum, or other toxins

Blood testing on Type C's shows that most nutrient levels are low. They need treatment for malabsorption and multivitamin supplementation.

Type D
COMMONLY OBSERVED CHARACTERISTICS
Reactive to sugar: hypoglycemic
Mildly aggressive
May be overweight
Irritable after eating sugar
Drowsy after meals
Nonviolent, but never reaches potential in life
Allergies

HAIR ELEMENT TEST LEVELS
Extremely high calcium
Elevated magnesium (also extremely high)
Depressed sodium
Depressed potassium
Depressed copper
Depressed zinc

Depressed manganese
Depressed chromium

Treatment for Type D's involves correcting the hypoglycemic and allergic reactions.

Applying These Patterns

The above pattern types were first identified about ten years ago. Since HRC regularly does hair analysis tests on all our clients, we began comparing our own clients' hair analysis test results to the mineral and trace metal abnormalities in the above four patterns. We consistently found that the deficiencies and symptoms named in these four types fit our clients' deficiencies and symptoms. Furthermore, we saw a gradual reduction of these symptoms as the biochemical imbalances were corrected. When you set out to apply these patterns to yourself, *do not expect a perfect fit*, but do recognize the clustering of your predominant characteristics, and of most of the mineral/toxic metal pattern listed. Your recovery depends on normalizing these abnormal levels. If you are young, the prognosis for fast recovery is much higher. I'm sorry to say that older bodies take more work and patience.

What You Need to Know
About Hair Analysis Tests

Hair analysis is often a better indicator than blood testing of deficiencies or toxic buildup of the minerals, trace elements, and toxic metals. That's because metals can be stored in tissues even when they don't show up in the blood. Here are the metals hair analysis can detect:

Arsenic
Cadmium
Calcium
Chromium
Copper
Lead
Magnesium
Manganese
Mercury
Nickel
Potassium

Selenium
Sodium
Zinc

You or your medical doctor, chiropractor, or nutritionist can send a sample of your hair to any of the laboratories listed in Appendix C. These labs have voluntarily accepted the guidelines for hair element analysis that were established by the Hair Analysis Standardization Board of the American Holistic Medical Institute.

The following preparations are necessary before you submit a hair sample for analysis:

- Do not submit dyed hair or hair that has a permanent wave less than one month old (a pubic hair sample may be substituted for scalp hair if necessary).
- Cut the hair as close to the scalp as possible, and discard all but the first one-and-a-half inches closest to the scalp.
- If possible, clip the hair from the nape of your neck.
- If you are ordering an analysis directly from the lab, place a total of one gram in a small envelope for submission. (A kit with a cardboard scale for weighing the hair can be obtained from the laboratory.) The results will come directly to you, in a printout. *Note:* Please take the results to a trained professional for interpretation. An untrained eye might misconstrue certain high readings, which actually may indicate storage of the mineral in question in the hair and soft tissues and an unavailability in the blood and bone. So, it is *vital* not to accept all the readings at face value. The lab will provide duplicate copies of the results and a computerized analysis.

  (If the lab test results were sent directly to your doctor, ask him or her for copies for your records.)

Reducing Toxic Metals in Your Body

Here is a brief summary of symptoms and treatment for the most common toxic metals.

ALUMINUM:
Aluminum toxicity has been associated with hyperactivity in children and with Alzheimer's disease. In early stages of aluminum

absorption, before the "tangles" of nerve fibers appear, aluminum levels can be lowered with magnesium. Your daily dosage should be 1,200 milligrams. Adding one cup of Epsom salts to your bathwater can also help bring high aluminum levels back to normal.

CADMIUM:

Cigarette paper contains cadmium, and so smokers inhale fumes from this metal with every cigarette. One pack contains 23 micrograms of cadmium. Excess intake of this metal can contribute to chronic bronchitis and/or emphysema. There is also a direct correlation between high blood pressure and cadmium intake. You can remove cadmium from your tissues with daily doses of zinc (40 mg), selenium (200 mcg), and calcium (1,200 mg).

LEAD:

Persons who work as house painters, garage mechanics, or at other jobs that expose them to lead are at high risk of accumulating toxic levels of this mineral. A lead buildup can impair your concentration and shorten your attention span. Your thinking may also become muddled and irritable. Megadoses of vitamin B_1 (200 mg daily) can help relieve these symptoms. Calcium (1,200 mg per day) also helps remove lead from tissues. However, the preferred treatment for lead toxicity is EDTA chelation therapy combined with several injections of vitamin B_1 (see mercury description for information about EDTA).

MERCURY:

Sugar lovers tend to have terrible teeth with lots of mercury fillings (as of this writing, *all* silver fillings being used are over half mercury!). Recent reports about the effects of the mercury contained in these fillings help explain why so many people also complain about aches and pains, depression, and fatigue. Many of our clients experienced dramatic improvement in their emotions and bodies after their mercury fillings were removed. It is important to treat with intravenous infusions of vitamin C to counteract the mercury the tissues have absorbed.

Mercury poisoning can cause suicidal depression, fatigue, memory loss, headache, vision loss, speech disorders, emotional instability, and confusion. (The expression "mad as a hatter" comes from the

EXCESS MANGANESE TIED NOT ONLY TO VIOLENT BEHAVIOR BUT ATTENTION DEFICIT DISORDER!

In a five-year study conducted by the chairman of psychiatry at the University of California, Irvine, levels of manganese were found to be over *400 percent* higher in the head hair of 63 percent of violent criminals (versus 11% of the nonviolent controls).

Researchers were even more surprised when three other studies reported that the hair of attention deficit (ADD) children had 100 percent higher amounts of manganese than non-ADD children! Scientists have now identified one major source of manganese: today's infant formulas contain forty to sixty times more manganese content than the manganese naturally present in mother's milk. Over thirty scientific papers now report significant reductions in aggressive and violent behavior by lowering the toxic element levels, and providing individualized nutrient treatment in such ADD children.

days when mercury vapor was used to clean hats. The cleaners, then called hatters, became "mad" as a result of their mercury exposure.) In some cases, mercury poisoning must be treated with EDTA chelation therapy. This involves intravenous administration of ethylenediamine tetra acetate, a substance that combines with metals like mercury, lead, and cadmium, and removes them from the body. Your doctor will have to determine how many treatments you need. For a list of physicians who use EDTA chelation therapy, contact the American College of Advancement in Medicine, 23121 Verdugo Drive, Suite 204, Laguna Hills, CA 92653, 714-583-7666.

Minerals That Can Be Toxic
Hair analysis will also indicate levels of copper and manganese (see Chapter 7 for a discussion of copper toxicity and treatment). Elevated levels of these two minerals should be confirmed by serum copper and serum manganese tests.

INFANT VACCINATION PROGRAMS
AND BEHAVIOR: ALWAYS A GOOD THING?

Infant vaccination programs: something responsible parents do for their children, right? Well, studies comparing the prevaccination era to today are beginning to come together, and it is a frightening picture. It appears quite possible that there is serious damage resulting from injecting all these live viral toxins into our infants to stave off disease. Science is now assessing our children's restlessness, aggressive behavior, attention deficit disorder, and even violence as possibly coming from vaccine-caused encephalitis (brain inflammation).

As background information, your brain functions via electrical impulses that jump across nerve synapses. And like electrical wiring, these nerve cells require insulation to function normally. This insulation is provided by myelin sheaths of fatty material that are laid down during the first five weeks of life. Experts believe that these viral injections can trigger an autoimmune reaction that attacks and prevents development of these myelin sheaths so that all future nerve impulses (messages) are damaged.

The battery of inoculations that is given to our infants at a time when they have no immune system protection nor myelin sheath protection could very well account for today's unstable, antisocial, and behaviorally disordered American kids. Here are just a few of the findings:

- Serious nervous system and other reactions to the measle mumps-rubella (MMR vaccines) have repeatedly been reported in medical literature. These reactions include encephalitis. The prestigious British Journal *Lancet* published a 1998 study by Andrew Wakefield, M.D., that is impressive in its linkage of "regressive developmental disorder" to MMR vaccinations. His newest study that is now in press also confirms the shocking neurological damage from MMR injections.
- The Dawbarris Law Firm of England has published a paper in which they report over six hundred instances of side effects following MMR vaccines, which were introduced in England in 1988. The side effects include autism, epilepsy, visual and hearing problems, and learning and behavioral problems in the older children.
- The *Physicians Desk Reference* on the MMR vaccine states that complications from MMR are encephalitis and optic neuritis. Reactions to dyptheria/pertussis/tetanus (DPT) vaccines include en-

cephalitis, convulsions, and brain damage, leading, in a sizable number of cases, to persistent diseases or death.

Harris Coulter, Ph.D., in his 1990 book *Vaccination, Social Violence & Criminality*, points out that vaccination-caused encephalitis can range from severe to extremely mild, but it still does long-term damage. The less serious cases are not mentally retarded, but they do suffer a loss of IQ. Instead of blindness, these children may have astigmatism or be dyslexic (i.e., have difficulty reading, spelling, or understanding numbers). Often there is a disturbance of sleep rhythm, and the children turn night into day.

Instead of being totally deaf, they may have mild hearing loss or chronic earaches—specifically otitis media or "glue ear," requiring drainage tubes. This type of otitis was unknown in American medical practice before the early fifties, the time when the pertussis vaccine was introduced. Now, over half of all American children have had otitis media by their first birthday, and over 90 percent by age six.

Dr. Coulter describes children with vaccination-caused encephalitis as having "low self-esteem . . . they are given to outbursts of rage. When combined with their tendency to compulsive behavior, this leads to many acts of impulsive violence." Dr. Coulter estimates that one out of five children have been injured by childhood vaccinations. This percentage is comparable to the 20 percent of American children who have been diagnosed as hyperactive.

If the possible danger posed by infant vaccination sounds preposterous to you still, let's look at the chronological events in the U.S. vaccination programs:

- The first vaccinations began in the late 1930s.
- The first handful of autistic children were documented in the early 1940s. Signs of autism are the inability to use words for language, isolation from people, spinning, staring, and aggressive behavior toward people and even objects.
- After World War II, as infant vaccination programs expanded, the number of autistic children increased greatly. The cases of autism in the United States have risen from a total of 11 cases in 1943 to over 250,000 today, and the number of children in special education classes because of hyperactivity, ADD, and dyslexia has risen from zero in the 1950s to about one million today. Ten million children are currently dyslexic.

- As the first generation of vaccinated children (from 1945) reached age nine in the 1950s, it was found that most had serious reading problems. (The popular *Why Johnny Can't Read* was published then.)
- In 1963, when these same children took college entrance exams and military service exams, their IQs were found to be lower than the previous generation, and IQ scores have been declining steadily ever since.
- As this same generation entered early adulthood, they created and have maintained a historically high incidence of violence. (Since 1960, violent crime has increased almost 400 percent—nine times greater than the growth of the U.S. population in that period, according to the FBI.) A large body of research on the neurologic status of violent persons links them to post-encephalitic (brain inflammation) conditions: hyperactivity, low IQ, allergies, seizure disorders, dyslexia.

And increasingly there seems to be a link between vaccination programs, behavior, and even illness, as documented by scientists worldwide:

- In 1975, Japan raised the age of pertussis (whooping cough) vaccination to two years (rather than giving the shot in early infancy, as in the United States), in order to give their babies' immune systems a chance to strengthen and mature. Since that time, there has been a dramatic decline in sudden infant deaths (SID), spinal meningitis, autism, violence, and other toxic vaccine effects in Japanese children.
- In 1979, Sweden banned the pertussis vaccine altogether, considering it both ineffective and dangerous. Today, Sweden maintains one of the lowest infant mortality rates in the world, and has far fewer instances of ADD than does the United States per capita.
- England and a host of other nations have a voluntary vaccination program that is not as stringently enforced as is the U.S. program of vaccination. All these countries have lower infant mortality rates than the United States. Sudden infant deaths were insignificant in the United States before the 1950s; today 8,000 crib deaths occur yearly.
- In 1999, the *New York Times* reported that the health minister

of France suspended all "Hepatitis B vaccinations in schools because of fears the vaccine causes neurological disorders." In the United States, we now give this vaccine to babies in hospitals within twenty-four hours after they are born. I was with my two-week-old granddaughter, Chrissie, and her parents when her pediatrician insisted on injecting her. Hepatitis B is a disease that can only be transmitted through infected blood, usually by IV drug users or sexually promiscuous adults. When we politely refused this vaccination, this doctor told us that Chrissie was not welcome at his office again. Yet the risk of an American infant contracting hepatitis B is far less than one in a million, according to the Centers for Disease Control! In 1996, there were more than three times as many reported hepatitis-B vaccine-associated serious adverse events as there were reported cases of the disease in children under age fourteen.

Weighing the Risks

By no means am I opposed to the use of all childhood vaccines, but like virtually all of the speakers at the 1997 National Vaccine Information Center Conference in Virginia, I decry the headlong rush into these programs without adequate safety screening. It is an established fact that the drug companies campaigning for more intensive use of vaccines have not tested them sufficiently or heeded the red flags being reported by the public.

One must weigh the risks against the facts: (1) No cases of polio have occurred in the United States since 1979 *except* in children who were inoculated with the *live polio virus*. (Parents must insist doctors use the *dead* polio virus to avoid this risk.) (2) The high-risk side effects from pertussis vaccine certainly can worry a parent about these injections.

Parents who choose to wait a few years until their children's immune systems and myelin sheaths are developed need to keep in mind that they are doing this because:

- Vaccines are showing immediate, sometimes fatal effects on infants.
- Vaccines have unknown long-term side effects, particularly postencephalitis brain damage in some.
- The protection from disease that vaccines provide decreases

over time, creating adult susceptibility of a far more serious nature.

Most childhood diseases for which we now inoculate are rare in this country. The balance appears to be tipping in favor of *not* risking neurological disease in your infant. Books, articles, and national organizations that will send you additional tapes and information are listed in Appendix D. After you gather the facts, you will have to make your own decision.

Fixing What's Broken

What can we do for the kids and adults who already live with neurological damage that leaves them hyper, agitated, irritable, or angry? Whatever the cause, we can address these symptoms by loading such brains with calming, natural chemicals, and we can build up the immune systems with substances that strengthen their capacity to protect us.

The Health Recovery Center formula for irritability, sudden anger, and violence incorporates amino acids and essential fatty acids known to calm the brain. At HRC we have seen the repeated success of this formula. My only caution, is that it seems to take a full two weeks before extremely agitated people calm down noticeably.

We include tryptophan in this formula based on some hard facts about the chemistry of anger and violence that arose from a 1982 study of two groups of murderers. The first group had committed unprovoked murders—their aggression was spontaneous. The second group only killed after much planning and premeditation. An analysis of the cerebral spinal fluid of both groups revealed that levels of a serotonin metabolite (hydroxyindoleactic acid or 5HIAA) were significantly *lower* among the unprovoked, spontaneous murderers (who acted because of too little serotonin to dampen and control their sudden anger) than the premeditated group (who simply brooded on the crime and planned to kill) or a group of normal noncriminal controls. Since serotonin is derived from tryptophan, we can conclude that calm, nonviolent chemistry requires an adequate intake of tryptophan plus B_3 and B_6, the nutrients that convert tryptophan to serotonin.

Another brain chemical with calming properties is GABA (gamma-aminobutyric acid). Valium and similar tranquilizers work by stimulating the GABA receptors in the brain.

THE HRC FORMULA FOR IRRITABILITY, SUDDEN ANGER, AND VIOLENCE©

Nutrient	Dose	Directions
Tryptophan*	500 mg	1 capsule 3 times daily: mid-morning, mid-afternoon, and at bedtime
Alpha waves (Bio-Recovery™)		1–2 capsules, 3 times daily:
• GABA	167 mg	mid-morning,
• Glycine	167 mg	mid-afternoon,
• Taurine	100 mg	and at bedtime
• Vitamin C (Ester C)	10 mg	
• Niacinamide	16.7 mg	
• Calcium	10 mg	
• Magnesium	25 mg	
• Vitamin B_6 (pyridoxine)	16.7 mg	
• Passion flower extract (6:1)	50 mg	
• Inositol	50 mg	
Niacinamide	500 mg	1 capsule daily, with food
Omega-3 fatty acids (Cold-water fish [EPA])	360 mg	1 capsule with breakfast 1 capsule with supper
Gamma-linolenic acid (GLA) (Omega-6 EFA)	300 mg	1 capsule daily, with food

Note: If you are already taking any of the above nutrients, do not exceed the amounts for your total dosage (see chart page 56).

*Tryptophan is available only by prescription in the United States and Canada. Your doctor can order it only from certain pharmacies. The two that we use are: Hopewell Pharmacy, 1-800-792-6670, and College Pharmacy, 1-800-888-9358.

Glycine is another amino acid that can reduce aggression when combined with inositol. Glycine strengthens the calming alpha brain waves and reduces excitatory beta waves. Taurine, another amino acid, helps to regulate the excitable tissues of the central nervous system.

The herbal passion flower extract is a formulation that also has a calming influence on the brain.

Calcium and magnesium also work to calm the brain and central nervous system.

The omega-3 essential fatty acids in the form of cold-water fish will calm and regulate the brain. There is compelling scientific evidence to show that gamma-linolenic acid (from omega-6 EFA) reverses hyperactivity. An English study of ten thousand hyperactive youngsters detected consistent abnormalities in their essential fatty acid availability. The findings were challenged by two groups of New Zealand psychiatrists. They then tested hyperactive children themselves—and came up with the same results: There was not enough omega-6 gamma-linolenic acid to load adequate prostaglandin E_1 (PGE1) in the brain. Recently, researchers at Purdue University have again proven the same research.

Doctors once believed that children outgrow hyperactivity in adolescence, but now we know that there is no magic age at which symptoms disappear. Many adults exhibit telltale signs of hyperactivity, including such nervous habits as nail biting, foot juggling, aggressiveness, unstable emotions, restless sleep, irritability, speaking with a louder or more high-pitched voice when stressed, and adult temper tantrums. *If you suspect neurological damage is causing some of your problems, plan to couple the formula for irritability, sudden anger, and violence with the formula to strengthen your immune system, found in the next chapter.*

But remember, when determining the uppermost safe dose for any nutrient in this book, do not increase beyond the highest recommended dosage of any *one* formula (see point 2, page 55).

Where Do You Fit In?

Now that you are familiar with the various problems that can underlie your sudden anger flare-ups, or your feelings of continual irritation or hyperactivity, it's time to determine the actions to take. You have *options*, so check the categories that best apply to you.

____ Correct hypoglycemia through diet and a nutritional regimen (review Chapter 3).

____ Replace essential fatty acids and restore high levels of calming neurotransmitters and other natural chemicals that quiet your brain and central nervous system (review Chapter 3 and take the formula on page 259).

_____ Invest in a hair analysis to check your levels of mineral and possible toxic metals.

_____ Contact a clinical ecologist to test you for chemical sensitivities. Have this doctor also check for candida-related complex (see Chapter 9).

_____ Consider strengthening your immune system if you have had the full childhood course of viral vaccinations (see Chapter 9).

Remember, the expert medical help you need can be obtained from the references in Appendix B, and the exact same nutrient formulas that we use at HRC can be sent to you within two days by calling 1-800-247-6237.

CHAPTER 9

Just Prop Me Up,
I'm Too Tired to Care
The Answers to What's Keeping You Fatigued

I
f you have faithfully changed your diet and applied the principles of the bio-repair program outlined so far, yet you know something is still missing, take heart. This chapter will alert you to several huge troublemakers that are notorious for wiping out your energy and mental clarity.

Jack, a frail forty-five-year-old carpenter, came to see me shortly after he had attempted suicide. He told me, "As a young man, I was friendly, outgoing, and full of anticipation for living. My problems began in Vietnam, where I was exposed to Agent Orange and subjected to the trauma of "kill or be killed" over many months. When I returned to the States I felt depressed and rudderless. I have never been able to overcome my fatigue and emptiness. I've spent twenty years going in and out of VA hospitals, to no avail. I'm just too tired to stay alive."

Jack made it plain that the lab tests I proposed would be his last stab at recovering his health. As expected, this testing revealed that he had very little immune system strength, most of which had probably been knocked out long ago by his exposure to Agent Orange. We found severe food allergies and chemical sensitivities. His candida score was extremely high. His CMV (cytomegalovirus— a herpes organism that creates fever, malaise, and joint-muscle pains) and Epstein-Barr (another herpeslike virus causing a mononucleosis-like infection) antibody levels were positive. Other tests showed he was severely malnourished. Unfortunately, we were unable to get information from the federal government on how to detoxify any residue of Agent Orange, the official position being "It didn't happen." As Vietnam veterans can't prove their symptoms are caused by Agent Orange, the government refuses to assist with solutions for this contamination.

Jack needed to rebuild his immune system from scratch by reducing the total load that was causing the breakdown (more on this later in this chapter). We used IV infusions containing high amounts of vitamin C to detoxify him. It was a slow process, but gradually, through correcting his many biochemical problems, Jack's long-lost stamina returned.

There are a number of reasons you might feel chronically fatigued. Like Jack, you may be reaping the effects of an unhealthy diet, or your symptoms may be caused by a "mixed infection" syndrome, meaning you are co-existing with bacterial or viral infections, parasites, or toxins that are weakening your immune system and your stamina, triggering a chronic fatigue syndrome in you. You may have severe food allergies or an overgrowth of *Candida albicans*, a fungal yeast that debilitates its many victims systematically. You may even be experiencing intense feelings of weakness and fatigue from daily exposure to strong electromagnetic fields.

I'll discuss each of these complex causes of chronic fatigue. We'll determine whether you are affected, and if you are, how to overcome these debilitating disorders. I have seen some dramatic recoveries among clients afflicted with such problems, so don't give up!

Chronic Fatigue Syndrome (CFS), or Running on Empty

Since the eighties, there has been a steadily growing number of people classified as having CFS. This exhausted state affects several million Americans, causing a lingering state of profound weakness and fatigue. The average length of their malaise is two years. During this time, only half of those afflicted with this immunodeficiency disorder are able to work regularly because of their illness.

In 1985, the *Annals of Internal Medicine* published a profile of common symptoms of chronic fatigue syndrome. Fatigue was the number-one complaint. Here are the others.

Symptom	Percent Affected
Easily fatigued	95
Fatigue alternating with periods of normalcy	70
Headache	80
Low-grade afternoon fever	78
Swollen lymph glands	70
Poor concentration	70
Sore throat	70
Depression	70
Allergies	65
Muscle aches/joint pains	50
Anxiety attacks	50
Mental confusion	50
Sleep disturbance	50
Abdominal problems	35
Weight loss	20
Skin rash	15

Besides ongoing fatigue, a majority of CFS sufferers experience memory loss and deficits in their ability to think and communicate, according to a 1990 article in *Medical World News*. Their MRI scans often show brain lesions similar to multiple sclerosis patterns. With so many diverse symptoms arising from this syndrome, nailing the culprits that give rise to it is no easy task. In his book *Solving the Puzzle of CFS*, Michael Rosenbaum, M.D., makes a strong case for CFS patients succumbing to a "mixed infection syndrome," which may involve a combination of synergistic viruses, yeasts, bacteria, and parasites.

DO I HAVE CHRONIC FATIGUE SYNDROME?

If you have wondered if your fatigue falls in the "normal" category or could be classified as "chronic," you will be interested in the 1994 revised definition of CFS by the Centers for Disease Control (which they offer for insurance purposes):

- A new onset of fatigue that causes a 50 percent reduction in one's activities for at least six months.
- Exclusion of other illnesses that cause fatigue.
- Eight of the following eleven signs and symptoms:

Mild fever (between 100°F to 102°F) or chills
Recurrent sore throat
Painful lymph nodes
Muscle weakness
Myalgia (muscle ache)
Prolonged fatigue from mild exercise
Recurrent headaches
Migratory arthralgia (pain switches from joint to joint)
Neuropsychological complaints (anxiety, low moods)
Sleep disturbance
Sudden onset of the symptom complex

If you have some of the above symptoms, you have a malfunctioning immune system. The big question is, *why* is your immune system failing you?

Diet and Chronic Fatigue

Over twenty-five years ago, a Russian research physician, Vladimir Dilman, found that carbohydrate intolerances and an increase in LDL levels in the blood led to a dysfunction of large scavenger cells (called macrophages) whose job it is to destroy harmful bacteria, viruses, fungi, cancer cells, and other cellular debris. We have already talked about Americans' high sugar intake, which creates abnormal blood sugar levels (Chapter 3), and their corresponding low intake of omega-3 fatty acids (Chapter 6), which, when increased, reduces LDL cholesterol (and triglycerides) and increases the good HDL cholesterol. So if you are running on empty, begin *at once* to make these changes:

- Systematically avoid all white flours, refined sugars, and white rice to boost your immune system. Also stabilize your blood sugar with daily glutamine (a 500 mg capsule) and 200 micrograms of chromium picolinate daily.

- Supplement the omega-3 and -6 essential fatty acids daily (use amounts found in your Balanced Emotions Basic Formula on page 43) and fortify your health by reloading all the essential vitamins and minerals.

Viruses and Chronic Fatigue

Concurrently with strengthening your immunity, you will want to know what viruses, bacteria, and fungi have won the first rounds in the battle with your immune system. Laboratory tests will provide your physician with information you need to defeat these invaders. The Epstein-Barr virus (EBV) has been detected in many CFS patients, as has the cytomegalovirus and human herpes virus Type VI (HHV-VI). Antibody blood titer tests for these can be routinely done by most labs.

Treating Viral Invaders Holistically

Luckily, these natural substances are extraordinary in their abilities to inhibit viral activity, and you'll find them in the formula for fighting viruses (page 267):

- Vitamin C (ascorbic acid) actually makes interferon (our bodies' natural antiviral and anticancer compound) at high doses. It should be taken in divided doses to "bowel tolerance" (until diarrhea is triggered).
- The antioxidants are free-radical scavengers. They boost immune response to viruses. These include: vitamins A and E, selenium, zinc, dimethyl-glycine, cysteine, glutathione, and methionine.
- The B-complex vitamins boost energy and act as co-enzymes to vital chemical reactions.
- The essential amino acids produce antibodies and stimulate T-lymphocyte cell activity.
- Alpha lipoic acid is so powerful that it has recently been shown to significantly inhibit replication of the HIV virus.
- Co-enzyme Q 10 plays a huge role in strengthening the immune system. Take 300 milligrams daily, in divided doses, to ward off cancer and protect against radiation damage from electromagnetic radiation. (A discussion of this real danger follows later in this chapter.)

THE HRC FORMULA FOR TREATING VIRAL INFECTIONS NATURALLY©		
Nutrient	Dose	Directions
Vitamin C (Ester C)	675 mg	3 capsules every four hours to bowel tolerance
Antioxidant complex (A, E, zinc, dimethyl glycine, cysteine, glutathione, methionine)		3 capsules with breakfast 3 capsules with supper
Bio-aminos		3 capsules twice daily on an empty stomach
Co-enzyme Q 10 (oil base)	100 mg	1 capsule 3 times daily with food
Pyridoxine (B$_6$)	250 mg	1 capsule daily with food
Lipoic acid	100 mg	1 capsule 3 times daily

Note: If you are already taking any of the above nutrients, do not exceed the amounts for your total dosage (see chart page 56).

© Copyright 1999 Health Recovery Center.™ All Rights Reserved.

- B$_6$ increases antibodies, thymus activity, and lymphocytes, all of which are needed to increase immune function.
- Herbs such as echinacea, gingko biloba, silymarin, and cat's claw also have antiviral properties. At HRC we have long used silymarin for treating liver damage due to alcoholism, and have seen an astoundingly quick reversal of all elevated liver readings.

Yeast Overgrowth (Candida) and Chronic Fatigue

Carol, a pleasant thirty-five-year-old teacher, had started taking antibiotics in college to clear her complexion. By the time we met ten years later, she was using them for recurring vaginal yeast infections and bouts with bronchitis. She complained of being tired all the time. Her concentration was so poor it was destroying her ability to teach. Food did not energize her. Instead, after eating a meal, she often found she could hardly stay awake. Her solution became skipping lunch and existing instead on coffee, cigarettes, and sugar snacks. Carol complained of ongoing sinus problems, itching ears, and constantly having to clear her throat. She felt cold most of the time. The chronic fatigue that had slowly engulfed her was gradually changing her life. She now slept nine or ten hours each night, yet she still felt exhausted and weak. At the time we met she was on more antibiotics in the hope of recovering her health. Symptoms pointed to a yeast invasion that now had the upper hand in her body.

Lab tests showed elevated levels of candida antibodies. Carol's immune system was fighting, but not winning, its war against candida yeast. These fungi had become systemic and were making trouble on multiple fronts. Her antithyroid antibody panel was also elevated, indicating her immune system was playing a role in killing off her thyroid as well as the candida yeast. (For unknown reasons, this occurs fairly often in our clients with candida.) Carol was cold and tired all the time, partly from having too little thyroid hormone circulating.

The good news is that all of this is *fixable.* A prescription for Armour thyroid will quickly deliver that missing hormone. And in the next pages I will describe a number of powerful nutritional weapons that knock out candida yeast.

A HISTORY OF THE FUNGUS
THAT LIVES IN OUR BODIES

It has been fifty years since the *Candida albicans* fungus was first identified as a cause of bodily infections under the right conditions. Slowly the medical community has become aware of candida's ability to proliferate and invade practically every organ of the body given the opportunity. According to public health experts, candida overgrowth may affect as many as 20 million Americans today.

Candida albicans is a microscopic plant about the size of a red blood cell. It is a cousin to the molds that live in damp basements and is related to the fungus that causes athlete's foot. The textbook *Medical Mycology* describes *Candida albicans* as "mild mannered creatures incapable of producing infections in normal, healthy individuals. [A yeast] can only cause trouble in the person with weakened defenses. . . . The clinical manifestations of candida infections are exceedingly variable . . . [and] account for the vast majority of . . . diseases caused by yeast."

The candida yeast normally inhabits the esophagus, gastrointestinal tract, and colon. But sometimes something occurs that allows the yeast to colonize far beyond the immune system's abilities to hold it in check with antibodies.

SIGNS OF CANDIDA YEAST INFECTION

Today's high technology is responsible for our current woes with fungal opportunists, mostly through our overuse of antibiotics. These destroy all the friendly flora in our intestinal tract, leaving behind only the candida yeast, which not only survive but flourish and multiply in their new environment. Our continued use of antibiotics, steroids, birth control pills, anti-inflammatory drugs, refined sugars, alcohol, and meats laced with antibiotics, all contribute to the steady invasion of candida yeast throughout our tissues and organs. With the right conditions, candida can reproduce quickly. When the body's immune system is impaired, this opportunist takes over. Signs of possible candida infestation include:

Bloating, swelling, or gas after eating
Frequent diarrhea or constipation
Recurring vaginal yeast infections
Recurring urinary tract infections
Feeling worse on damp, muggy days or in moldy places
Feeling light-headed from a small amount of wine or beer
Recurring sinus infections or fungal infections of the nails
Chronic fatigue and fogginess
Past heavy use of antibiotics that preceded any of the above
    symptoms

DIAGNOSING CANDIDIASIS

The doctors who have worked with me at Health Recovery Center have considered patient history as important as the laboratory studies in diagnosing candida. In the final analysis, the most definitive test may be the patient's response to an antifungal drug like Diflucan or nystatin combined with an anticandida diet.

Some doctors still adhere to the old (and incorrect) view that candida yeast accounts for only disorders in the intestinal tract, not for disorders occurring elsewhere in the body. Since they do not employ blood tests that show candida, these doctors may tell you it doesn't exist. If your M.D. dismisses the notion that candida may be to blame for otherwise unexplained symptoms, encourage him to seek medical proof through a lab test. If you have a yeast-related illness, your immune system is busy making high amounts of candida antibodies in an effort to control the overgrowth, and these antibody levels can be measured with a blood test.

The test we use to detect *Candida albicans* is called the candida-antibody panel. It measures levels of three different antibodies: IgG, IgA, IgM. Normally, these levels are 100 MONA (measure of normal activity) units or below. In people with candidiasis, one or more of the antibody counts is elevated over 100 units, showing us the immune system is fighting the yeast. Of these three antibody measures, the IgG signifies either a past or ongoing infection, IgA shows current mucosal or vaginal candidiasis, and IgM is the best indicator of current candida infestation.

The lab we use for this analysis is Immuno Diagnostic Laboratories (see Appendix C for address and telephone). This test's only drawback is that it assumes your immune system is still in the business of sending out candida antibodies. Yet in some chronic long-time sufferers, this immunal activity has finally "dried up"—in exhaustion and defeat. This is a situation where the case history and current symptoms speak more strongly than the testing, and a trial run of medication, nutritional antifungals, and diet are in order.

The Candida Questionnaire and Score Sheet on page 271 was designed by William Crook, M.D., who has long led the battle to elevate awareness of this crippling disease. The questionnaire is designed for *adults*; the scoring system is not appropriate for children. It lists factors in your medical history that promote the growth of *Candida albicans* (Section A) and the symptoms commonly found in persons with yeast-related illness (Sections B and C).

CANDIDA QUESTIONNAIRE AND SCORE SHEET

For each "yes" answer in Section A, circle the point score in that section. Total your score and record it in the box at the end of the section. Then move on to Sections B and C and score as directed.

Filling out and scoring this questionnaire should help you and your physician evaluate the possible role of yeasts in contributing to your health problems, but it will not provide an automatic diagnosis.

Section A: History

	POINT SCORE
1. Have you taken tetracyclines (Sumycin, Panmycin, Vibramycin, Minocin, etc.) or other antibiotics for acne for one month (or longer)?	35
2. Have you, at any time in your life, taken other broad-spectrum antibiotics* for respiratory, urinary, or other infections (for two months or longer, or in shorter courses four or more times in a one-year period)?	35
3. Have you taken a broad-spectrum antibiotic drug*—even a single course?	6
4. Have you, at any time in your life, been bothered by persistent prostatitis, vaginitis, or other problems affecting your reproductive organs?	25
5. Have you been pregnant . . .	
Two or more times?	5
One time?	3
6. Have you taken birth control . . .	
For more than two years?	15
For six months to two years?	8
7. Have you taken prednisone, Decadron, or other cortisone-type drugs . . .	
For more than two weeks?	15
For two weeks or less?	6
8. Does exposure to perfumes, insecticides, fabric, shop odors, or other chemicals provoke . . .	
Moderate to severe symptoms?	20
Mild symptoms?	5
9. Are your symptoms worse on damp, muggy days or in moldy places?	20

*Including Keflex, ampicillin, amoxicillin, Ceclor, Bactrim, and Septra. Such antibiotics kill off the "good germs" while they're killing off those that cause infection.

10. Have you had athlete's foot, ringworm, jock itch, or other chronic fungus infections of the skin or nails?

    Have such infections been . . .

Severe or persistent?	20
Mild to moderate?	10

11. Do you crave sugar?   10

12. Do you crave breads?   10

13. Do you crave alcoholic beverages?   10

14. Does tobacco smoke *really* bother you?   10

TOTAL SCORE, SECTION A

Section B: Major Symptoms

For each symptom that is present, enter the appropriate figure in the point score column:

If a symptom is occasional or mild	score 3 points
If a symptom is frequent and/or moderately severe	score 6 points
If a symptom is severe and/or disabling	score 9 points

POINT SCORE

1. Fatigue or lethargy

2. Feeling of being drained

3. Poor memory

4. Feeling spacey or unreal

5. Inability to make decisions

6. Numbness, burning, or tingling

7. Insomnia

8. Muscle aches

9. Muscle weakness or paralysis

10. Pain and/or swelling in joints

POINT SCORE

11. Abdominal pain

12. Constipation

13. Diarrhea

14. Bloating, belching, or intestinal gas

15. Troublesome vaginal burning, itching, or discharge

16. Prostatitis

17. Impotence

18. Loss of sexual desire or feeling

19. Endometriosis or infertility

20. Cramps and/or other menstrual irregularities

21. Premenstrual tension

22. Attacks of anxiety or crying

23. Cold hands or feet and/or chilliness

24. Shaking or irritable when hungry

TOTAL SCORE, SECTION B

Section C: Major Symptoms†

For each symptom that is present, enter the appropriate figure in the point score column:

If a symptom is occasional or mild	score 1 point
If a symptom is frequent and/or moderately severe	score 2 points
If a symptom is severe and/or persistent	score 3 points

1. Drowsiness

2. Irritability or jitteriness

3. Uncoordination

†While the symptoms in this section commonly occur in patients with yeast-connected illness, they also commonly occur in patients who do not have candida.

4. Inability to concentrate

5. Frequent mood swings

6. Headache

7. Dizziness/loss of balance

8. Pressure above ears, feeling of head swelling

9. Tendency to bruise easily

10. Chronic rashes or itching

11. Psoriasis or recurrent hives

12. Indigestion or heartburn

13. Food sensitivity or intolerance

14. Mucus in stools

15. Rectal itching

16. Dry mouth or throat

17. Rash or blisters in mouth

18. Bad breath

19. Foot, hair, or body odor not relieved by washing

20. Nasal congestion or postnasal drip

21. Nasal itching

22. Sore throat

23. Laryngitis, loss of voice

24. Cough or recurrent bronchitis

25. Pain or tightness in chest

26. Wheezing or shortness of breath

27. Urinary frequency, urgency, or incontinence	
28. Burning on urination	
29. Spots in front of eyes or erratic vision	
30. Burning or tearing of eyes	
31. Recurrent infections or fluid in ears	
32. Ear pain or deafness	
TOTAL SCORE, SECTION C	
TOTAL SCORE, SECTION B	
TOTAL SCORE, SECTION A	

GRAND TOTAL SCORE

The grand total score will help you and your physician decide if your health problems are yeast-connected. Scores in women will run higher, as seven items in the questionnaire apply exclusively to women, while only two apply exclusively to men.

- Yeast-connected health problems are almost certainly present in women with scores over 150 and in men with scores over 140.
- Yeast-connected health problems are probably present in women with scores over 120 and in men with scores over 90.
- Yeast-connected health problems are possibly present in women with scores over 60 and in men with scores over 40.
- With scores of less than 60 in women and 40 in men, yeasts are less likely to be the cause of health problems.

TREATING CANDIDA

When they are first told about the protocol for treating candida, our clients at HRC are almost too exhausted to take on the major changes required. So, to you many tired souls, I beg you to look at how out of control your life has become because of these tiny yeast invaders, and don't even *think* you might permit yourself to host these destroyers any longer. Muster your innermost being to take charge, and I guarantee that you will fully regain your health and energy.

Ideally, your first step is to partner with your physician. I know from the hundreds who have called after reading my first book that some of you will not be dealing with a sympathetic doctor. The problem is, you need help *now*; you can't wait for your doctor's knowledge to evolve and grow. To get the name of a doctor in your area who will treat you, telephone the International Health Foundation at 1-901-660-7090 or the American Academy of Environmental Medicine at 1-215-862-4544.

I also know from past experience that some of you are living in rural areas or cannot afford medical costs at this time. For you, your recovery may have to exclude the one or two common drugs used to treat candida: nystatin and Diflucan. This does not rule out your success. It just means you will need to pay exacting attention to (1) changing your diet, (2) taking the nutritional supplements, (3) testing for food allergies *at home*, and (4) removing as many chemical exposures as you can from your life. (Food allergies and reactions to chemicals often result from yeast-related disorders, because you no longer have a strong immune system to prevent these reactions. Both help to keep you feeling tired and sick.)

Your Candida Diet

If you are already on the low-carbohydrate diet (the first hypoglycemic diet in Chapter 3) you are halfway there. If not, please switch immediately! Then there are only a few adjustments you should make for your candida diet. For the first three weeks, you need to avoid these in addition:

- fruit and fruit juices
- cheeses (moldy cheeses like blue cheese are the very worst)
- vinegar-containing foods (i.e., salad dressings, mustard, catsup, relishes, sauerkraut, condiments, and sauces)
- mushrooms
- melons
- leftover foods (mold grows quickly, even in the refrigerator)
- breads
- peanuts

After three weeks test your tolerance to these foods by eating each separately. Then watch for a flare up of symptoms, especially fatigue. If you remain symptom-free, you can return them to your diet.

Permanently avoid all refined sugars, milk sugars, and high-carbohydrate, simple-sugar foods. Eat fresh foods, not boxed or canned. Eliminate all foods that you suspect may cause allergic reactions until you have tested them. (Instructions on this are found later in this chapter.) Of course, eliminate the use of all antibiotics, steroids, immune-suppressing drugs, and birth-control pills, unless you have a medical emergency that requires these drugs.

Your Nutritional Regimen

The HCR formula for candida control (page 278) offers a two-pronged attack to destroy the candida and to rebuild your immune system. The following natural substances included in the formula are powerful nondrug yeast destroyers.

- Wild oregano* is probably the most powerful antifungal agent available. It can destroy even resistant fungal yeast forms, as well as the mutated fungi that result from antibiotic overuse. Jonathan Wright, M.D., has found wild oregano to be as effective as the drug nystatin. Dr. Cass Ingram, Ph.D., authored an entire book on oregano, *The Cure is in the Cupboard*, after using it himself to recover from candida.
- Citrus seed extract is an antifungal agent that fights candida fungi in the intestinal tract. It is also effective against other intestinal parasites, such as giardiasis.
- Caprylic acid has been shown to heal the intestinal tract and to eliminate or greatly reduce the candida growth in the intestinal tract within sixteen days.
- Kyolic garlic extract is a powerful antiviral, antibacterial, and antifungal herb. In a study reported in the *Journal of the American Chemical Society*, one milligram of allicin (the main constituent of garlic) proved equal to fifteen standard units of penicillin!
- *Lactobacillus acidophilus* is the name of the friendly bacteria that normally inhabit your intestines. Candida fungus can grow and thrive there only when antibiotics have wiped out much of your acidophilus flora. It is important to replace these "good guys" as you clear out the candida yeast.

---

* The pure wild oregano from Europe is *not* the spice you find in supermarkets. That imitation is a Mexican plant of *no* value against yeast. Pure oil of oregano can be obtained from 1-800-247-6237.

THE HRC FORMULA FOR CANDIDA CONTROL©		
Nutrient	**Dose**	**Directions**
Oregano extract	700 mg	2 capsules at breakfast 2 capsules at lunch 2 capsules at supper and several drops of oregano oil super strength under the tongue twice daily.
Citrus seed extract	250 mg	1 capsule with each meal
Caprylic acid (Time-released or enteric-coated capsules)	1,000 mg	1 capsule with each meal
Kyolic garlic extract	600 mg	2 capsules with each meal
Lactobacillus acidophilus (nondairy)	1 billion lactobacillus *(Live culture)*	3 capsules with each meal
Vitamin C (Ester C)	675 mg	2 capsules with each meal
Antioxidant complex		3 capsules with breakfast 3 capsules with supper
Co-enzyme Q10 (oil base)	100 mg	1 capsule, 3 times daily
B_6 (pyridoxine)	250 mg	1 capsule daily with food

Note: If you are already taking any of the above nutrients, do not exceed the amounts for your total dosage (see chart page 56).

© *Copyright 1999 Health Recovery Center.™ All Rights Reserved.*

- Hydrochloric acid with betaine will completely inhibit the growth of *Candida albicans* at a pH of 4.5. (*Note:* HCl capsules are already on your daily nutrient list to increase absorption of foods and nutrients.)

In the HRC formula for candida control, we also combine yeast fighters with strong immune system builders, including: vitamin C; an antioxidant complex of A, E, selenium, zinc, dimethyl glycine, cysteine, glutathione, and methionine; co-enzyme Q10; and B$_6$. *The formula should be used faithfully for* two months *to eliminate candida yeast.*

Food Allergies and Chronic Fatigue

I know of nothing more bewitching (on a daily basis) than our abiding addiction to the foods that hurt us. Have you ever stood in front of your refrigerator after a big meal, searching? We want that certain food that produces an allergic/addictive response—the mild lift or high. Never mind that it zaps our energy later. Actually, most allergic persons aren't even aware of their need for a "fix." They simply bring home these foods every shopping trip.

Back in the 1950s, Theron Randolph, M.D., a brilliant allergist, made breakthrough discoveries on how foods can act like drugs for many of us. They can mimic the same cravings, produce a high, and create a demand for more of the same substance to satisfy our addiction. If we don't maintain our daily "supply," we experience a withdrawal reaction. From years of experience I can tell you that getting allergic-addicted clients off their favorite foods is a hazardous job indeed! I have seen tears rolling down women's cheeks as I demanded they abandon dairy products. I have been told by alcoholics who had stopped drinking that giving up wheat was not possible. While they no longer drank fermented grain, they *had* to have their pizzas, cereals, breads, or crackers every day. The mere suggestion that they give these up turned them surly. Yet they were complaining of fatigue; feeling depressed, muddled, headachey, or hyper, and they had intermittent cravings for sugar or alcohol. Food allergies often affect the brain as well as causing a general malaise of aches and pains.

You cannot feel emotionally stable if you are a slave to your food addictions. Life becomes a roller coaster of emotional ups and downs, depending on where you are in the cycle of craving, stimulation, and withdrawal. Take another look at the chart on pages 239–40, "The Ups and Downs of Addiction," to remind you of how addiction works.

WHY SOME FOODS MAKE YOU FEEL GOOD

You are not properly metabolizing the foods you crave. It may be as simple as not having sufficient digestive enzymes to break down and absorb these substances normally, or as complex as a leaky gut causing intestinal permeability. The antigens that attack undigested foreign food particles also release a psychoactive chemical in the brain that produces an endorphin effect. This mild high convinces us we love the food in question. We experience withdrawal symptoms when we don't have our "favorite" food, and we experience a relief from our withdrawal symptoms when we load up on these substances our bodies "crave."

Addictive foods have another effect on us: They store extra water weight. When we eliminate these troublemakers, we magically shed several pounds without dieting!

ARE YOU FOOD ALLERGIC?

Maladaptive responses commonly occur after ingesting cow's milk, wheat, eggs, cane sugar, corn, and chocolate. Predisposing factors are nutritional deficiencies; infestation of candida; autoimmune illness; thyroid, liver, or adrenal disorders; or digestive problems. The American College of Allergy and Immunology has cited the following medical conditions as provoked or caused by food allergy:

- attention deficit
- bronchial asthma
- bronchitis
- chronic diarrhea
- chronic fatigue syndrome
- depression
- headaches (migraine and non-migraine)
- hyperactivity
- insomnia
- learning disorders
- sleep disorders
- tension-fatigue syndrome

The self-screening test on page 281 (designed by George Kroker, M.D.) will give you a good idea of foods to which you may be allergic. Follow these instructions:

1. Complete all five parts.
2. In part five, circle any foods you listed in part three.
3. Women only: In part five circle any foods you listed in part four.
4. In part five, circle any heading above a section that contains foods eaten six or seven days per week.

Screening Test for Food Allergies

1. List a typical day's meals and snacks:

BREAKFAST	LUNCH	DINNER	SNACKS

2. List your three most favorite foods that you ate regularly before starting this program:

_____

3. Do you crave or binge on any foods? If so, which ones?

_____

4. (For women) Do you crave or binge on foods premenstrually? If so, which ones?

_____

5. Food Questionnaire

How many days in one week do you eat the following foods:
(Write the number of days in the parentheses following the food.)

WHEAT/YEAST

Bread	( )	Spaghetti	( )
Rolls	( )	Casseroles	( )
Muffins	( )	Pizza	( )
Sandwiches	( )	Breakfast cereal	( )
Bagels	( )	Crackers	( )
Pasta	( )	Cookies	( )
Macaroni	( )	Canned soup	( )
Noodles	( )	Pastries	( )

CORN

Popcorn	( )
Lunch meat	( )
Tacos	( )
Cornflakes	( )
Corn (vegetable)	( )
Pancake syrup	( )

OTHER GRAINS

Rice	( )
Oatmeal	( )
Other: ____	( )

DAIRY

Milk	( )
Cheese	( )
Yogurt	( )
Ice cream	( )
Coffee creamer	( )
Margarine	( )
Butter	( )
Cream cheese	( )
Cottage cheese	( )

EGGS

Scrambled, omelet, etc.	( )
Mayonnaise	( )
French toast	( )

MISCELLANEOUS

Vinegar	( )
Salad dressing	( )
Mushrooms	( )
Soy sauce	( )
Raisins	( )
Dates	( )
Prunes	( )
Ketchup	( )
Mustard	( )
Peanuts	( )
Other nuts:	
____	( )
Dessert:	

____	( )
Jell-O	( )
Jelly/jam	( )
Sweet 'N Low	( )
Equal	( )

BEEF

Beef roast	( )
Hamburger	( )
Steak	( )

PORK

Ham	( )
Bacon	( )
Sausage	( )
Pork chops	( )

OTHER PROTEIN

Chicken	( )
Turkey	( )
Fish:	
____	( )
____	( )
Soy/tofu	( )
Hot dogs	( )

BEVERAGES

Diet soda: ____	( )
Alcoholic beverages	( )
Soda:	
____	( )
Coffee	( )
Tea	( )
Fruit juice	( )

SNACKS

Potato chips	( )
Chocolate	( )

FRUIT

Apples	( )
Bananas	( )
Oranges	( )
Pears	( )
Melon	( )

Grapefruit	( )	_____	( )
Grapes	( )	Lettuce salads	( )
Pineapple	( )	Potatoes/french fries	( )
Other:		SPICES	
_____	( )	Onion	( )
_____	( )	Garlic	( )
VEGETABLES		Pepper	( )
Tomato	( )	Dry mustard	( )
Green pepper	( )	Basil	( )
Peas	( )	Paprika	( )
Green beans	( )	Rosemary	( )
Other beans:		Ginger	( )
_____	( )	Parsley	( )
Carrots	( )	Oregano	( )
Celery	( )	Cinnamon	( )
Broccoli	( )	Mint	( )
Cabbage/coleslaw	( )	Other:	
Cauliflower	( )	_____	( )
Other:		_____	( )

The foods you have circled are the ones most likely to trigger addictive cravings and delayed allergic reactions.

You can get expert medical help with diagnosing and treating food allergies by contacting a physician who specializes in clinical ecology. For a list of qualified physicians in your area, call the American Academy of Environmental Medicine at 215-862-4544.

You can take some steps to control food allergies on your own. Remove them from your diet; don't buy them when you shop; and remove them from your cupboards and refrigerator. Replace them with foods you don't often eat.

For more information on food allergies/addiction, refer to the reading list in Appendix D.

BE YOUR OWN DETECTIVE:
THE ELIMINATION DIET

One effective way to confirm that a specific food is causing you problems is to stop eating it for at least one week. This isn't as easy as it sounds, because if you are allergic/addictive, you may develop withdrawal symptoms as your body pleads for its usual fix of these foods. Symptoms vary from person to person, and can include headache or fatigue during the first days. Back and joint aches may develop on the third day and persist for a day or two. Among the "psychological" symptoms of withdrawal are anxiety, confusion, depression, and mood swings. *Note:* If you are chemically sensitive, during this week try to avoid exposure to fresh paint, new synthetic carpets, cleaning solutions, gas stoves, tobacco smoke, auto exhaust, perfumes, and shopping malls (which are filled with fumes from the formaldehyde in new clothing, furniture, and fabrics). You want clear reactions based on the substance you are testing. You won't know if the food is causing the allergy if you are reacting to other chemicals that set off your symptoms. Also, if you smoke: Do not smoke during an elimination diet. Cigarettes are loaded with chemicals that keep allergic users in a chronically reactive state, and you won't be able to see the effects of the diet while you continue to smoke.

By the end of the week, withdrawal agonies, if any, will have ceased. After that, reintroducing the suspected food(s) should produce noticeable symptoms. This is your body's way of telling you whether it can tolerate the food.

To test yourself, follow these directions:

1. Test only one food per meal.

2. Make a whole meal of the test food. For example, if you suspect that dairy products are the source of your problems, eat only cheese, milk, yogurt, and cottage cheese; if wheat is the suspected culprit, limit yourself to hot wheat cereal, wheat toast, pancakes, or bread. Don't butter your bread unless you are certain that dairy products (which include butter) are not a problem for you.

3. Take your pulse just before eating the food you are testing. Take it again five minutes after you finish, and again twenty-five minutes later. A pulse twelve or more beats per minute faster or slower than what is normal for you suggests an allergic reaction to the food you are testing.

4. Make a note of any changes in how you feel physically and emotionally. (Reactions usually occur within the first hour, although some may be delayed.) Be aware that if your brain chemistry is altered because of a reaction to the food, you may not be able to think

clearly enough to accurately assess and record your reaction. I learned how difficult this can be when, after a five-day total fast (except for spring water), I tested eggs at lunch. I soon felt very sleepy and decided to take a short nap. A half hour later, I realized I was lying on the couch instead of driving back to my office. At first, I was in such a fog that I had no idea why I had dozed off at noon. As the grip of the allergic response subsided, I realized that the eggs were responsible for my reaction.

5. If possible, test the suspect foods when someone else is around. This way, if you are too muddled by an allergic reaction, your companion will be able to observe your behavior and relate it to the food you tested. The day I tested wheat, I had a meeting with colleagues scheduled for afterward. After downing a stack of pancakes, I hurried off to the meeting. Driving a familiar route, I took a wrong turn not just once but twice! I never connected my mistakes to the possibility that my brain was losing its smarts in response to the wheat. When I finally arrived, I delivered my report in a halting voice, struggling to think clearly. I was mortified by my performance. Suddenly a close friend began to laugh. "You must be in reaction. What did you eat this morning?" That embarrassing experience told me in no uncertain terms that wheat was not good for me.

6. Any uncomfortable symptoms can be partially relieved by taking two tablets of Alka-Seltzer Gold. Milk of magnesia can also help eliminate food-related problems. (Follow the directions on the label.)

7. Be sure to avoid any chemical exposure while testing a food, and get plenty of fresh air. Drink only spring water, deep-well water, or water that has been filtered—just not tap water, which is full of chemicals. One of our Health Recovery Center clients discovered that the groin pain that had plagued him for years disappeared when he stopped using chlorinated water. He later found that he could turn the pain on and off by switching from spring to tap water. I also have noticed that allergic people don't feel well when they drink city water treated with chlorine and other chemicals.

You can also identify food allergies through a blood test your doctor can order from Great Smokies Diagnostic Laboratories. This lab test assesses immediate and delayed reactions to ninety-six common foods. See Appendix C for the lab's complete address and telephone number.

STAYING FREE OF FOOD ALLERGY/ADDICTION
AND REPAIRING YOUR DAMAGED DIGESTIVE TRACT

Identifying the foods that undermine your equilibrium is only half the battle. These foods will remain appealing to you because they promise an instant high. Your heartbeat probably won't quicken at the thought of eating green beans in the future—but the very word "pizza" or —— (insert the name of your favorite food) can start you salivating. And that is the anticipation of the promised high.

Still, there are steps you can take to keep your brain and body in balance so you don't continually crave a fix to pull you out of fatigue. The formula on this page is designed to repair your compromised intestinal tract so you can better handle the digestion and assimilation of foods without adverse reactions.

THE HRC FOOD ALLERGY REPAIR FORMULA©		
Nutrient	**Dose**	**Directions/Purpose**
Pantothenic acid	500 mg	2 capsules 3 times daily with food
Zinc picolinate	25 mg	1 capsule 2 times daily with food
Glutamine powder	¼ tsp (1 gram)	3 grams 2 times daily on an empty stomach
Quercetin	300 mg	2 capsules 3 times daily with food
Pancreatic enzymes		2 capsules daily between meals

Note: If you are already taking any of the above nutrients, do not exceed the amounts for your total dosage.

Pantothenic acid works to repair the intestine, while glutamine powder reduces inflammation. Quercetin inhibits allergic/inflammatory reactions.

© Copyright 1999 Health Recovery Center.™ All Rights Reserved.

Why You Overreact to Stress

All of our immune systems have a breaking point. Imagine that your body is a ship loaded with heavy boxes. Each box represents a stress in your life. Your body has a threshold capacity for multiple stresses, but if you insist on overloading that capacity, your emotional and physical health will suffer. The chart on page 288 illustrates the building-block concept of stress overload. Each box in the chart represents a piece of what may be your total "load":

- food allergies
- your sensitivity to dust, molds, and pollens, or to auto exhaust or chemicals on the job
- your high intake of refined sugars
- cigarettes and caffeine
- candida overgrowth
- personal life stresses (e.g., a divorce, a death, or a relationship ending)

Stacked together, these boxes are the total overload that is buckling your immune system and causing your physical and emotional instability. You must jettison some of them in order to lower the threshold under the level that triggers mayhem in your health.

ASSESSING YOUR PERSONAL STRESS LOAD

How overloaded is your immune system? You can make an educated guess by listing on a separate sheet of paper the various "boxes" that you are carrying on your own "ship." Make up your mind to toss some of them over the side so your immune system can finally defend you properly. Appendix D has a list of excellent books containing more information on food and chemical sensitivities, controlling candida, and proven therapies that help us heal from the emotional stresses of life. For right now, start targeting the two hot "boxes" that cause you instant stress: cigarettes and caffeine.

TOSS OUT YOUR NICOTINE!

Cigarettes contain hundreds of chemicals that sap your health and weaken your immune system. I know you are resolved to make meaningful changes to stabilize your health—and kicking the cigarette habit will be a major step forward. Giving up cigarettes can be

BUILDING-BLOCK CONCEPT OF IMMUNE SYSTEM
BREAKDOWN FROM STRESS OVERLOAD

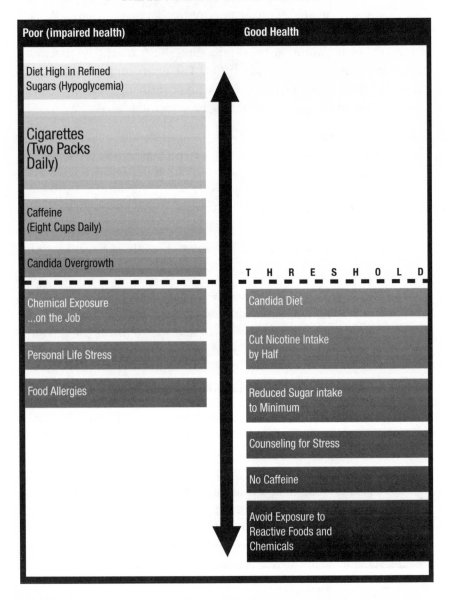

done. Millions of ex-smokers have done it. They were no stronger than you are now, and you have the advantage of a strategy that works. I've seen it succeed over and over. If you let it, it will work for you. (You can't afford not to.)

Use the following steps:

1. Set a target date to quit, two weeks from today.
2. Continue to avoid refined sugars, junk food, and caffeine.
3. Stay with (or embark on) your exercise program. It will help counteract any weight gain when you stop smoking.
4. Over the two weeks leading to your quit date, cut down on cigarettes. This is easier if you take sodium/potassium bicarbonate (Alka-Seltzer Gold) to alkalize your system and reduce your nicotine cravings. Take two tablets every four hours, but no more than eight tablets in any twenty-four-hour period.
5. Avoid red meats, cranberries, plums, and prunes (they promote the acidity you are trying to neutralize with Alka-Seltzer Gold).
6. Drink at least six glasses of water a day.

The Smokers Formula

Certain nutrients help to rid your system of nicotine and reduce your cravings. Read through the following descriptions to see how these nutrients can help you before you start the Quitting Smoking Formula offered on page 290.

- Lobelia is an herb that can help reduce your craving for nicotine.
- The Alpha Wave* formula contains three amino acids that have a calming and centering effect: GABA*, glycine*, and taurine*. (Smoking a cigarette has a stress-reducing effect, lowering reactions to outside stimuli by altering brain neurotransmitters.) GABA (gamma-aminobutyric acid) has a soothing effect on the brain. Glycine strengthens the calming alpha brain waves and reduces excitatory beta waves. Taurine helps to regulate and quiet the excitable tissues of the brain and nervous system.
- Glutamine* is in the formula to counteract the high sugar content of cigarettes. Tobacco is cured with beet, corn, and cane sugars. The sugar content of cigarettes can run as high as 70 percent. Hypoglycemic smokers will never bring their blood sugar under control if they regularly introduce these sugars into

* If you already take any of these amino acids in your daily regimen, do not duplicate.

THE HRC QUITTING SMOKING FORMULA©		
Nutrient	**Dose**	**Directions**
Lobelia	375 mg	1 capsule 3 times daily
Alpha waves (Bio-Recovery™)		2 capsules 3 times daily
• GABA	167 mg	
• Glycine	167 mg	
• Taurine	100 mg	
• Vitamin C (Ester C)	10 mg	
• Niacinamide	16.7 mg	
• Calcium	10 mg	
• Magnesium	25 mg	
• Vitamin B_6 (pyridoxine)	16.7 mg	
• Passion flower extract (6:1)	50 mg	
• Inositol	50 mg	
B complex*		1 capsule with food
Zinc picolinate*	25 mg	1 capsule with food
Glutamine*	500 mg	1 capsule 3 times daily on an empty stomach

Note: If you are already taking any of the above nutrients, do not exceed the amounts for your total dosage (see chart page 56).

Refer to your nutrient replacement list (page 56) to determine whether you need to add more of this nutrient to achieve the level suggested here.

© Copyright 1999 Health Recovery Center.™ All Rights Reserved.

their bloodstream. Glutamine, an alternative source of glucose for the brain, alleviates hypoglycemic reactions among smokers.

- B complex vitamins help allay the nervousness that develops as nicotine leaves your system. It also replenishes vitamin B_1 (thiamine), which cigarettes are known to seriously deplete.
- Zinc levels are usually deficient because your body uses a lot of zinc to prevent the buildup of cadmium, a metal contained in cigarette papers (it makes them white). Increase your total load of zinc to 50 milligrams daily for six weeks.

- Calcium and magnesium both calm your nervous system and brain.
- Inositol, a B vitamin, has strong antianxiety properties.

Current Prescription Gimmicks:
Nicotine Patches, Gum, or Antidepressants

We have watched clients switch from being addicted to cigarettes to being hooked on the nicotine patch. Because the patch delivers its nicotine even in your sleep, it often doesn't lead to total freedom from nicotine. On the other hand, Nicorette gum can be used only as needed to quench nicotine cravings. And it no longer requires a prescription. A 1987 study in the *Journal of the American Medical Association* showed Nicorette gum doubled the success rate of quitting and minimized weight gain over the period studied. Though it is still feeding you nicotine, the gum is a better choice than the patch.

The antidepressant drug Wellbutrin (recently renamed Zyban) is being sold on prescription as a potential help for smokers. We have seen this drug benefit some clients but produce irritability and angry outbursts in others. My advice is don't trade one drug for another; they are hard on your immune system.

Whatever way you choose to beat this addiction, you *can* do it. The real secret is to keep up your strong resolve. Do not, for one moment longer, give that pack of deadly chemicals any power over you. Don't let this drug undo the gains you're making by following your seven-week restoration plan.

Set a stop date and *go for it!*

Electromagnetic Fields and CFS

Before ending this chapter on chronic fatigue, I want to talk about a cause that remains unknown to many of you. Indeed, we may be well into the twenty-first century before Americans will accept what scientists are telling us about our changing environment, both within and around us.

This century has seen drastic changes in our electromagnetic environment. Electromagnetic fields (EMF) vibrating at 60 hertz now surround nearly every person, from appliances at home to machines at work. Over 500,000 miles of high-voltage power lines cover the United States. The airwaves are full of low, medium, and high frequencies. The density of radio waves around us is now 200 million times the natural level reaching us from the sun. Today it is common for us to spend many hours absorbing the magnetic fields of computers and TV signals.

Robert Becker, M.D., whose life's work involves the effects of electrical fields on humans, has written a brilliant book, *The Body Electric*, that I strongly recommend to you. In it he shares a myriad of international studies linking the effects these magnetic fields are having on us. These exposures can cause prolonged stress reactions leading to chronic fatigue and exhaustion. Scientists have found that subliminal activation of the stress response is one of the most important effects that electromagnetic fields have upon life. Dr. Becker says: "The sites of the greatest changes (due to electromagnetic fields) are the brain's hypothalamus and cortex. The hypothalamus links the emotional centers, the pituitary gland, the pleasure center, and the autonomic system, the single most important part of the brain for homeostasis and a crucial link in the stress response. Any interference with cortical activity of course disrupts logical and associational thought."

At one point, Dr. Becker collaborated in a study with an English physician who had noticed that people living near high-voltage lines were prone to depression. The study mapped the addresses of 598 suicides in relation to the location of such power lines. The magnetic fields averaged 22 percent higher at suicide addresses, and the strongest magnetic fields contained 40 percent more suicide locations than randomly selected houses!

Other scientists have found startling results when researching the impact of electrical fields. Researchers at the University of Kansas in Wichita studied electropollution coming from their two airports' radar beams. They plotted the cancer incidence for the whole city, and found it was highest where the residents were exposed to both radar beams.

An Alabama public health researcher found a surge of birth defects among children of radar-exposed army pilots at Fort Rucker in Alabama. Nineteen radar emitters were in use at the time of the birth defect report, and these pilots regularly flew helicopters whose Plexiglas bubbles left them completely exposed to this radiation.

Researchers now link birth defects to the use of electric blankets.

These blankets emit the most powerful electromagnetic field of any household appliance! Furthermore, an alarming number of miscarriages and birth defects have been documented nationwide, including pregnant women working in computerized offices where malfunctioning terminals emitted enormous amounts of electromagnetic field waves.

England has moved to restrict the use of cellular phones, because exposure to a person's head of thousands of microwatts has been shown to do brain damage. Way back in 1971, the USSR's Institute of Labor and Occupational Diseases identified a series of such symptoms (from EMF exposure) that they called microwave sickness. They are:

> chronic excitation of the nervous system (stress syndrome)
> high blood pressure
> headache
> dizziness
> sleeplessness
> irritability
> anxiety
> stomach pain
> nervous tension
> inability to concentrate
> hair loss
> increased incidence of appendicitis
> cataracts
> reproductive problems
> cancer

Such chronic symptoms eventually lead to adrenal exhaustion and ischemic heart disease.

Unfortunately, the changes in our electromagnetic environment are not going away, so there are some obvious and practical things to do for yourself and your family.

LIMITING OUR EXPOSURE TO EMFS

Here's what we need to do to best protect ourselves from the electromagnetic fields in our environment:

1. Don't settle your family into an apartment or house that is close to high-voltage power lines.
2. If you are pregnant, do *not* work at an unshielded computer terminal for those nine months.
3. If you know you have high exposure to electromagnetic fields on your job, and you are experiencing ongoing fatigue and other signs of "microwave sickness," change your job quickly.
4. Don't use electric blankets.
5. Keep your cellular phone turned off, and use it only in emergencies. Limit your cellular calls to less than ten minutes.

What you should bear in mind is that many wondrous EMF developments are happening around us. And the growing knowledge of electromagnetic energy is doing much good for humanity! An example is magnetic resonance imaging (MRI), which provides a sensational new window into the structure and function of the human brain and body. The future will bring even more exciting discoveries. We have no reason to fear electromagnetic field energies *as long as we are cautious about shielding our bodies from the potential damage of high exposures.* In the next decades, we can expect to learn much more about how to safely coexist with these powerful, invisible fields.

Checklist

We have now covered many of the possibilities for ongoing fatigue. You've taken appropriate steps to identify the most likely areas of trouble for you:

____ chronic bacterial or viral infection
____ *Candida albicans* overgrowth
____ food allergies
____ chemical sensitivities (review Chapter 8)
____ exhausted adrenals (review Chapter 5)
____ hypothyroidism (review Chapter 6)
____ low histamine levels (review Chapter 7)
____ effects of electromagnetic field exposures

Almost all of these conditions should be confirmed with lab tests and treated medically. I urge you to make an appointment with your physician ASAP. (See Appendix B for the organizations that can refer you to doctors who specialize in these problems.)

But even before you get medical help, stay with your healthy, sugar-free diet; keep your promise to kick cigarettes; and use the appropriate nutrient formulas to restore your immune system and digestive tract. Ultimately, it is your own body's "inner healer" that is doing the repair. So be a little patient . . . it will happen!

PART FOUR

Keeping Your Emotional Balance for Life

CHAPTER 10

Feeling Good and Living Long
The "Lazarus Effect" of Natural Hormone Restoration

By now you are reaping major rewards from making smart changes in your diet and reloading the missing nutrients that your brain and nervous system depend on for top performance.

You feel good, so you may think your hardest work is behind you. If only Mother Nature played fair! Problem is, our bodies have been genetically programmed: We peak sexually early on, we reproduce, and then our bodies start to self-destruct as the aging clock accelerates.

In *The Melatonin Miracle*, Dr. Walter Pierpaoli, M.D., defines aging and how it occurs:

> Aging is actually the loss of the body's ability to adapt to its environment. Our bodies are constantly forced to respond to various stresses and stimuli such as adjusting to temperature change, fighting off a virus, or even just knowing when it's time to sleep and wake. Think of your body as a rubber band. When we're young and strong our bodies can easily bounce back from the force of these stresses, but as we age, we increasingly lose our ability to rapidly adapt to new situations—in short, we lose our resiliency. Like an old, worn-out rubber band, it takes longer and longer to bounce back.

Up until a few years ago, scientists could only speculate on how to interrupt and slow down this aging process. Today, the field of antiaging medicine offers cutting-edge scientific answers. In a sentence: *The declining substances that signify the occurrence of the aging process in our bodies are our hormone levels.* Thousands of studies now record this downward spiral in hormone production, which usually starts when we're in our twenties or thirties. These hormones are the source of our youth, vigor, stamina, sexual interest and performance, energy, memory, immune system, and mental sharpness.

This chapter is for those who want to maintain their emotional, mental, and physical health throughout their lives and who are willing to do what it takes to grow younger with hormones and to add decades to their life span. To those who are willing to just let nature take her course, let me remind you (while there is still time) that you are agreeing to slowly become frail and weak, lose your mental capacity, and, finally, become dependent on others. To me, that is a fate far worse than death. And I am speaking not from the role of researcher but from my own life experience. Next year (as of this writing) I will be seventy years old. I continue to work full-time: directing the Health Recovery Center, writing books and articles, and lecturing. I take most of the eight hormones that I will discuss in this chapter, and I *love* the benefits they give me. Truthfully, I can think of no better insurance against an unknown future than to stay vigorous and mentally alert with hormonal rejuvenations, taken in consultation with your doctor first. But let me convince you with facts.

Rewinding the Aging Clock

There are eight incredible hormones to which nature has assigned the task of maintaining our peak potential. When taken together, they can work toward and create a personal blueprint for age reversal. In combination, they control virtually all of the body functions, including our metabolism and our immune and reproductive systems. They determine how we age by controlling our physical and mental health. We start to decline physically and mentally as the levels of these hormones decrease with aging. Their loss saps our energy and vitality, and ultimately takes decades off life. These super-hormones are:

Hormone	Location in body
Melatonin	Made in the pineal gland, which houses the body's aging clock

Hormone	Location in body
DHEA	Produced in the adrenal glands, brain, and skin
Pregnenolone	Synthesized from cholesterol and produced in the brain and adrenal cortex; it is the parent hormone for DHEA, testosterone, estrogen, and progesterin
Estrogen	Produced in the ovaries and adrenal glands; in men, small amounts of estrogen are produced in the adrenals
Progesterone	Produced in the corpus luteum of the ovaries, the adrenals, and the placenta of pregnant women
Testosterone	Manufactured in the testes and adrenal glands; in women, small amounts are produced in the ovaries
Thyroid	Produced in the thyroid gland, which is located at the front of the neck
Human growth hormone	Made in the pituitary gland, which is called the body's master gland

Some of these hormones are already well known, not only to the medical community but to the general public as well. Estrogen, progesterin, thyroid, and testosterone replacement have been available for years (these require a prescription from a doctor). Others have just recently broken into print: melatonin, DHEA, and pregnenolone all have brand-new breakthrough research that is exciting—and none of them are prescription drugs: They are classified as *natural substances*.

Human growth hormone, or HGH, is in a class by itself, and whether you need a prescription to increase your HGH is dependent on your age. Your own natural supply can often be stimulated to much higher levels simply by taking a combination of certain amino acids together with niacin, another growth-hormone-releasing nutrient (more about this later).

Let's examine each of these powerhouses for what they do. Then you can target this information to your own needs. I'll tell you what symptoms you will notice if your levels lag behind normal, and how to confirm your body's hormone supply with laboratory

LOCATION OF HORMONE GLANDS

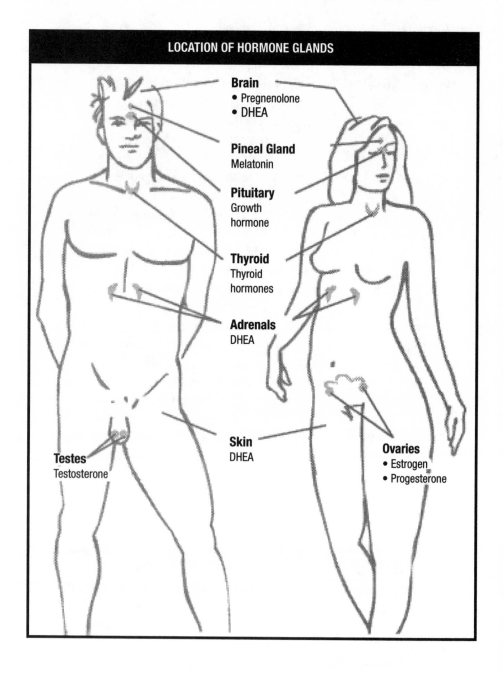

Brain
- Pregnenolone
- DHEA

Pineal Gland
Melatonin

Pituitary
Growth
hormone

Thyroid
Thyroid
hormones

Adrenals
DHEA

Skin
DHEA

Testes
Testosterone

Ovaries
- Estrogen
- Progesterone

testing. Although this is the ideal approach scientifically, I am aware that half of the U.S. population is now dabbling with melatonin and DHEA. If you are one of these experimenters, let me give you *all* the facts so you can make sure you are proceeding down the right path. *Note:* To correctly balance your multiple hormone therapies, contact the American Academy of Anti-Aging Medicine for a medical referral, or call any of the physicians specializing in anti-aging who are listed in Appendix B.

MELATONIN AND OUR AGING CLOCK

In the eighties, the Swiss scientist Walter Pierpaoli, M.D., discovered that we have a pea-sized gland deep in our brains that controls the aging process. The discovery of the pineal gland changed forever our understanding of how we age. Dr. Pierpaoli proved that all of the endocrine glands in the human body are in constant communication with each other and with the immune system, and that if the communication is severed, we stop developing normally. He suspected that melatonin, secreted by the pineal gland, may be the master control because of its regulation of a function critical to our survival: the sleep/wake cycle. He noted that rapid physical and mental disability follow the precipitous decline of this hormone. His experimentation with rats revealed shocking changes in the melatonin-treated animals: They lived 30 percent longer (the equivalent of over a hundred years of human life) than the control rats, and their bodies retained their strength and youthful appearance to the end.

In subsequent experiments, Dr. Pierpaoli transplanted the pineal glands of old mice into young animals and vice versa. Again the results were astounding. The old pineal glands rapidly aged their young recipients, causing premature death, while the young pineal glands rejuvenated the old mice, improving their immune system, creating a youthful and vigorous appearance, and prolonging their lives another 30 percent—to about 105 years in human terms!

Since the eighties, hundreds of studies have been done on melatonin. And their findings point to a "fountain of youth" hormone that can reset our aging clocks and turn back the ravages of time!

Melatonin is one of the most powerful antioxidants ever discovered. Unlike vitamin E, it crosses the blood-brain barrier, and its presence in our cells prevents any chemical damage from oxidation, one of the main reasons for aging. Melatonin protects the DNA-containing nucleus of cells. By protecting DNA, melatonin protects the integrity of the cell's "blueprint." A damaged cell with intact DNA *can* repair itself, but a cell with damaged DNA often cannot fix even minor damage. If you immediately recognize that I am describing a major preventative against cancer, you are absolutely right. Melatonin protects against this chromosomal damage that otherwise results in that dreaded disease.

Its role with the immune system is equally impressive. Melatonin will "reset" your immune system when it has been under siege from infections, cancer, stress, and so on. Such attacks disrupt its rhythms and diminish its effectiveness. Any disruption in our immune system's twenty-four-hour rhythm lowers our immunity, leaving us prone to more illnesses.

Melatonin protects our thymus, one of the fundamental organs of the immune system. It is within the thymus that T-cells are manufactured to protect our bodies against invaders. The thymus tends to shrivel as we age until, in old age, it is virtually gone. Melatonin rejuvenates the thymus gland to protect our immunity, and so guards us against the many diseases of old age. Melatonin's success in prevention and reversal of breast cancer has been confirmed in countless new studies. Taking melatonin is a far better preventative of breast cancer than taking pictures of it with mammograms.

Unfortunately, by age sixty we are producing only *half* of the melatonin that we did when we were in our twenties! Yet today, it is possible to alter the built-in programming. From an evolutionary standpoint, we are programmed to become obsolete once our reproductive years are behind us. All body systems receive their marching orders from our lagging hormonal systems, which eventually leads to their (and thus, our) destruction.

Yet now we can use the results of science and research to nip body breakdown in the bud. By restoring melatonin levels, as well as adrenal DHEA hormones and human growth hormones, we are marking the beginnings of an "ageless society."

Is It Safe?

Melatonin is incredibly safe. It has been tested in human volunteers at 6,000 milligrams (6 g) per night for a month. (A typical dose is

1 to 5 mg, depending on age.) The only side effects were some residual sleepiness and stomach discomfort. Government scientists tried unsuccessfully to find what a lethal dose of melatonin would be in animals, but they couldn't make a high enough concentrate to kill even a mouse! More good news about this hormone is that using it nightly will not alter or damage in any way your own natural production of melatonin.

Nature's Sleeping Pill

Melatonin's most common attribute is its regulation of our sleep/wake cycle. Not only does it deliver sound sleep, but it provides a buffer against the buildup of corticosteroids, stress hormones. This protection against stress-induced brain damage results in feeling calmer, more revitalized, and more productive when we are awake.

How often have we heard our elderly parents complain of their inability to sleep well? I remember my own mother regularly spending her nights gazing out her window into the night. The very blackness around her would have triggered the sleep hormone in a younger body. Such sleep disruption seriously impairs functioning in many ways: The following day we feel irritable, and even depressed, as a result of the confusion in our body rhythms.

But sleep disorders are no longer a necessary part of aging. With melatonin, we can turn back the body's aging clock and restore normal body rhythms.

How to Take Melatonin

Our strategy calls for returning melatonin levels to where they were when we were in our twenties. Doing this is fairly simple. The chart on page 306 suggests the typical dose in each age decade. Because no two people have exactly the same needs, you will have to experiment to see if the dose suggested creates sound sleep for you. Take your melatonin about a half hour before bedtime, and from that point on, stop any stimulating projects in which you might be involved.

If you find yourself still waking up during the night, increase your melatonin by 2 milligrams each night until you are sleeping well and feel rested in the morning.

MELATONIN DOSAGE

Age*	Dose
40–45	½–1 mg
45–55	1–2 mg
55–65	2–3 mg
65–75+	3–5 mg or more as needed

Note: To avoid jet lag, use melatonin to reset your biological rhythms, so that your body clock will let you sleep at your new bedtime. Simply take 3 to 5 milligrams of melatonin at bedtime in your new destination. Continue to do this for your entire stay. You may need to take an additional 3 to 5 milligrams if you find yourself waking too early in your new environs. Just adjust your dose to your own needs. Upon returning home, continue the higher dosage at bedtime until your body readjusts to the time change.

DHEA: THE ANTIAGING SUPER-HORMONE

If you think melatonin sounds like a miracle substance, get set to hear about one that is even *more* dazzling!

DHEA (dehydroepiandrosterone) is an adrenal hormone that has finally caught the attention of the medical community, although it has been known since the thirties. The volume of DHEA research, currently done or in progress, is now monumental—as are the claims being made about it. DHEA is a steroid hormone similar in structure to estrogen, progesterone, and testosterone but with its own powerful biological effects.

DHEA levels drop steadily as we age, peaking between twenty-five and thirty years and then falling 2 percent per year (20% per decade). Just before death due to old age, the DHEA level is virtually nonexistent. Researchers in the world's leading universities are proving this hormone has multiple abilities:

- DHEA is a potent anticancer protector.
- DHEA protects against heart disease by preventing blood clots (it's a natural blood thinner) and by lowering cholesterol.
- DHEA sharpens memory.

*People aged thirty-nine and younger usually have enough natural melatonin.

- DHEA greatly improves the immune system.
- DHEA protects against bone loss by providing ongoing natural estrogen.
- DHEA has shown good results against autoimmune diseases.
- DHEA has strong antidiabetic properties.
- DHEA increases strength and endurance.
- DHEA lifts fatigue and depression and increases feelings of well-being.

You can see why DHEA's tremendous promise in so many areas is making it a popular choice in today's antiaging arsenal. Its powerful effects can change both your present stamina and drive, and your future health and survival.

I started taking DHEA about five years ago, when it was still available only by prescription. My personal experience can be described in one word: stamina. I now need less sleep, have more energy, and don't run down as easily. At the end of my workday, I can enjoy evening outings (socializing, attending meetings, shopping) whereas before I was content to sink into my easy chair to read or watch TV. Before taking DHEA, my self-talk had been, "I'm not young anymore, so it's okay to be tired every night." Now, that thought never crosses my mind. For the astounding reversal of that aging mentality, I can thank DHEA, a truly magic potion that resupplies the powerful adrenal hormones that I had in my youth. Now, let's talk about DHEA's more important antiaging aspects.

DHEA's Cancer-Fighting Effects
Due to their strong immune systems, young people are less likely to get cancer. A sixty-five-year-old is fifty times more likely to develop cancer than a twenty-five-year-old. For this, we can blame our immune systems gradually switching off with age.

A large number of animal studies have shown that DHEA inhibits the development of tumors in the liver, breast, lung, colon, and lymph tissues, and is now even being used by physicians in conjunction with chemotherapy. According to oncologist William Regelson, M.D., in *The Superhormone Promise*, DHEA blocks an enzyme called glucose 6 phosphate dehydrogenase that otherwise causes a chemical reaction with the enzyme NADPH, generating oxygen-activated free radicals in the body. When this combination is not blocked, dormant carcinogens activate into cancers. A long-term study of five thousand women found that their DHEA levels fell drastically over nine years before their onset of clinically proven breast cancer. The researchers concluded that the highest risk factor for breast cancer is a low level of DHEA.

Heart Disease and DHEA

Research at the University of California has proved that, for every microgram per cc increase in blood levels of DHEA, death by all causes diminished *36 percent*. In those age fifty to seventy years, there was a 48 percent decrease in heart attack deaths!

Another study, reported in the *New England Journal of Medicine*, tracked 242 men from fifty to seventy-nine years of age and concluded that "Those individuals with higher DHEAs levels lived longer and had a much lower risk of heart disease."

DHEA and Diabetes

Researchers have discovered a critical link between insulin, the hormone regulating the metabolism of sugars and starches, and DHEA levels. Adult-onset diabetes occurs when the body's tissues develop a resistance to insulin, causing glucose to remain in the blood at high levels. This condition (known as Type II diabetes) occurs with aging in about 14 percent of the population. Studies in humans show DHEA enhances tissue insulin sensitivity and uptake, offering a great potential for staving off the onset of this diabetes.

Insulin resistance also stiffens and injures blood vessels, interfering with their ability to pump blood and leading to arteries clogged with plaque and lethal blood clots. Dr. John Nestler at the Medical College of Virginia has linked the decline in DHEA and the corresponding rise in diabetes to damage of the cardiovascular system, triggering heart disease. His clinical studies confirm that taking DHEA normalizes insulin and reduces high blood sugar (diabetes).

DHEA Protects Against Stress

DHEA protects, or acts as a buffer, against corticosteroids, the stress hormones. Stress triggers the outpouring of these steroid hormones, and over time, with the decreasing levels of DHEA, our bodies become less able to clear them from the bloodstream. The result is ongoing anxiousness and tension. Research shows that even young people, when under chronic or extreme stress, experience severe drops in DHEA to levels similar to much older persons, as the ongoing stress exhausts their supply of DHEA.

If you have lived with a lot of stress in your life, you can expect your DHEA levels to be diminished. A simple lab test will confirm what your current levels are. Replacing DHEA will help you feel much calmer and far more able to handle the upcoming stresses of life.

Brain Performance and DHEA

If all DHEA could do for us was slow the aging process; stave off cancer, heart disease, and diabetes; and reduce our stress levels, it would still make tremendous sense for us to take it. But there is even frosting on the cake: DHEA's positive effects on our brains.

Taking DHEA on a daily basis influences many brain chemicals. For example, DHEA interacts with GABA (gamma-aminobutyric acid) and serotonin to relax and calm us. Hundreds of studies show DHEA successfully lifts depression, improves libido, and raises low moods. It creates a sense of well-being, improves energy levels, and enhances clarity of thought and memory. Any other biochemical regimen that you are on will only improve in effectiveness by bringing your DHEA levels up to speed.

How to Determine DHEA Dosing

DHEA is derived from substances normally present in the human body, so it is classified by the FDA as a nutritional supplement, not a drug, under the Dietary Supplement, Health and Education Act of 1995. Since it is natural to human physiology, DHEA is very safe when used properly at naturally occurring levels.

Have your physician check your DHEA levels with either a blood test or a noninvasive saliva test. It is a smart move to get this kind of baseline reading before you begin taking DHEA, although some doctors simply assume that most older persons have low levels and will simply start them on a 5, 15, or 25 milligram dose and then observe how they feel. But by getting a lab reading, you can compare your range with the normal range of persons twenty to thirty years old— the level you are aiming to resurrect. Most physicians experienced in prescribing DHEA will raise the dosage gradually. A second lab test one month later should confirm attainment of the youthful levels you want.

If you are over forty and are buying DHEA over-the-counter with no medical direction, I advise you to START WITH A LOW DOSE. DHEA comes in a 15 milligram time-released tablet that is typically a pretty safe dose, and it duplicates the body's gradual release of DHEA into the system. (This product is available from Bio-Recovery at 1-800-247-6237.) Make sure the DHEA you buy clearly states that it is pure, pharmaceutical-grade (this means that it is 99% pure DHEA). *Note:* If you have liver damage, purchase the sublingual pill form that dissolves under the tongue and goes directly into the bloodstream, bypassing the liver.

Getting a general idea of the right DHEA dosage for you depends on your gender and age:

- Men and women under age thirty usually need no additional DHEA unless they are living with an autoimmune disease or experiencing severe stress. Even so, check out your need first with a lab test.
- Men forty years of age and older may need 25 to 75 milligrams per day.
- Women forty years of age and older may need 15 to 50 milligrams per day.
- Men and women past sixty-five may need even higher amounts. Compare your own lab reading with the levels for a twenty- to twenty-five-year-old and adjust accordingly.

My personal recommendation is to adjust and sustain your DHEA hormones at a twenty-five-year-old's level. Be cautious; do not exceed these physiological parameters. There is no doubt in my mind that this miracle hormone will prove invaluable in your antiaging arsenal.

Is It Safe?

Even though DHEA is classified as a steroid, it has *none* of the problems associated with the anabolic steroids sometimes used by athletes. Your body's regulation of testosterone, progesterone, and estrogen is enhanced, not distorted, by DHEA. DHEA has been reported to be safe in humans in daily doses of 2,000 milligrams and higher. Dr. William Regelson has stated, "You can't kill an animal with DHEA. . . . There is NO lethal dose." Still, side effects *do* occur with overdosing in excessive amounts. (*Note:* These are always reversible by simply stopping your regimen.) The most common side effects with high doses of DHEA are:

acne
facial hair growth in women
voice deepening
mood changes, irritability
overstimulation (especially for those on thyroid medications, who may find the combination of DHEA and thyroid overstimulating)
insomnia
fatigue

Rare reports include headache, aggressiveness, and menstrual irregularity.

It has been theorized, but not proved, that in high doses DHEA could have an influence on hormone-sensitive cancers. We know DHEA increases levels of other hormones, but so far only positive results have been documented. For instance, DHEA raises estrogen, preventing bone loss in postmenopausal women, and converts into supplemental testosterone for older males. Present research shows substantial evidence that DHEA actually prevents cancer, and there is no evidence that moderate-range doses (5 to 30 mg) have any kinds of serious effects.

As no clinical studies exist for using DHEA during pregnancy or breast feeding, it is not advised you do so.

Some well-known clinicians who use DHEA regularly have these (sometimes contradictory) comments:

- Allen Gaby, M.D., editor of *Nutrition and Healing* and *Townsend Letter for Doctors*: "Higher doses may, in a minority of cases, lead to irritability, insomnia, and overstimulation. It's very uncommon to have hair growth. Acne is possible in large doses."
- Edmund Chein, M.D., Palm Springs, California: "I have not

seen side effects when DHEA is replaced in the physiological range [at levels that are normal to our bodies]."

- Ron Van Vollenhoven, M.D., Ph.D., Stanford University Medical Center, California: "In our experience [of] having treated a large number of women with 50 to 200 milligrams of DHEA for close to three years, there have been no major side effects. . . . Blood tests in the patients we have followed on DHEA have been okay, without any apparent changes in liver enzymes."

- Eric Braverman, M.D., Princeton, New Jersey: "Side effects we've seen in higher doses are acne and facial hair in women, sometimes on the chin. . . . Positive effects that we've seen include improved well-being, not all the time but commonly, and improved libido."

And please bear in mind that while over four thousand studies have reported DHEA's benefits, the *long-term* results of studies on humans are still not in; it's too early for this data.

PREGNENOLONE:
THE ULTIMATE HORMONE PRECURSOR

This hormone is believed to be the most potent memory enhancer of all time. It also appears to make us happier, as well as smarter. Yet I suspect you have never heard of it, even though its initial study goes back to the 1940s. Researchers at that time found that a 50 milligram daily dose of pregnenolone increased the coping skills of a group of factory workers, dramatically lowering their fatigue and increasing their productivity. And there were no undesirable side effects! Despite these results, pregnenolone was never promoted because, like other super hormones, it is a *natural* substance produced by the human body and therefore unpatentable. No drug company could get rich on it as a drug, so its development was abandoned for many years.

The chart on page 313 shows how pregnenolone provides the hormonal "raw material" in our bodies. At least 150 steroid hormones are made from pregnenolone, so it is the father of all hormone precursors. It is synthesized from cholesterol, that precious lipid compound that serves as the building block of all steroids and is vital for their production. Drugs that block cholesterol availability contribute to serious deficiencies of pregnenolone. Symptoms that

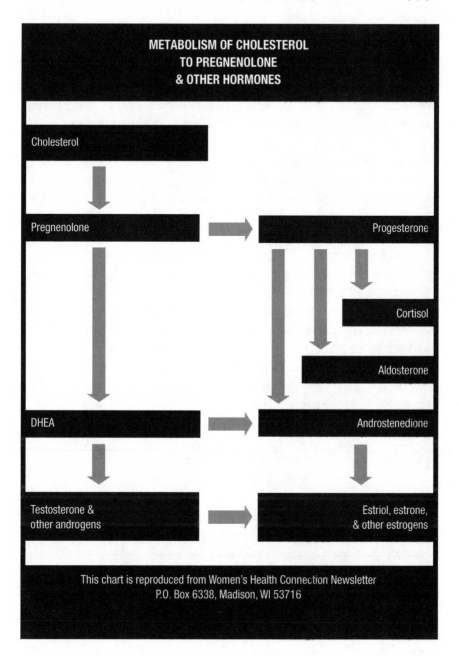

**METABOLISM OF CHOLESTEROL
TO PREGNENOLONE
& OTHER HORMONES**

Cholesterol

Pregnenolone   Progesterone

Cortisol

Aldosterone

DHEA   Androstenedione

Testosterone &   Estriol, estrone,
other androgens   & other estrogens

This chart is reproduced from Women's Health Connection Newsletter
P.O. Box 6338, Madison, WI 53716

you can expect from a lack of pregnenolone are impaired brain functioning and mood disorders that can even lead to suicide! Recent studies conclude that low serum levels of this hormone result in serious memory and behavioral disorders, and that giving pregnenolone significantly improves memory function. This improvement happens not over days or weeks, but within *three hours*.

When Rahmahwhati Sih, Ph.D., from the St. Louis University Medical School, conducted several tests with pregnenolone, he found that only three hours after a 500 milligram dose, both men and women showed improved memories, although the nature of their increased abilities differed with the sexes. Men improved more in three-dimensional thinking; women in verbal recall.

John Morley, M.D., who specializes in gerontology, has this to say about pregnenolone: "Pregnenolone . . . is clearly and by far the most potent of the neurosteroids for improving memory by light-years, and it has a much broader memory response than any of the other neurosteroids. This makes it almost an ideal agent for looking at memory and the consequences of the age-related deterioration of memory."

But progressive loss of memory is not all that changes with age. There is commonly a steady decline in mood, even to the point of depression. Antidepressants cannot address the deficiency in brain steroid hormones that is occurring. Since pregnenolone can deliver a constant, daylong sense of well-being, consider this hormone replacement as a first choice for treating your depression.

How to Take Pregnenolone

If you're wondering whether this hormone is for you, let me give you some clues. As with the other antiaging hormones, pregnenolone levels drop with age. *By age seventy-five, you can expect to have 60 percent less in your body than you did at age forty.* Pregnenolone levels can be measured by a lab test, if you wish. But if you already feel you are losing your sharpness and quick memory, you can purchase pregnenolone over-the-counter in health food stores and pharmacies or by calling Bio-Recovery at 1-800-247-6237. The usual dose is 50 milligrams daily taken in the *morning*. Taking your dosage in the evening is unwise, as it stimulates your mental function. If, after you have taken pregnenolone for a period of time, you are concerned because you are still getting sleepy in the late afternoon, you might want to try splitting your dose and take the second half just before lunch.

Is It Safe?

The standard 50 milligram dose has not been found to cause any undesirable side effects. In fact, its promise as an inhibitor of fatigue, especially in high stress situations, is impressive. Unfortunately, further testing with high doses and long-term usage has yet to occur. We do know that the calming effect of low doses (50 mg) may be overturned when high amounts are used. Because pregnenolone stimulates the central nervous system, you could experience irritability and anxiety from elevated doses. No human studies exist on pregnant women, so it is best to avoid using this hormone during this time. Do remember to take pregnenolone in the *morning*, so its stimulating effect does not interfere with sleep.

ESTROGEN: THE MOST POPULAR DRUG FOR WOMEN IN THE UNITED STATES

Do you remember when you first heard about estrogen? To a woman, its promises seemed wondrous! This is the hormone that fills out our round, soft feminine bodies, keeps the muscle tone in our breasts, enhances our sex drive, orchestrates our menstrual cycles, and staves off the dreaded changes of menopause and the osteoporosis of old age. How could we afford to snub our noses at such a miracle?

It has been forty years since estrogen came to market in the form of Premarin, made from mares' urine. At first we believed the only disadvantages to taking estrogen were weight gain, breakthrough uterine bleeding, bloating from fluid retention, and experiencing PMS-type symptoms like irritability and headaches.

But gradually, warnings of estrogen's carcinogenic nature began to appear.

Is It Safe?

The *New England Journal of Medicine* reported that women on estrogen had a 32 to 46 percent increased risk of breast cancer, based on data from the famous long-term Nurses' Health Study conducted by the Harvard Medical School. The sheer size of this study (725,550 women) makes the conclusions persuasive. (This study also showed that women who took estrogen plus a synthetic progestin actually had a higher rate of cancer than those taking estrogen alone.)

All of the outcry that arose over the *Journal*'s report drew attention away from a study reported in the *American Journal of Epidemiology* that showed long-term estrogen therapy also increased the risk of fatal ovarian cancer. This seven-year study included over 240,000 pre- and postmenopausal women. It found women who used estrogen for six to eight years had a 40 percent higher risk of fatal ovarian cancer. And women who used estrogen eleven or more years had a 70 percent higher risk.

Since breast, uterine, and ovarian cancers account for 41 percent of the cancers in American women, we clearly needed to come up with an alternative to estrogen that would provide all the antiaging benefits without the potentially carcinogenic effects of estrogen. And there *is* one.

Estriol: A Safer Kind of Estrogen
There is another form of estrogen, estriol, which is a weak estrogen, able to provide all the antiaging benefits without the risk of cancer. Most of a woman's natural estriol is converted in the liver from the two potent estrogens, estradiol and estrone. (Those two are the potential killers.) A Medical College of Georgia study has proven that estriol at high doses is perfectly safe, and is able to modify menopausal symptoms and reverse vaginal atrophy at doses between 2 to 8 milligrams daily.

In a five-year study at eleven hospitals in Germany in the mid-eighties, gynecologists found that estriol therapy was successful in 92 percent of all cases of hot flashes. Depressive moods saw an overall 57 percent improvement. Forgetfulness, memory loss, lack of concentration, irritability, and heart palpitations also improved toward normal.

The University of Nebraska Medical Center has also been testing estriol as a preventative for human breast cancer. They found women with breast cancer have much lower levels of estriol relative to estradiol and estrone than did women without breast cancer.

The Ideal Estrogen Formula
Dr. Jonathan V. Wright, a physician in Kent, Washington, first began using high doses of estriol but soon found the level that protected women against osteoporosis often resulted in nausea. That's when he hit upon his now famous tri-estrogen formula, which added

10 percent each of estrone and estradiol and lowered the amount of estriol to 80 percent. This stopped the nausea but gave protection against osteoporosis.

Experientially this formula is very safe and able to deliver as many benefits as the carcinogenic version of estrogen. However, your doctor will need to prescribe TriEst according to *your* particular needs: For mild to moderate estrogen deficiencies, the dose is 1.25 milligrams TriEst, taken twice daily. For moderate to severe symptoms, 2.5 milligrams TriEst should be taken twice daily.

I strongly recommend adding progesterone (see discussion of progesterone that follows), as Mother Nature designed estrogen and progesterone to work together. Natural progesterone and TriEst can be compounded into capsules or creams by ordering from pharmacists at Women's International Pharmacy, Madison, Wisconsin, 1-800-279-5708.

PROGESTERONE: THE FEEL-GOOD HORMONE

For many years scientists have virtually ignored progesterone, choosing to focus on estrogen as women's wonder hormone in preventing bone loss. New studies now tell us that estrogen doesn't rebuild bone, progesterone does.

Bone loss can occur even in young women with normal estrogen levels—if their progesterone is deficient. Progesterone levels begin to decline at age thirty, and after menopause, production of progesterone is virtually nonexistent! Eventually researchers even documented that without progesterone to remove estrogen buildup of the uterine lining, up to one third of women taking estrogen were developing uterine cancer.

This research alarmed so many in the mid-1970s that estrogen abruptly fell from favor. Quickly the drug companies rushed in to solve our problems . . . but the synthetic progesterone that appeared had side effects of bloating, moodiness, and headaches. The *Physicians Desk Reference* says adverse reactions to Provera and other synthetic progestins include the risk of birth defects, breast cancer, and runaway blood clots (embolisms) that lodge in the lungs or the brain. Yet this synthetic progesterone, progestin, is still the overwhelming prescription written for progesterone replacement. It is *not* the best choice.

The Ideal Form of Progesterone

In 1995, the *Journal of the American Medical Association* reported a major clinical trial comparing natural oral progesterone with synthetic progestin. The natural hormone won hands down in protecting the heart, raising HDL levels, and protecting against uterine cancer. As I mentioned, natural progesterone is also a fabulous bone builder. You will stand straight and tall in your seventies and eighties because it actually forms new bone, and this natural hormone does not create moodiness, bloating, or other negative symptoms.

Is It Safe?

Natural progesterone replacement is perfectly safe, but adverse effects of Provera and other synthetic progestins (synthetic analogues of progesterone) are downright alarming. Besides the increased risk of birth defects, cancer, and blood clots, the *Physicians Desk Reference* tells us that reactions can include cerebral hemorrhage, uterine tumors, loss of scalp hair, and depression (to mention just a sampling). Synthetic progesterone is not readily broken down by the liver for excretion in the bile and urine, unlike natural progesterone. Instead, it stays in the body for an abnormally long time, occupying the progesterone receptor sites of the true hormones but incapable of doing most of its jobs. *I would not consider taking a synthetic progesterone under any circumstance.*

Taking Natural Progesterone

Natural progesterone cream is not on prescription. Many thousands of women buy it over-the-counter. A monthly guide for using the natural cream has been suggested by John Lee, M.D., a recognized expert on its use. He recommends using 1 ounce of natural progesterone cream (half a 2-oz jar) each month. This equals out to one quarter teaspoon daily, *skipping the first seven days of the month.* If you are already in menopause and concerned about severe osteoporosis, use a full 2-ounce jar (or possibly more) per month. Again, skip the first seven days, and take two daily doses of half a teaspoon each, or 1 teaspoon daily. Natural progesterone cream is well-absorbed through the skin, and is diffused throughout the body by the bloodstream.

The Benefits You Can Expect "Naturally"

Natural progesterone:

- stimulates osteoblast-mediated bone-building (which means you'll never lose inches in height).
- is a natural diuretic.
- helps use your fat for energy.
- is a natural antidepressant.
- restores your libido.
- helps normalize blood sugar levels.
- restores normal cell oxygen levels.
- protects against breast cancer and endometrial cancer.
- protects against breast fibrocysts.
- helps thyroid hormone action.

A note of caution, however: Taking progesterone alone (without estriol) veers from nature's blueprint. Women need *both* of these magical hormones in our "feeling good/antiaging" arsenal.

TESTOSTERONE: A NEGLECTED HORMONE

For many of you, the very mention of the hormone testosterone conjures up visions of aggression, sexuality, and even lust. I'll bet you don't know that this hormone lowers cholesterol, protects against heart disease, improves memory, prevents osteoporosis, builds muscle, enhances the sex drive, and elevates one's mood. This powerful hormone is important for *both* men and women, and its importance has been grossly overlooked by both sexes.

Dr. William Regelson points out that "testosterone is responsible for the sex drive in both men and women; it is the hormone that stimulates our desire for sexual activity and orgasm . . . that makes us desire sex in the first place!" A man who is low in testosterone may well be able to physically engage in sex, but he simply may not care enough to pursue it. The popular drug Viagra can now guarantee your physical sexual performance, but without adequate testosterone you'll still have very little emotional desire to have sex.

For most of the twentieth century, research has concentrated on women's hormones. Very little was known about the male hormonal aging clock. Men are just beginning to replace their waning testosterone levels now. Experts predict that replacing this male hormone will be as common for men in the next five years as taking estrogen is for women.

Male Menopause, or "Andropause"

The decline in testosterone, the dominant hormone in a man's body, produces many physical and emotional problems we used to shrug off as symptoms of aging. Loss of libido, fatigue, muscle weakness, loss of well-being, and even bone loss are all part of this hormone depletion. Testosterone is so intertwined with the male ego that many men cannot accept the fact that its level in their bodies is running low. The good news is that this decline, although inevitable in all of us, is neither irreversible nor irreparable!

Here are some new research facts to convince you it's worth the effort to supplement your testosterone supply.

- In 1996, *The New England Journal of Medicine* reported the amazing news that taking testosterone will significantly enhance muscle size even in men who do not exercise.
- The University of Washington in Seattle reported that in men aged sixty and over who were getting testosterone injections once weekly, there was a significant increase in lean body mass (losing fat and gaining muscle) without any dieting.
- A double-blind study at the Oregon Health Sciences University showed that men on testosterone patches for three months showed improved brain functioning involving visual spatial abilities. This is an area where young men dominate women in their ability, and we now believe that testosterone is the key to that dominance.
- Gerald Phillips, M.D., a Columbia University researcher, has studied men undergoing coronary angiography, comparing their degree of atherosclerosis (narrowing of the arteries) and HDL levels to their levels of testosterone. He concluded: "In men, the higher the testosterone, the less coronary artery disease."
- Maurice Lesser, M.D., studied the effect of testosterone in cases of angina pectoris, which is either a spasm or an arterial blockage in the heart that causes intense pain. The testos-

terone injections had a remarkable result: Out of one hundred cases, ninety-one showed "moderate to marked" improvement in chest pain, meaning both the frequency and the severity of the attacks were reduced.

So obviously, sexual desire and enjoyment are not the only reasons for replacing testosterone. It is another magic antiaging substance that most of us unwittingly lose as we age.

Testosterone: A *Female* Sex Hormone

What do you think is the most devastating effect of a woman's loss of testosterone? It's her loss of libido, a symptom of menopause that is all too common.

Barbara Sherwin, M.D., of McGill University in Montreal, has over the past ten years led the research on women's need for this hormone. Her studies show that taking testosterone has a dramatic effect on the female libido.

And women get even more protection from taking testosterone *after* menopause. That's when we suffer a severe decrease in these natural androgens, the very substances that are protective against breast cancer. We know that progesterone, the other female hormone, offers protection against breast cancer, but testosterone is a thousand times more protective than progesterone!

C. W. Lovell, M.D., working at the Baton Rouge Menopause Clinic, has treated four thousand patients with a combination of estrogen (estradiol) and testosterone. By doing so, he reduced the incidence of breast cancer in his clients to less than half that of the national average. Another statistic on cancer is that one cancer is discovered for every one hundred mammograms done. In those patients on testosterone, there is only one cancer found in every one thousand mammograms done . . . a decrease of 90 percent!

Testosterone has also been found to grow new bone in postmenopausal women over a nine-week course of study combining estrogen and testosterone.

My own experience with testosterone is one that sometimes gets mentioned in women's magazine articles. I am, by nature, a soft-spoken, feminine type, but testosterone gives me a take-charge attitude that is extremely helpful in running a business. There's no doubt in my mind that a smidgen of this "male" hormone puts a lot of zest and energy back into us during our aging years. If only you could just walk into your drugstore and get this hormone like some of the others, but it's not that simple.

Is It Safe?

Though testosterone is an important hormone in your arsenal against aging, certain warnings are in order: The common low-dose replacement in women almost never causes problems, but higher doses may result in some masculine traits, such as deepening voice, unwanted hair growth, increase in blood pressure, and risk of heart disease. Men worry about testosterone increasing the risk of prostate cancer (the second most common cancer in men). There are two theories about this: As testosterone has the ability to stimulate prostate cells, there may be some danger of either aggravating a benign prostate growth, or of promoting an undetected prostate cancer. Currently, this is speculation, not fact, and regular ultrasounds and PSA lab tests will keep any such possibilities in check. Two antiaging physicians, Edmund Chein and L. Cass Terry, have monitored over eight hundred patients on full hormone replacement (including testosterone) and have seen *no* cancer, nor any rise in PSA levels. But dosage is important: Do not take if your levels are normal, and do not take in amounts above a replacement level, to avoid atrophying of the testicles, fluid retention, and lowered sperm count and semen volume. Testosterone replacement is worthwhile for men who have entered male menopause. Signs of such male menopause are reduction in libido, difficulty with erection, lessened sexual satisfaction, fatigue, and the traditional pot belly that happens to middle-aged men.

WARNING: Be sure your doctor does not prescribe methyl-testosterone. The United States is the only country still using this *synthetic* hormone. Doctors in Europe won't touch it because it is harmful to the liver.

How to Take Testosterone—Safely

Your doctor probably isn't going to suggest taking testosterone to you. If you are a woman, your physician may even be a little shocked at your request unless he or she is into life-extension therapies.

There are clinics nationwide that specialize in thwarting aging, but the average family doctor may know less of this research than you. So let me give you some direction.

First, it is important to check your level of free or unbound testosterone with a lab test to determine how much you might need before embarking on a replacement regimen. Second, taking testosterone orally (by mouth) can cause liver damage. So do not accept any such prescription. Testosterone creams and gels are sold by compounding pharmacies such as Women's International Pharmacy (see Appendix C). There is also a sublingual pill that you dissolve under the tongue, so it absorbs right into your bloodstream and bypasses the liver. The FDA has recently approved a patch for men, which offers a steady delivery of this hormone, and certainly beats injections for comfort. But women should take care not to use the testosterone patch, as it delivers too high a dose. Women should start with the *lowest* dose of cream or gel and rub it directly into the skin on the arms, stomach, or thighs. Effects are usually noticeable within three to five days. Dosages can be adjusted upward gradually to give the result that is right for you.

THYROID HORMONE

We have already looked closely at the role of the thyroid hormone in Chapter 6, when we discussed depression. If you found you scored high in the Hypothyroidism Checklist, page 199, you have a fairly common problem. It is estimated that one in ten women and one in twenty men over fifty have some symptoms of low thyroid. If you suspect this hormone is under par in you, it is essential to your rejuvenation program to have the lab work done and restore your thyroid levels to normal.

In a recent *Journal of the American Medical Association* article, researchers at Johns Hopkins University urged doctors to routinely test patients over thirty-five for thyroid abnormalities, as they leads to high cholesterol levels, depression, and weight gain. I suggest you ask for this lab panel if your doctor fails to suggest it.

Natural Thyroid Beats Synthetic

The likelihood of being prescribed Synthroid, a synthetic form of thyroid, rather than the natural desiccated hormone made from animal thyroid, is almost predictable. Only a small number of physicians are aware of the advantage of duplicating nature by combining T3 and T4 in the desiccated (Armour) thyroid. For all the facts, read Dr. Broda Barnes's book *Hypothyroid: The Unsuspected Illness* or Steven Langer's *Solving the Puzzle of Illness*.

If you suspect you have thyroid abnormalities, reread the information in Chapter 6 and do the at-home test (page 201) to confirm or rule out thyroid problems.

Is It Safe?

Providing you *need* thyroid—and only your physician can confirm that for you—taking thyroid is not only safe but essential to staying healthy. Remember, it is a lifelong commitment. Stopping thyroid maintenance will result in a sudden or gradual return of symptoms. You may find that your dosage levels fluctuate from cold to warm seasons. Paying attention to symptoms such as consistently feeling overheated or chilled will help you to better regulate your body's thyroid needs.

HUMAN GROWTH HORMONE: DISCOVERING THE LAZARUS EFFECT

Are you ready for the wildest research revelations in the whole anti-aging field, the accomplishments of the human growth hormone? If ever science has been close to stumbling on immortality, discovering the effects of replacing the human growth hormone (HGH) levels comes closest.

The study that opened the floodgates to thousands of research papers was published in 1990 in the *New England Journal of Medicine*. During this study, twelve aging men (between ages sixty-one and eighty-one) shed their flabby, fat-laden bodies and became younger, stronger versions of themselves. The study claimed that "The effect of six months of HGH on lean body mass and adipose-tissue mass were equivalent in magnitude to the changes that occurred during ten to twenty years of aging." In other words, aging was *reversed*! But that's only the beginning of what this pituitary hormone will do for you. The list of benefits keeps growing with the research.

Fifteen years ago, endocrinology texts declared that the growth hormone had no effect at all on adults. At that time, it was used only to increase underdeveloped children's growth to normal size. The fact that we all lose our levels of HGH starting in our twenties, and that by age sixty our HGH production is cut in half, and by age sixty-five half of the population is partially or wholly deficient in the growth hormone, did not register as a marker for aging until just a few years ago. Little did science suspect that this amazing substance, if taken by adults, would offer a fountain of youth:

- An effective antiobesity solution
- Cosmetic surgery in a bottle; it works to remove facial wrinkles, plump up skin contours, replace extracellular water, and restore skin elasticity
- A new lease on life mentally and emotionally, reviving energy, relieving stress and anxiety, restoring deep, restful sleep, and sharpening memory and IQ
- A restoration to normal of shrinking organs (brain, heart, liver, kidneys), and a concurrent reversal of wear-and-tear that has occurred with those aging organs.

If all of this sounds like fiction to you, let me get right down to specifics. I want you to know just what researchers have found, how safe (or unsafe) HGH is, who needs it most, and how you can increase your own HGH availability wisely and successfully for the rest of your life.

The Fat-to-Muscle Miracle

It's certainly no secret that America is fattening up at an alarming rate. Unfortunately, the more fat we carry, the less growth hormone we release. Those who are apple-shaped (with a fat accumulation around the middle) have a far greater risk of diabetes and heart disease, as well as the loss of HGH, than pear-shaped persons (with a fat accumulation around the hips and thighs). So the shape of your body can clue you in to your individual HGH needs.

Over two hundred persons who received a low dose (.3 to .7 IU of growth hormone twice daily) reported no adverse effects in a 1997 study by L. Cass Terry, M.D. Over 75 percent noted body-fat loss, muscle gain, greater strength, and higher energy levels. Skin texture improved, as did skin thickness and elasticity.

Photographs in the June 1997 issue of *Life Extension*, an international monthly periodical on antiaging research, show remarkable changes in an aging couple after six months of HGH treatment. Their formerly sagging, lumpy bodies had totally changed into muscular and curvaceous shapes. Their hair was thicker and facial muscles tauter. They looked twenty years younger in every way. No plastic surgeon could accomplish all of these changes. Yet what we are looking at is only the outside of the package.

HGH Effects on the Brain

Have you lost your zest for life? Do you feel depressed or anxiety-riddled? Are you living with low vitality and a fading interest in staying alive? The growth hormone can do something about all this. Pioneering researchers in Sweden, Denmark, and England noted such marked changes in self-esteem and well-being in their patients on HGH that they started calling it the "Lazarus Effect," a biblical reference to Lazarus, who was brought back to life. Benzt-Ak Bengtsson, M.D., at Sahlgrenska Hospital in Sweden, says of these clients: "We woke them up. With some patients it was like giving them a kick in the back. Their lives changed within a few weeks." Researchers at St. Thomas Hospital in London noted that their patients, before using the growth hormone, shared "poor energy, emotional liability, low mood, and social isolation." Some were so disturbed—full of anxiety, depression, and a loss of self-control—that they warranted intervention. Yet on HGH, these abnormalities of mood and energy cleared up. HGH crosses the blood-brain barrier and proceeds to raise endorphin levels, creating its own natural high. It also lowers dopamine, too much of which produces agitation.

Bengtsson's work with growth hormone patients documents a reversal of fatigue and depression. The rehydration of body tissues adds vitality, in the same way that watering drooping flowers perks them up. HGH has also proved its worth in reversing chronic fatigue syndrome by lifting energy levels to new highs.

Stress Relief from HGH

You probably have already seen that the ability to rebound from the stresses of life gradually fades with age. Thierry Hertoghe, M.D., an expert on hormonal deficiency, tells us: "Overanxiety or hyper-emotionality is a sign of growth hormone deficiency. Androgens help both men and women calm down, but you don't get the calmness that you do with GH. Of all the hormones I work with, growth hormone relaxes the individual most."

He describes his own reactions upon taking growth hormone: "In the past year, I've been in difficult situations but I haven't experienced the stress that usually goes along with this, like not sleeping well, waking up in the middle of the night worrying, [or] getting up in the morning feeling like I haven't slept. That has all gone away."

Memory and Growth Hormone

HGH has been proven to reverse the decline in memory and in cognitive abilities. Dutch researcher Jan Berend Deijem, M.D., and his colleagues found that a lack of growth hormone is associated with impairment of both short-term and long-term memory and of iconic memory (the ability to process flashes of information) as well as perceptual motor skills such as hand-eye coordination. And they were able to actually correlate the levels of growth hormone present to the aging patient's IQ.

Growth hormone may well be able to reverse our aging brain's shrinking size. The growth factors stimulate neurons to regrow dendritic connections. Glial cells, which nourish the neurons, can also regenerate. The University of California at Berkeley has successfully carried out these experiments on rats, turning their old brains into young ones and even increasing their cortex growth!

Can HGH Increase Life Span?

As long as we can continually fight and win our battles with disease, we will stay alive and healthy. But as our immune systems slowly fail us, we start losing the war. *There is a vital connection between maintaining high immunity and our levels of growth hormone.*

The primary weapon of the immune system is our thymus gland. It provides us with all the immunity factors we need to fight off disease. It also shrivels as we age, as do our defenses against invading illnesses. The growth hormone boosts our thymus gland, reviving it and reversing this shrinkage.

For years it has been a common belief that nothing can stop the shriveling of the aging thymus. But Dr. Keith Kelley, a University of Illinois researcher, has disproved the notion that nothing will reactivate this life-protecting gland by injecting HGH into old rats whose thymus had all but disappeared. The GH cells caused their thymus glands to grow back to the size of young rats. Other studies by Vincent Giampapa, M.D., have shown an increase in the size of human thymus glands. This researcher explains that HGH jump starts the older cells, causing them to repair themselves and reproduce more quickly.

Greg Fahy, Ph.D., a researcher in cellular physiology, explains: "I think that a lot of aging can be explained by deficits in growth hormone. I don't think that even people working in the field see the whole picture.... If you put all the pieces of evidence together, it suggests that growth hormone is even more central to the aging process than most people [suspected]."

With increased immunity we avoid disease and live much longer. How long still remains to be seen, but there is no doubt we have stumbled on a way to rejuvenate our immune systems as well as our brains.

How to Say "No" to Aging!

At any point after the second decade of life you can take specific steps to replace this precious hormone. In doing so, you halt physical and mental decay and prolong your life substantially because you have restored your body's immune system. Depending on your age and your levels of HGH, you will either choose to (1) boost your own production of HGH by taking growth hormone releasers (certain aminos and niacin), and/or GHB (gamma-hydroxybutrate); or (2) take the actual HGH by daily injection.

First, however, you need to assess your current level of HGH by measuring the somatomedin C (IGF-I), which is the body's growth hormone marker. This blood test can be done in your doctor's office, or it can be ordered through the Life Extension Foundation by calling 1-800-841-5433 or faxing them at 1-954-761-9199 and requesting a requisition form and information on the blood draw station nearest you. You will be sent the results along with the recommendation that you work closely with your physician in evaluating the test's outcome. Your doctor's task will be to raise your IGF-I to a level normal for a thirty- to forty-year-old, which would be somewhere in the high 200s or low 300s. There are two paths you can take: either taking GH releasers or injecting actual HGH, as described earlier.

BOOSTING PRODUCTION OF HGH WITH GROWTH HORMONE RELEASERS

Many of you may be able to up your waning growth hormone levels by taking certain natural substances in fairly large amounts that will cause increased secretion of growth hormone. Providing that your pituitary gland still stocks ample growth hormone, you will be able to increase its output to levels that have a definite effect on your body and mind.

The amino acid arginine is already used intravenously (15 to 30 g) as a medical test to provoke the pituitary into producing HGH. In the eighties, Durk Pearson and Sandy Shaw, an author/researcher team, extolled (and became living proof of) the combination of combining arginine (5 to 10 g) with the amino ornithine (2½ to 5 g) at bedtime to jump-start an outpouring of growth hormone while you sleep.

A 1981 Italian study found the combination of lysine and arginine at 1,200 milligrams each (or, 1 g plus 200 mg) was ten times as efficient as arginine alone in raising HGH levels in teenagers. Unfortunately, in men over sixty-five, these two aminos did nothing. In other words, there was little growth hormone left to trigger a response.

Glutamine in 2 gram doses has been shown to raise HGH levels more than four times higher than a placebo *at any age*, according to a 1995 study at Louisiana State College of Medicine conducted by Dr. Thomas Wellbourne.

Niacin (or B₃) at 500 milligrams also has proved effective in releasing HGH, according to Pearson and Shaw in their 1990 report "GH Releasers: An Update Review."

GHB (gamma-hydroxybutrate), the newest entry, is a precursor of GABA (gamma-aminobutyric acid). GABA regulates the anterior pituitary gland, which secretes growth hormone. While GHB is one of the most powerful simulators of HGH known to date, it is not currently available in the United States.

To figure out the most promising combination of growth hormone releasers, we rely on the experts who have worked with hundreds of patients increasing their growth hormone levels with natural formulas. One of these is Vincent Giampapa, M.D., director of the Longevity Institute International in Montclair, New Jersey. His recommendation, based on his own research and observation, is a combination of the following four aminos, all taken at bedtime:

Ornithine, 1 gram
Arginine, 2 grams
Lysine, 1 gram
Glutamine, 1 gram

After a few weeks, increase all doses to 2 grams each. (One tsp. of powder is equal to 2.5 g.)

Ronald Klatz, M.D., author of *Grow Young with HGH*, suggests a variation on the above formula. He claims it boosts growth hormone levels up to 20 percent higher.

Arginine, 3 grams
Lysine, 3 grams
Glutamine, 3 grams
GHB, 500 milligrams to 1 gram

Increase these aminos (but *not* the GHB) one gram per week, to 5 grams each, or 15 grams total, taken at bedtime. This level of amino acid intake is equivalent to two eggs and is completely safe to ingest.

The table on page 331 is the growth hormone releasers formula we suggest at HCR that you take.

ARE GH RELEASERS SAFE? You must always be concerned with keeping your body from shutting down its own natural supply of hormones because of your new regimen's daily interference with your body's built-in feedback mechanism. Experts recommend taking your amino formula every day for a period of three weeks, and then *cycling off* for one week. In that way the feedback mechanism doesn't shut down. Our bodies will reset their feedback mechanisms during that week off.

Second, if you are taking the amino acid formula to release your own growth hormone, be aware that aminos are not good to take if you have a damaged liver. If you suspect you have elevated liver readings, have a chemistry profile lab test done to check it out.

Last, taking niacin if you are diabetic may raise your glucose levels and call for an adjustment in your insulin. See your doctor for specific medical advice.

THE HRC GROWTH HORMONE RELEASERS FORMULA©

Nutrient	Dose	Directions
Arginine +*^	3 g	Take together in powder form at bedtime (1 tsp = 2½ g)
Lysine +*^	3 g	
Glutamine +*^	3 g	
Ornithine ^	1 g	
Niacin	500 mg	1 capsule at bedtime

Note: If you are already taking any of the above nutrients, do not exceed the amounts for your total dosage (see chart page 56).

+ *After one week at this level, increase arginine, lysine, and glutamine to 4 grams, and increase ornithine to 2 grams.*
* *After the second week at 4 grams, increase arginine, lysine, and glutamine to 5 grams.*
^ *After three weeks, skip the fourth week entirely so your body can adjust and reset its own cycled feedback mechanism.*

© *Copyright 1999 Health Recovery Center.™ All Rights Reserved.*

THE FUTURE OF GROWTH HORMONE RELEASERS: There are several drug GH releasers presently undergoing clinical drug trials. When approved, these oral agents will mean you can just pop a pill to stimulate the production of your growth hormone! The time for these wondrous drugs is within the next five to seven years (as of this writing).

TAKING ACTUAL HGH BY DAILY INJECTION

But what if you are in the one third of our aging population that has practically no growth hormone of your own to stimulate? If you are running on empty, then the growth hormone releasers just described are not for you. (Remember, a lab test will answer the important question of how much, if any, HGH you have right now.) The good news for you is that the FDA has now approved the use of actual growth hormone, so you can put back what you lost. These shots of growth hormone will thrill you with their ability to reverse the trappings of aging.

A 1995 study by Hans DeBoer at the University Hospital of Amsterdam established a growth hormone dose that is 40 to 60 percent lower than previous studies by monitoring the amount of extracellular water that returns with growth hormone rehydration. (Normal rehydration and extracellular water occurs at 1.10 IU or 3 mg. Three mg is equal to 1 IU.) Dr. DeBoer's suggested starting dose was .50 international unit (1½ mg) daily. This dose may be raised *monthly* by .50 international unit a day until 1.10 is reached. However, Swedish researcher Dr. Bengtsson believes a daily .50 international unit is a sufficient amount of hormone for those over sixty.

The ideal replacement dose for those under sixty would be one that brings up the growth hormone level to that of a healthy thirty- to forty-year-old person. The doctor you choose to work with should have expertise in antiaging medicine, a new and rapidly growing field (a list of such physicians is found in Appendix B).

Researchers seem to agree that the most satisfactory approach now in use is twice-daily injections, totaling between 4 and 8 international units weekly, skipping the seventh day so as not to atrophy the pituitary gland. The consensus seems to be that .50 per day is an appropriate starting point and monthly increases should *stop* at an optimum 1.10 daily. Monitor the growth hormone marker IGF-I (with lab testing) and keep the levels in the high 200s or low 300 IGF-I units.

IS IT SAFE TO INJECT HGH? Noticeable side effects may occur in doses of 2 international units daily or more, and a 1996 Danish study concluded that 2 seemed too high for most adults. Researchers say that in studies using doses substantially over 1.10 international units daily, lower extremity edema, joint pain, and carpal tunnel syndrome developed. (These side effects disappeared when the dosage was cut in half.)

Other side effects at higher doses are: enlargement of male breasts, diabetes, and fluid retention. Fortunately, we are entering the HGH replacement era at the right time. The mistakes of overdosing have already been made, recognized, and corrected downward. Scientists have come to understand that the right HGH dose is simply a *replacement* dose, and not a pharmacological level such as that which bodybuilders and athletes would seek.

Last, researchers also have questioned whether cancer is a possible risk with growth hormone replacement. Researchers Edmund Chein and L. Cass Terry have treated over eight hundred patients in an older age group where cancers would be expected to occur but have seen no cases. Still, Dr. Chein stresses the importance of rebalancing all of your declining hormones: estrogen, progesterone, testosterone, DHEA, melatonin, and so on. This equilibrium restores your body's youthful ability to fight disease and optimize health.

BRACE YOURSELF FOR THE PRICE TAG!

Growth hormones don't come cheap. In the United States, the yearly cost for adults may run up to $9,000 per year or $800 per month (plus doctor's visits, blood tests, and total costs for replacing other antiaging hormones like DHEA, melatonin, etc.).

If you choose to get your HGH from a clinic in Mexico, such as the Cancun Renaissance Rejuvenation Center, you can save on your prescription. Mexico sells quality growth hormone over-the-counter in drugstores. As of this writing, the same growth hormone costs about $43 for 4 international units, saving you about $200 to $400 per month or $2,400 to $4,800 per year.

The Swiss Rejuvenation Centre Incorporated in the Bahamas supplies growth hormone by mail order directly to customers in the United States at about $25 per international unit. The recommended dosage of .50 to 1.10 would cost $75 to $150 per week, or $4,300 to $8,600 per year. But total fees are over $12,000 yearly because all on-going lab work must be done through this corporation. For more information, contact Sonoma Diagnostic Inc., at 1-800-635-3021.

THE FUTURE OF HGH

At this writing, the search for the perfect growth hormone capsule or patch continues worldwide. The latest speculation is that there remains yet another undiscovered hormone that is the key regulator of growth hormone release. A 1996 article in *Science* presents the research that supports this theory. Now all we have to do is find it!

Total Repair: Your Bright Future

What you have learned from this book represents the basic knowledge you need to live a stable, healthy, and amazingly long life. We are standing at the brink of many wondrous scientific breakthroughs, yet we can't discount all the powerful research already at our fingertips. By now I hope you have come to understand and appreciate the foundation of knowledge upon which this book is based.

If you have not yet set out to apply these pages to your own personal needs, I urge you to begin today. You have nothing to lose, and so much to gain, by restoring yourself to optimal health. Begin today, and in the weeks and months ahead, you and I together will set you firmly on the path to wellness and stable emotions.

A Final Word

In writing this book, I had in mind each of you who have been struggling for sensible, scientific answers to your needs. It is imperative that you find a good doctor who will do your lab tests for you and guide you along the way. I know from the responses to my first book that this doesn't always happen, so I have listed physician-referral agencies in Appendix B. I also extend our own medical services to you. You may call us at the Health Recovery Center, 1-800-554-9155 or 1-612-827-7800. We've had nineteen years of experience with the problems I've described, and we are here to help.

A final word about accessing the nutrient formulas in this book. You may do so by calling 1-800-247-6237. Bio-Recovery will ship what you need by two-day air.

Get started now. . . . I wish you Godspeed.

APPENDIX A

Chapter References

INTRODUCTION

D. Mossberg, et al., "Clinical Conditions in Alcoholics During Long-Term Abstinence," *Alcoholism, Clinical and Experimental Research* 8, no. 2 (March/April 1984): 250.

CHAPTER ONE

Abram Hoffer, *Orthomolecular Medicine for Physicians* (New Canaan, Conn.: Keats Publishing, 1989), 37.

Ancel Keys, et al., *The Biology of Human Starvation* (Minneapolis: University of Minnesota Press, 1950).

David Garner and Paul Garfunkel, eds., *Handbook for Psychotherapy: Anorexia and Bulemia* (New York: Guilford Press, 1985), 327, 394.

Linus Pauling in His Own Words: Selections from Writings, Speeches, and Interviews, edited by Barbara Marinacci (New York: Simon and Schuster, 1995).

Linus Pauling, "Varying the Concentration of Substances Normally Found in the Human Body," *Science* 160 (1968): 265.

David F. Horrobin, *Medical Hypothesis* 6 (1980): 785–800.

Jean Barilea, M.S., ed., *The Good Fats & Oils, Vol. II* (New Canaan, Conn.: Keats Publishing, 1992–93), 92–93.

E. R. Gardner, R. C. Hall, "Medical Screening of Psychiatric Patients," *Journal of Orthomolecular Psychiatry* 9 (1980): 207–15.

M. Kitahara, "Dietary Tryptophan Ratio and Suicide in the United Kingdom, Ireland, the U.S., Canada, Australia and New Zealand," *Omega Journal of Death and Dying* 18 (1987): 71–76.

P. D. Delgado, et al., "Serotonin Function and the Mechanism of Antidepressant Action," *Archives General Psychiatry* 47 (1990): 411–18.

P. Niskamen, et al., "The Daily Rhythm of Plasma, Tryptophan and Tyrosine in Depression," *British Journal Psychiatry* 128 (1976): 67–73.

CHAPTER TWO

Daphne Roe, *Drug Induced Nutritional Deficiencies* (Westport, Conn.: AVI Publishing, 1976).

Crocetti and Guthrie, *Eating Behavior and Associated Nutrient Quality of Diets* (Anarem Systems Research Corporation, 1982).

David Classen, et al., *Journal of American Medical Association* (January 1997): 301–306.

F. R. Klenner, "Significance of High Daily Intake of Ascorbic Acid in Preventive Medicine," *Journal of the International Academy of Preventive Medicine* 1 (1974): 45–69.

H. Tao and H. Fox, "Measurement of Urinary Pantothenic Acid Excretion of Alcoholic Patients," *Journal of Nutritional Science* 22 (1976): 333–37.

R. Passwater, "Evening Primrose Oil," in J. Barilla, editor, *The Nutrition Superbook: The Good Fats and Oils* (New Canaan, CT: Keats Publishing Co., 1995).

J. Levine, et al., "Double Blind, Controlled Trial of Inositol Treatment of Depression," *American Journal of Psychiatry* 152 (1995): 792–94.

J. Benjamin, et al., "Double Blind Placebo Controlled Crossover Trial of Inositol Treatment for Panic Disorder," *American Journal of Psychiatry* 152 (1995): 1084–86.

J. E. Pizzorno and M. T. Murray, *A Textbook of Natural Medicine* (Seattle, Wash.: Bastyr University Publications, 1995).

Gregory Kelly, "Hydrochloric Acid: Physiological Functions and Clinical Implications," *Alternative Medicine Review* 2, no. 2 (March 1997).

J. E. Pizzorno and M. T. Murray, "Heidelberg PH Capsule Gastric Analysis," *A Textbook of Natural Medicine* (Seattle, Wash.: Bastyr University Publications, 1995).

CHAPTER THREE

George Mann, Sc.D., M.D., ed., *Coronary Heart Disease: The Dietary Sense and Nonsense* (London: Janus Publ. Co.), 60–75.

G. Dhopeshworker, *Nutrition and Brain Development* (New York: Plenum, 1983), 23.

F. Hale, et al., "Post-Prandial Hypoglycemia," *Journal of Biological Psychiatry* 17 (1982): 125–30.

A. Keys, "Letter-Normal Plasma Cholesterol in a Man Who Eats 25 Eggs a Day," *New England Journal of Medicine* 325 (1991): 584.

T. E. Strangberg, V. V. Salonna, and V. A. Naukkareenen, et al., "A Long-Term Mortality After 5-Year Multi Factorial Primary Prevention of Cardiovascular Diseases in Middle-Aged Men," *Journal of American Medical Association* 266 (1991): 1225.

Cass Ingram, N.D., "Eat Right to Live Long," in *American Curative Medicine* (Hiawatha, Iowa: Cedar Graphics, 1989), 142.

CHAPTER FOUR

Charles Darwin, *The Expression of the Emotions in Man and Animals* (New York: The Philosophical Library, 1955).

Candace Pert, *Molecules of Emotions: Why You Feel the Way You Feel* (New York: Scribner 1997).

Eric Braverman, M.D., *The Healing Nutrients Within* (New Canaan, Conn.: Keats Publishing, 1997), 23.

Eric Braverman, M.D., and Carl Pfeiffer, "Suicide and Biochemistry," *Biological Psychiatry* 20 (1985): 123–24.

Carl Pfeiffer, *Mental and Elemental Nutrients: A Physical Guide to Nutrition and Health Care* (New Canaan, Conn.: Keats Publishing, 1975), 402–408.

H. Beckman, et al., "DL Phenylalanine VS Imipramine: A Double Blind Controlled Study," *Archiv Fur Psychiatre Und Nerven Krankhleiten* 227 (1979): 49–58.

H. Van Praag, "Depression, Suicide, and the Metabolism of Serotonin in the Brain," *Journal of Affective Disorders* 4 (1982): 275–90.

J. Fernstrom and R. Wurtman, "Brain Serotonin Content: Physiological Dependence on Plasma Tryptophan Levels," *Science* 173 (1971): 149–52.

Oberleas, et al., *Psychopharmacology Bulletin* (July 1997).

A. A. Ronaghy, *Chemical Engineering News* (July 10, 1972).

L. M. Klevay, "Changing Patterns of Disease: Some Nutritional Remarks," *Journal of American College of Nutrition* 3 (1984): 149–58.

CHAPTER FIVE

M. J. Hoes, et al., "Hyperventilation Syndrome, Treatment with Tryptophan and Pyridoxine," *Journal of Orthomolecular Psychiatry* 10, no. 1 (1981): 7–15.

D. Benton and R. Cork, "The Impact of Selenium Supplementation on Decreasing Anxiety," *Biological Psychiatry* 29, no. 11 (June 1991): 1092–98.

Carl Pfeiffer, *Nutrition and Mental Illness* (Rochester, Vt.: Healing Arts Press, 1975), 40–42.

Melvyn R. Werbach, *Nutritional Influences on Mental Illness: A Source-book of Clinical Research* (Tarzana, Calif.: Third Line Press, 1991), 48–55.

R. G. Kay, et al., "A Syndrome of Acute Zinc Deficiency During Parental Alimentation in Man," *American Surgery* 183 (1976): 331–40.

R. Vadnal et al., "Role of Inositol in Treatment of Psychiatric Disorders: Basic and Chemical Aspects," *CNS Drugs* 7, no. 1 (January 1997): 6–16.

Mendel Fux, et al., "Inositol Treatment of Obsessive-Compulsive Disorder," *American Journal of Psychiatry* 153 (September 1996): 1219–21.

J. Benjamin, et al., "Double Blind Controlled, Crossover Trial for Inositol Treatment for Panic Disorder," *American Journal of Psychiatry* 152 (1995): 1084–86.

O. W. Wendel, et al., "Glycolytic Activity in Schizophrenia," in *Orthomolecular Psychiatry*, eds. D. Hawkins and L. Pauling (San Francisco: W. H. Freeman, 1973).

L. C. Abbey, "Agoraphobia," *Journal of Orthomolecular Psychiatry* 11 (1982): 243–59.

R. T. Stanko, et al., "Body Composition, Energy Utilization and Nitrogen Metabolism with a 4.25 Ml/d Low-energy Diet Supplement with Pyruvate," *American Journal of Clinical Nutrition* 56, no. 4 (October 1992): 630–35.

CHAPTER SIX

Pat Lazarus and Abram Hoffer, *Healing the Mind the Natural Way* (New York: Putnam Publishing Group, 1995), 147–48.

Roger Greenberg and Seymour Fisher, "Examining Antidepressant Effectiveness: Findings, Ambiguities and Some Vexing Puzzles," *The Limits of Biological Treatments of Psychological Distress* (Hillsdale, NJ: 1989), 1–37.

Martin Teicher, Carol Glod, and Jonathan Cole, "Emergence of Intense Suicidal Preoccupations During Fluoxetine Treatment," *American Journal of Psychiatry*, 147: 207–210.

Gary Null, Ph.D., *Nutrition of the Mind* (New York: Four Walls, Eight Windows, 1995), 58.

Peter Breggin, M.D., *Toxic Psychiatry* (New York: St. Martin's Press, 1994), 179.

Peter Breggin, M.D., *Talking Back to Prozac* (New York: St. Martin's Press, 1994), 64.

Ibid., 47.

Donald Rudin, *The Omega-3 Phenomenon* (New York: Rawson Associates, 1987).

C. M. Reading, "Latent Pernicious Anemia," *Medical Journal Association* 1, no. 91 (1975).

T. L. Perry, et al., "Hereditary Mental Depression and Parkinsonism with Taurine Deficiency," *Archives of Neurology* 32 (1975): 108.

Eric Braverman, M.D., *The Healing Nutrients Within* (New Canaan, Conn: Keats Publishing, 1997).

Dorothy Gaev, Ph. D., "Nutritional Aspects of Manic Depressive Disorders," *Nutritional and Dietary Consultant* (August 1988): 12–13.

R. E. Banks, et al., "Incorporation of Inositol into the Phosphornositides of Lympho Blastoid Cell Lines Established from Bipolar Manic-Depressive Patients," *Journal of Affective Disorders*, no. 1 (May 19, 1990): 1–8.

T. Donaldson, "Body Clocks and Aging," *Anti-Aging News* 4, no. 7 (July 1984).

A. A. Fierro, "Natural Low Dose Lithium Supplementation in Manic Depressive Disease," *Nutrition Perspectives* (Jan. 1988): 10–11.

D. A. Dick, et al., "Plasma Vanadium Concentrations in Manic-Depressive Illness," *Journal of Physiology* 310 (1981): 27.

G. T. Naylor, "Vanadium and Manic Depressive Psychosis," *Nutritional Health* 3, no. 1–2 (1984): 79–85.

J. Brzyinski, "Alteration of Brain Noradrenaline, Dopamine and 5 Hydroxy Tryptamine Levels During Vanadium Poisoning," *Journal of Pharmacological Pharmacy* 31 (1979): 393–98.

D. A. Dick, et al., *Psychiatry Medicine* 12 (1982): 533–37.

Z. A. Leitner, "Nutritional Studies in a Mental Hospital," *Lancet* 1 (1956): 565–67.

G. Milner, "Ascorbic Acid in Chronic Psychiatric Patients: A Controlled Trial," *British Journal of Psychiatry* 109 (1963): 294–99.

"Vanadium, Vitamin C and Depression," *Nutritional Review* 40, no. 10 (1981): 293–95, quoted in M. R. Werbach, M.D., *Nutritional Influences on Mental Illness: A Sourcebook of Clinical Research* (Tarzana, CA: Third Line Press, 1991), 84.

J. Levine, et al., "Double Blind, Controlled Trial of Inositol," *American Journal of Psychiatry* 152 (1995): 792–94.

A. Gelenberg, et al., "Tyrosine for the Treatment of Depression," *American Journal of Psychiatry* 137, no. 5 (1980): 622–23.

I. Goldberg, "Tyrosine in Depression," *Lancet* 2 (1980): 364.

H. Beckman, et al., "L-Phenylalanine Versus Imipramine: A Double-Blind Controlled Study," *Archives fur Psychiatre und Nerven Krankheiten* 227 (1979): 49–58.

H. Beckman, "Phenylalanine in Affective Disorders," *Advanced Biological Psychiatry* 10 (1983): 137–47.

R. Bunevicius, et al., "Effects of Thyroxine As Compared with Thyroxine plus Triiodothyronine in Patients with Hypothyroidism," *New England Journal of Medicine* 340 (1999): 424–29.

C. J. Glueck, et al., "Improvement in Symptoms of Depression and in an Index of Life Stressors Accompanying Treatment of Severe Hypertriglyceridemia," *Biological Psychiatry* 34, no. 4 (1993): 240–52.

David Horrobin, *Clinical Uses of Essential Fatty Acids* (Montreal: Eden Press, 1982).

Charles Bates, *Essential Fatty Acids and Immunity in Mental Health* (Tacoma, Wash.: Life Sciences Press, 1987), 104–108.

"Hypomagnesemia: Physical and Psychiatric Symptoms," *Journal of American Medical Association* 224, no. 13 (1973): 1749–51.

L. E. Reiser and M. F. Reiser, "Endocrine Disorders" in *Comprehensive Textbook of Psychiatry IV*, H. I. Kaplan and B. J. Sodock, eds. (Baltimore, Md.: Williams and Wilkins, 1985), 1167–78.

Stephen Langer and James F. Scheer, *Solved: The Riddle of Illness*, 2nd ed. (New Canaan, Conn.: Keats Publishing, 1995).

C. Jovon, et al., "Psychiatric Symptomology in Patients with Primary Hyperthyroidism," *Journal of Medical Science* 91, no. 1: (1986): 77–87.

W. L. Webb, "Electrolyte and Fluid Imbalance: Neuropsychiatric Manifestations," *Psychosomatics* 22, no. 3 (1981): 199–203.

F. A. Meyers and E. Jawetz, *Review of Medical Pharmacology*, 1983.

D. Mossberg, et al., "Clinical Conditions in Alcoholics During Long Term Abstinence," *Alcoholism, Clinical and Experimental Research* 8, no. 2 (March/April 1984): 250.

CHAPTER SEVEN

Eva Edelman, *Natural Healing for Schizophrenia: A Compendium of Nutritional Methods* (Eugene, Ore.: Borage Books, 1996), 48–49.

Carl Pfeiffer, Richard Mailloux, and Linda Forsythe, *The Schizophrenias: Ours to Conquer* (Wichita, Kans.: Bio-Communications Press, 1988), 55–160.

Linus Pauling and David Hawkins, eds., *Orthomolecular Psychology: Treatment of Schizophrenia* (San Francisco: W. H. Freeman, 1973).

J. Yarijura-Tobias, "L-Tryptophan in Obsessive-Compulsive Disorders," *American Journal of Psychiatry* 10 (November 1977): 1298–99.

R. Vadnel, et al., "Role of Inositol in Treatment of Psychiatric Disorders: Basic and Chemical Aspects," *CNS DRUGS* 7, no. 1 (January 1997): 6–16.

Russell Jaffe, M.D., Ph.D., "Are Histamine Values Going Up? If So, So What?" *International Clinical Nutritional Review* (January 1992).

CHAPTER EIGHT

Select Committee on Nutrition and Human Needs, U.S. Senate Dietary Goals for the U.S., Washington D.C.: Government Printing Office, 1977.

H. Okuyama, "Effects of Dietary Essential Fatty Acid Balance on Behavior and Chronic Disease," *Polyunsaturated Fatty Acids Human Nutrition*, U. Bracco and R. J. Deckelbaum, eds., Nestlé Nutrition Workshop Series 28 (New York: Raven Press, 1992).

T. Hamazaki, et al., *Journal of Clinical Investigations* 97 (1996): 1129–1134.

Dr. William Walsh, Ph.D., Letter to the editor, *Townsend Letter for Doctors* (August 1992).

William Walsh, "Chemical Imbalances and Criminal Violence: Results of Two Controlled Studies in California Institutions," unpublished manuscript (Chicago: Health Research Institute, 1987).

Louis Gottschalk, et al., "Abnormalities in Hair Trace Elements as Indicators of Aberrant Behavior," *Comprehensive Psychiatry* 32, no. 3 (May/June 1991): 229–237.

V. J. Singh, et al., "Antibodies to Myelin Basic Protein in Children with Autistic Behavior," *Brain Behavior and Immunity* 7 (1993): 1197–1203.

G. M. Fenichel, "Neurological Complications of Immunization," *Annals of Neurology* 12 (1982): 119–28.

F. White, "Measles Vaccine Associated Encephalitis in Canada," *Lancet* 2 (1983): 683–84.

Harris Coulter Ph.D., *Vaccination, Social Violence & Criminality: The Medical Assault on the American Brain* (Berkeley, Calif.: North Atlantic Books, 1990).

Harold Buttram, "Measles, Mumps, Rubella Vaccine as a Potential Cause of Encephalitis (Brain Inflamation) in Children," *Townsend Letter for Doctors* (December 1997): 100–102.

Vera Scheibner, *Vaccination: 100 Years of Orthodox Research Shows that Vaccines Represent a Medical Assault on the Immune System* (Santa Fe, NM: New Atlantean Press, 1993), 35–49.

W. Herbert, "The Case of the Missing Hormones," *Science News* (October 30, 1982): 282.

I. Colquhoun and S. Bundy, "A Lack of Essential Fatty Acids as a Possible Cause of Hyperactivity in Children," *Medical Hypotheses* 7 (1981): 637–639.

E. A. Mitchell, et al., "Clinical Characteristics and Serum Essential Fatty Acid Levels in Hyperactive Children," *Clinical Pediatrics* 26 (1987): 406–411.

CHAPTER NINE

Paul Yanick, "Chronic Fatigue Syndrome and Immune Suppression," *Townsend Letter for Doctors* (April 1994): 288–91.

C. D. Truss, "The Role of Candida Albicans in Human Illness," *Journal of Orthomolecular Psychiatry* 10 (1981): 228–38.

Dr. Illingworth, et al., "Inhibition of Low Density Lipoprotein Synthesis by Dietary Omega 3 Fatty Acids in Humans," *Arteriosclerosis* 4 (1984): 270–75.

John Trowbridge and Morton Walker, *The Yeast Syndrome* (New York: Bantam Books, 1986).

M. Rosenbaum and M. Susser, *Solving the Puzzle of CFS* (Tacoma, Wash.: Life Sciences Press, 1996), 34–44.

J. C. Stiles, et al., "The Inhibition of Candida Albicans by Oregano," *Journal of Applied Nutrition* 47 (1995): 96–101.

Cass Ingram, *The Cure Is in the Cupboard* (New Hyde Park, N.Y.: Purity Products, 1997).

William Crook, *The Yeast Connection: A Medical Breakthrough* (Jackson, Tenn.: Professional Books, 1997), 249.

William Philpott, *Brain Allergies: The Psychonutrient Connection* (New Canaan, Conn.: Keats Publishing, 1987).

Marshall Mandell, *Dr. Mandell's 5-Day Allergy Relief System* (New York: Crowell, 1974).

Robert Becker, *The Body Electric* (New York: William Morrow, 1985).

Richard Gerber, *Vibrational Medicine* (Santa Fe, N. Mex.: Bear and Co., 1988).

CHAPTER TEN

Walter Pierpaoli, D. Bulian, and A. Dall'ara, "A Circadian Melatonin and Young to Old Grafting Postpone Aging and Maintain Juvenile Conditions of Reproductive Functions in Mice and Rats," *EXP Gerontology.* Abstract: Third International Symposium on Neurobiology and Neuroendocrinology of Aging (1996).

William Regelson and Carol Colman, *The Superhormone Promise* (New York: Simon and Schuster, 1996), 218–46.

Walter Pierpaoli and William Regelson, *The Melatonin Miracle* (New York: Simon and Schuster, 1995).

Ray Sahelian, *DHEA: A Practical Guide* (Garden City Park, N.Y.: Avery, 1996).

William Campbell-Douglas, *Second Opinion* 6, no. 10 (October 1996): 2–5.

E. Barrett-Connor and D. Goodman-Gruen, "The Epidemiology of DHEAS and Cardiovascular Disease," *Annals of New York Academy of Sciences* 774 (1995): 259–270.

A Morales, et al, "Effect of Replacement Dose of DHEA in Men and Women of Advancing Age," *Journal of Clinical Endocrine Metabolism* 78 (1994): 1360–1367.

Regelson and Colman, *Superhormone Promise*, 68–70.

C. W. Boone, G. J. Kelloff, and W. C. Malone, "Identification of cancer preventative agents and their evaluation in animal models and human clinical trials: A review," *Cancer Research* 50 (1990): 2–9.

A. R. Gaby, "DHEA: The hormone that does it all," *Holistic Medicine* (Spring, 1993): 19–23.

E. B. Connor, K. T. Khaw, and S. S. Yen, "A prospective study of DHEA—sulfate, mortality and cardiovascular disease," *New England Journal of Medicine*, Vol. 315, No. 24 (December 1986): 1519–1524.

J. E. Nestler, J. N. Clore, and W. G. Blackard, "Dehydro-epiandrosterone (DHEA): The Missing Link between Hyperinsulinism and Atherosclerosis," *FASEB Journal* 6 (1992): 3073–3075.

M. Majewska, "Neuronal Actions of DHEA: Possible Roles in Brain Development, Aging, Memory and Affect," *Annals of NY Academy of Science* 774 (1996): 111–20.

"The Super Hormone for the Brain, Pregnenolone," *Women's Health Connection* 5, no. 3 (1997): 1–4.

William Regelson and Carol Colman, *The Superhormone Promise* (New York: Simon and Schuster, 1995), 106–107.

V. A. Tzingournis, M. F. Asku, and R. B. Greenblatt, "Estriol in the Management of Menopause," *Journal of American Medical Association* 239, no. 16 (April 1978): 1638–41.

C. Lauritzen, "Results of a 5 Year Perspective Study of Estriol Succinate Treatment in Patients with Climacteric Complaints," *Hormone Metabolism Research* 19 (1987): 579–84.

"Pathophysiologic Considerations in the Treatment of Menopausal Patients with Estrogens: The Role of Estriol in the Prevention of Mammary Carcinoma," *Acta Endocrinol Suppl.* (Copenhagen, Denmark) (1980): 233.

G. A. Cousert, et al., "The Use of Estrogens and Progestins and the Rush of Breast Cancer in Postmenopausal Women," *New England Journal of Medicine* (June 1995): 1589–94.

"Estrogen Replacement Therapy and Fatal Ovarian Cancer," *American Journal of Epidemiology* (May 1995). Reprinted in *Life Extension Newsletter* 9, no. 1 (January 1996): 47.

John R. Lee, *Natural Progesterone: The Multiple Roles of a Remarkable Hormone* (Sebastopcol, Calif.: BLL Publishing, 1993).

John R. Lee, "Osteoporosis Reversal: The Role of Progesterone," *International Clinical Nutritional Review* 10 (1990): 384–391.

J. C. Prior, "Progesterone as a Bonetrophic Hormone," *Endocrine Review* 11 (1990): 386–98.

H. M. Lenron, et al., "Inhibition of Radiogenic Mammary Carcinoma in Rats by Estriol or Tamoxifen," *Cancer* 63 (1989): 1685–92.

Carol Kahn, "The Growing Impact of Growth Hormone," *Life Extension Newsletter* (June 1997): 28–34.

Dr. Julian Whitaker, "Use of Natural Progesterone Over Provera," *Health and Healing Newsletter* 3, no. 3 (March 1993): 3–4.

J. Tenover: "Effects of Testosterone Supplementation in the Aging Male," *Journal of Clinical Endocrinology and Metabolism* 75 (1992): 1092–98.

William Campbell Douglass, "A Neglected Hormone—Testosterone for Men and Women, Part 1," *Second Opinion* 5, no. 3 (March 1995): 1–5.

Regelson and Colman, *Superhormone Promise*, 203–18.

B. A. Bengtsson, et al., "Treatment of Adults with Growth Hormone GH Deficiency with Recombinant Human GH," *Journal of Clinical Endocrinol Metabolism* 76, no. 2 (February 1993): 309–17.

Carol Kahn, "The Growing Impact of Growth Hormone," *Life Extension* (June 1997): 28–34.

Ronald Klatz, *Grow Young with HGH* (New York: HarperCollins, 1997), 139.

J. B. Deijen, et al., "Cognitive Impairments and Mood Disturbances in Growth Hormone Deficient Men." Manuscript in preparation. For research see Ronald Klatz, *Grow Young with HGH* (New York: HarperCollins, 1997), 142.

J. O. Jorgensen, et al., "Growth Hormone vs Placebo Treatment for 1 Year in Growth Hormone Deficient Adults: Increase in Exercise Capacity and Normalization of Body Composition," *Clinical Endocrinology* 45, no. 6 (December 1996): 681–88.

Ronald Klatz, *Grow Young with HGH* (New York: HarperCollins, 1997), 84.

K.W. Kelley, et al., "GH Pituitary Adenoma Implants Can Reverse Thymic Aging," *Proceedings of the National Academy of Sciences* 83 (1986): 5663–67.

V. Giampapa, R. Klatz, B. DiBernard, and F. Kovarik, "Biomarker Matrix Protocol," *Advances in Anti-Aging Medicine* 1 (New York: Mary Ann Liebert, 1996).

D. Rudman, et al., "Effects of Human Growth Hormone in Men Over 60 Years Old," *New England Journal of Medicine* 323, no. 1 (July 1990): 1–6.

H. De Boer, et al., "The Optimal Growth Hormone Replacement Dose in Adults, Derived From Bioimpedance Analysis," *Journal of Clinical Endocrinology and Metabolism* 80, no. 7 (1995): 2069–2076.

A. Tsidori, et al., "A Study of Growth Hormone Release in Man After Oral Administration of Amino Acids," *Current Medical Research and Opinion* 1, no. 7 (1981): 475–81.

D. Pearson and S. Shaw, "GH Releasers: An Update Review," *Life Extension Newsletter* 3, no. 2 (July–August 1990).

Jiro Takahara, et al., "Stimulatory Effects of Gamma-hydroxybutyric Acid on Growth Hormone and Prolactin in Humans," *Journal of Clinical Endocrinology and Metabolism* 44 (1977): 1014–17.

Medical References

ALTERNATIVE MEDICINE RESOURCES

American Academy of Environmental Medicine (AAEM)
P.O. Box CN 1001-8001
New Hope, PA 18938
Office: 1-316-684-5500
Fax: 1-316-684-5009

American College for Advancement in Medicine (ACAM)
23121 Verdugo Drive, Suite 204
P.O. Box 3427
Laguna Hills, CA 92654
Office: 1-949-583-7666
Fax: 1-949-455-9679

American Association of Naturopathic Physicians
601 Valley, Suite 105
Seattle, WA 98109
Office: 1-206-298-0126
Referrals: 1-206-298-0125
Web site: www.naturopathic.org
(FYI: Naturopathic physicians must have four years of education in basic
biomedical sciences with emphasis on preventive and natural therapies
and on diagnosing and treating chronic disease.)

American Holistic Health Association
P.O. Box 17400
Anaheim, CA 92817-7400

Office: 1-714-779-6152
Web site: www.ahha.org
(FYI: Holistic practioners include medical, chiropractic, and osteopathic
doctors.)

American Holistic Medical Association (AHMA)
4101 Boone Trail
Raleigh, NC 27607
Office: 1-703-556-9728

Broda Barnes Research Foundation
P.O. Box 98
Trumbill, CT 06611
1-703-261-2101

International Health Foundation (IHF)
P.O. Box 3494
Jackson, TN 38303
Office: 1-901-660-7090

Holistic Health Guide (a New Age journal)
42 Pleasant Street
Watertown, MA 02172
Office: 1-617-926-0200
Fax: 1-617-926-5562

Journal of Orthomolecular Medicine
16 Florence Avenue
Toronto, Ontario, Canada M2N-1E9
Office: 1-416-733-2117
(FYI: This group supplies names of orthomolecular physicians and psychia-
trists in Canada and the United States.)

ORTHOMOLECULAR PSYCHIATRY

Well Mind Association of Greater Washington
18606 New Hampshire Avenue
Ashton, MD 20861-9789
Office: 1-301-774-6617
Fax: 1-301-774-0536

VACCINATION INFORMATION

National Vaccine Information Center
(Dissatisfied Parents Together)

1-800-909-SHOT
1-800-909-7468

Vaccine Research Institute (Jo Szczesny)
1-847-564-1403
(A four-minute recorded message is available twenty-four hours a day to learn how to access the research on vaccine health hazards.)

Vaccine Network (attn: Chris Abel)
3411 Winnetka Avenue North
Crystal, MN 55427
1-612-593-9440

Mothering Magazine
P.O. Box 1690
Santa Fe, NM 87505
1-505-984-8116
1-505-986-8335
(FYI: From this publication you can receive a booklet collection of articles by physicians and parents on immunization.)

NATIONAL ANTI-AGING ORGANIZATIONS

The American Academy of Anti-Aging Medicine (4 M)
1341 W. Fullerton, Suite 111
Chicago, IL 60614
Office: 1-773-528-4333
Fax: 1-773-528-5390

Life Extension Foundation
P.O. Box 229120
Hollywood, FL 33022
Office: 1-800-841-5433
Fax: 1-954-761-9199

PHYSICIAN SPECIALISTS IN ANTI-AGING

Allen Ahlschier, M.D.
San Antonio, Texas
1-210-653-2708

Benjamin Rothstein, D.O.
Baltimore, Maryland
1-410-484-2121

Chong Park, M.D.
Montclair, New Jersey
1-973-746-3535

Eric Braverman, M.D.
Princeton, New Jersey
1-609-921-1842

E. W. McDonagh, D.O.
Kansas City, Missouri
1-816-453-5940

Jonathan Wright, M.D.
Kent, Washington
1-253-854-4900

Julian Whitaker, M.D.
Newport Beach, California
1-949-851-1550

L. Cass Terry, M.D., Ph.D.
Milwaukee, Wisconsin
1-414-454-5204
1-414-259-0469 (fax)

L. Stephen Coles, M.D, Ph.D.
Marina del Rey, California
1-310-827-3920

L. Terry Chappell, M.D.
Bluffton, Ohio
1-419-358-4627
1-800-788-4627

R. Arnold Smith, Jr., M.D.
Greenwood, Mississippi
1-800-720-8933

Ronald Hoffman, M.D.
New York, New York
1-212-779-1744

Roman Rozencwaig, M.D.
Montreal, Quebec
1-514-487-0439

Stephen Sinatra, M.D, FACC
Manchester, Connecticut
1-860-643-5161

Recommended Laboratories

Company	Tests Performed
Bio Center Laboratory 3100 North Hillside Avenue Wichita, KS 67219 1-316-684-7784 1-800-494-7785 1-316-682-2062 (fax)	Pyrroles Serum histamine Serum zinc Serum copper Amino acid assays
Doctors Data Inc. P.O. Box 111 170 West Roosevelt Road West Chicago, IL 60185 1-800-323-2784 1-630-231-9190 (fax)	Hair analysis
Immuno Diagnostic Laboratories (IDL) 10930 Bigge Street P.O. Box 5755 San Leandro, CA 94577 1-510-635-4555 1-800-888-1113	Anti-candida panel FAMA, T3U, T4, FTI, TSH (thyroid panel)
Great Smokies Diagnostic Laboratories 63 Zillicoa Street Asheville, NC 28801-1074 1-828-253-0621	Food allergy profile Salivary hormonal assay

Company	Tests Performed
Spectra Cell Laboratories, Inc. 7051 Portwest Drive, Suite 100 Houston, TX 77024 1-713-621-3101 1-713-863-8104 (fax)	B complex profile 1500 FIA-comprehensive 3000 Antioxidant profile 1400
SmithKline Beecham Clinical Laboratories 600 W. County Road D. New Brighton, MN 55112 1-612-635-1500	Glucose tolerance test Chemistry profile Pyruvate Lactic acid
Aatron Laboratories 12832 South Chadron Avenue Hawthorn, CA 90250 1-800-433-9750	Amino acid assays

NATIONAL NUTRIENT DISTRIBUTOR

Company	Products
Bio-Recovery Inc. 3255 Hennepin Avenue South Minneapolis, MN 55408 1-800-247-6237 1-888-900-0709	All formulas in this book
Purity Products 1804 Plaza Avenue New Hyde Park, NY 11040 1-800-769-7837	Oregano
Women's International Pharmacy Madison, WI 1-800-279-5708	TriEst, natural progesterone, testosterone compounding
Sonoma Diagnostic, Inc. 1-800-635-3021	Growth hormone

Suggested Reading

HYPOGLYCEMIA

Low Blood Sugar and You, by Carlton Fredricks (New York: Constellation International, 1969).

Pure, White, and Deadly, by John Yudkin (New York: Viking, 1986).

The Sugar Trap and How to Avoid It, by Beatrice Trum Hunter (Boston: Houghton Mifflin, 1982).

Sugar Blues, by William Dufty (New York: Warner, 1976).

Hypoglycemia: The Disease Your Doctor Won't Treat, by Harvey Ross and Jeraldine Saunders (New York: Kensington, 1996).

Get the Sugar Out, by Ann Louise Gittleman, M.S. (New York: Crown Trade Paperbacks, 1996).

Feed Your Body Right, by Lendon Smith (New York: M. Evans, 1994).

Lick the Sugar Habit, by Nancy Appleton (Garden City Park, N.Y.: Avery Publishing Group, 1996).

ALLERGIES

Allergies and Your Family, by Doris Rapp, M.D. (New York: Sterling Publishing Co., 1981).

Brain Allergies: The Psychonutrient Connection, by William Philpott and Dwight Kalita (New Canaan, Conn.: Keats Publishing, 1980).

The Type 1/Type 2 Allergy Relief Program, by Alan Levin (Los Angeles: Tarcher, 1983).

Human Ecology and Susceptibility to the Chemical Environment, by Theron Randolph (Springfield, Ill.: Charles Thomas, 1962).

Coping with Your Allergies, by Natalie Golos (New York: Simon and Schuster, 1979).

Is This Your Child, by Doris Rapp, M.D. (New York: William Morrow, 1991).

Superimmunity for Kids, by Leo Galland, M.D., and Diane Buchman (New York: Dutton, 1988).

Chemical Sensitivity, by William Rea, M.D. (Boca Raton, Fla.: Lewis Publishers, 1992).

An Alternative Approach to Allergies, by Theron Randolph, M.D., and Ralph Moss (New York: Lippincott & Crowell, 1980).

NUTRITION

Diet for a Small Planet, by Frances Moore Lappe (New York: Ballantine, 1971).

Mental and Elemental Nutrients, by Carl Pfeiffer (New Canaan, Conn.: Keats Publishing, 1975).

Four Pillars of Healing, by Leo Galland (New York: Random House, 1997).

Psychodietetics, by Emanuel Cheraskin (New York: Ringdorf-Bantam, 1976).

Nutrition Against Disease, by Roger Williams (New York: Pitman, 1971).

Medical Applications of Clinical Nutrition, by Jeffrey Bland, ed. (New Canaan, Conn.: Keats Publishing, 1983).

Wellness Against All Odds, by Sherry Rogers, M.D. (Syracuse, New York: Prestige Publishing, 1994).

Total Wellness, by Joseph Pizzorno, M.D. (Rocklin, Calif.: Prima Publishing, 1996).

The Nutrition Super Book, edited by Jean Barilla (New Canaan, Conn.: Keats Publishing, 1995).

Dr. Wright's Guide to Healing with Nutrition, by Jonathan Wright, M.D. (New Canaan, Conn.: Keats Publishing, 1990).

The Healing Nutrients Within, by Eric Braverman, M.D. (New Canaan, Conn.: Keats Publishing, 1997).

Excitotoxins: The Taste That Kills, by Russell Blaylock, M.D. (Santa Fe, N. Mex.: Santa Fe Health Press, 1995).

Feed Your Body Right, by Lendon Smith, M.D. (New York: M. Evans, 1994).

Nutrition and the Mind, by Gary Null, Ph.D. (New York: Four Walls Eight Windows, 1995).

Eat Right 4 Your Type, by Peter J. D'Adamo (New York: G. P. Putnam's Sons, 1996).

The Omega-3 Phenomenon, by Donald Rudin, M.D. (New York: Rawson Associates, 1987).

DEPRESSION

The Way Up from Down, by Priscilla Slagle (New York: Random House, 1987).

Health and Light, by John Ott (New York: Simon and Schuster, 1973)

CANDIDA

The Yeast Connection, by William Crook (Jackson, Tenn.: Professional Books, 1983).

The Yeast Syndrome, by John Towbridge and Morton Walker (New York: Bantam Books, 1986).

The Missing Diagnosis, by Orien Truss (self-published, 1983). Obtain from P.O. Box 26508, Birmingham, AL 35226.

The Yeast Connection Handbook, by William Crook, M.D. (Jackson, Tenn.: Professional Books, 1997).

Beyond Antibiotics, by Michael Schmidt, M.D., Lendon Smith, M.D., and Keith Sehnert, M.D. (Berkeley, Calif.: North Atlantic Books, 1994).

Digestive Wellness, by Elizabeth Lipski, M.S. (New Canaan, Conn.: Keats Publishing, 1996).

ANTI-AGING

Stop Aging Now, by Jean Carper (New York: HarperCollins, 1995).

Resetting the Clock, by Elmer Cranton and W. Fryer (New York: M. Evans and Co., 1996).

Grow Young with HGH, by Ronald Klatz (New York: HarperCollins, 1997).

The Superhormone Promise, by William Regelson and Carol Colman (New York: Simon and Schuster, 1996).

CHILDHOOD VACCINATIONS

Vaccinations, Sociopathy and Criminality: The Medical Assault on the American Brain, by Harris L. Coulter (Berkeley, Calif.: North American Books, 1990).

DPT: A Shot in the Dark, by Harris L. Coulter and Barbara Fisher Brace (San Diego: Jovanovich Publishers, 1985).

Immunization: The Reality Behind the Myth, by W. James (Granberry, Mass.: Bergin and Garvey Publishers, 1988).

APPENDIX E

An Easy, Where-to-Find-It Tests and Formulas Locator

Formulas:

INDEX

Aatron Laboratories, 250
Acetaldehyde, 116
Acetylcholine, 49, 120, 153, 229
  manic depression and, 172–173
Acid (LSD), 218
ACTH, 109
Addiction, ups and downs of, 239, 279
Adrenal cortex stress profile, 152
Adrenal glands, 49, 83, 85–87, 90, 301, 302
  exhaustion of, 152
Adrenaline, 64–65, 73, 85, 112, 118, 119, 143–145, 159, 177, 184, 235
Agent Orange, 262, 263
Aging, 9, 299–300
  antioxidants and, 50
  see also Hormones
Agoraphobics, 145
Agriculture, U.S. Department of (USDA), 41
Airborne chemicals, 15
ALA (alpha-linolenic acid), 52
Alanine, described, 116
Alcohol
  as cause of depression, 6, 207–208
  craving for, 85
  histamine and, 225
  hypoglycemia and, 69
Alcoholism, 4–6, 34
  amino acids and, 116, 117

Detox Formula, 208, 209
genetic history and, 39
nationality and, 37
Aldehydes, 146
Alka-Seltzer Gold, 244, 285, 289
Allergies
  food. *See* Food allergies
  genetic history and, 38
Allicin, 277
Alpha brain waves, 112, 113
Alpha lipoic acid, 266, 267
Alternative Approach to Allergies, An (Randolph), 238–239
Aluminum, 121
  toxicity, 251–252
Alzheimer's disease, 251
American Academy of Anti-Aging Medicine, 303, 347
American Academy of Environmental Medicine (AAEM), 162, 212, 245, 276, 283, 345
American Association of Naturopathic Physicians, 345
American College for Advancement in Medicine (ACAM), 73, 253, 345
American College of Allergy and Immunology, 280
American Heart Association, 187
American Heart Institute, 80

ABOUT THE AUTHOR

Joan Mathews Larson, Ph.D., is the author of the national bestseller *Seven Weeks to Sobriety*. She holds a doctorate in nutrition and is the founder and executive director of the highly esteemed Health Recovery Center in Minneapolis, Minnesota.

It was the loss of her seventeen-year-old son to suicide that fueled her ongoing search for more effective solutions to emotional healing. Her clinic has now successfully treated several thousand people over a twenty-year period. She lives in Minneapolis.